FOREVER IN THE SHADOW OF HITLER?

D0060812

FOREVER IN THE SHADOW OF HITLER?

ORIGINAL DOCUMENTS OF THE <u>HISTORIKERSTREIT</u>, THE CONTROVERSY CONCERNING THE SINGULARITY OF THE HOLOCAUST

JAMES KNOWLTON AND TRUETT CATES
Translators

HUMANITIES PRESS
New Jersey

Originally published in German as *Historikerstreit: Die Dokumentation der Kontroverse um die Einzigartigkeit der nationalsozialistischen Judenvernichtung*, © R. Piper GmbH & Co., Munich.

English translation first published 1993 by Humanities Press International, Inc., Atlantic Highlands, New Jersey 07716.

This English translation ©1993 by Humanities Press International, Inc.

Library of Congress Cataloging-in-Publication Data

Historikerstreit. English.
    Forever in the shadow of Hitler? : the dispute about the
Germans' understanding of history, original documents
of the Historikerstreit, the controversy concerning the singularity
of the Holocaust / translated by James Knowlton and Truett Cates.
      p.   cm.
    Translation of: Historikerstreit.
    Includes bibliographical references and index.
    ISBN 0-391-03811-7 (cloth).—ISBN 0-391-03784-6 (pbk.)
    1. Holocaust, Jewish (1939–1945)—Historiography. 2. Historians—
Germany (West)
D804.3.H5713 1993
940.53′18′072—dc20   92-23763
                                    CIP

A catalog record for this book is available from the British Library

All rights reserved. No part of this publication may be reproduced or transmitted, in any form or by any means, without written permission from the publisher.

Printed in the United States of America

CONTENTS

APPENDIX: Notes on the *Historikerstreit*

PUBLISHER'S NOTE
TO THE ENGLISH EDITION

The task of translating this work has not been easy and our translators have had to make some editorial decisions concerning the form of the English text.

The first concerns the way in which a few of the writers quote one another. Throughout the volume material is contained within quotation marks, often quoting from another piece contained within this volume. In a few instances close examination will reveal slight variations between the original text and the quoted text. Where this occurs it reflects the German original.

Another problem was the result of revisions made to some texts following their original publication. All this material had appeared in print, in German, before the compilation of this work; both the original position papers, and the responses. However, where the response quotes a text which was subsequently revised, it obviously quotes the pre-revision version. No attempt has been made to enforce consistency where this occurs.

It will be noted that there are inconsistencies between the various contributors' quotations of pieces from Ernst Nolte's *Between Historical Legend and Revisionism? The Third Reich in the Perspective of 1980*. This has occurred because Nolte's work was published both in German and English. Nolte made some revisions for the English version of his text and the respondents here have sometimes quoted from the German and sometimes from the edited English version. In this volume we have retranslated Nolte's German text as published in the German edition of this book, leaving it unaltered.

Finally, there are also quotations from material not published in this volume. Page citations in these articles—whether to material published in this volume or to articles or papers published elsewhere—refer to the original page numbers.

The full German title of this book was *Historikerstreit: Die Dokumentation der Kontroverse um die Einzigartigkeit der nationalsozialistischen Judenvernichtung*. No attempt has been made to translate it for use in this English-language edition.

EDITORIAL PREFACE

This book contains only texts that have already been published. They were printed without editorial changes. Only obvious misprints and typographical errors have been changed.

The sole exceptions to this rule are the "Notes" printed in the appendix; they are by Joachim Fest, Jürgen Habermas, Andreas Hillgruber, Ernst Nolte, and Michael Stürmer.

We would like to thank all those who contributed to this project for their willingness to make the compromises that made possible the shared goal of a documentation of this controversy in one volume.

Responsibility for the content of the individual texts lies with the authors.

THE GERMAN PUBLISHER

ERNST NOLTE

Between Historical Legend and Revisionism? The Third Reich in the Perspective of 1980

If in 1980 residents of a distant star were to come to earth to find out about the history of mankind and about the German Third Reich, they would have to conclude that the Third Reich is still alive thirty-five years after its downfall. Not in the sense that countless people hold it in longing memory. Nor that large memorial celebrations attract great masses. Nor that a powerful party is intent upon Nazi restoration. Quite the contrary: The feeble attempts to re-create a Nazi party at best offer material for sensational reporting, and the "Hitler waves" that repeatedly pop up serve less to glorify the führer of the Third Reich than to present him as a figure who is fascinating precisely because of his strangeness.

And yet, a film [*Holocaust*] that focused on the greatest atrocity of the Third Reich exerted a powerful influence on large masses of people in the United States and in the Federal Republic of Germany. For years, the best-known school of social analysis has referred to the Third Reich as a part of its foundation. Prominent politicians of the Federal Republic are forced to resign or jeopardize their careers if they can be connected in even the slightest way to the Third Reich. A statement such as "The majority of the SA members in the years around 1933, despite their blood-curdling songs, were not motivated by criminal intentions" is seen as a dangerous trivialization of what really happened. And in numerous popular publications of the United States, SA and SS members are portrayed as being ceaselessly occupied with plundering houses, torturing prisoners, and raping women.

However, nothing even vaguely similar can be demonstrated thirty-five years after the fall of the second French Empire. The reign of Napoleon III had long since become an object of historical inquiry, no matter how vehement the attacks during the early 1970s were. Of course it was quite different thirty-five years after the collapse of the first empire. Around 1850, the Napoleon legend had been long since established, and memories of the emperor had been transformed into a positive image that could be utilized by a powerful party in its political battles—despite the fact that

1

after 1815 opinions about the Corsican could hardly have been more negative than opinions about Hitler after 1945. In fact this legend, which had already made Napoleon's nephew the president of the republic, was to become the national legend in the Deuxième Empire. Thus the Napoleon legend had an essentially positive character. In stark contrast to this, the vividness of the Third Reich, with the exception of a few areas on the lunatic fringe, has a thoroughly negative character. And there are good reasons for this.

The first, most compelling, and most generally accepted is that the Third Reich was guilty of beginning the greatest and bloodiest war in the history of mankind. Hitler's refusal to negotiate, to step down, or to capitulate brought this war to such a catastrophic conclusion that, at least for the Germans, its memory will remain inextinguishable. Hitler's moral condemnations of the survivors makes a condemnation of Hitler a necessity of life in today's Germany.

Moreover, the Third Reich, when viewed from the perspective of a westernized consumer-oriented society, appears grotesquely antiquated and reactionary. One only has to think of the motto *Blut und Boden* [Blood and Soil], of the talk about the peasantry as the lifeblood of the folk, of the characterization of Blacks as "half-apes," of the uniforms that were everywhere in evidence, of the glorification of hierarchy and discipline, of the songs praising the war, of the subordinate role of women, who supposedly never uttered doubts that their sphere of life was the home, or that they, on the "battlefield of childbirth," would make their contribution to the people's struggle for its place in the sun. And when people talked about "democracy," they did not mean a participatory or direct kind but rather "Germanic" democracy, that is, assent to an autocratic leadership.

Also, the acts of violence perpetrated by the Third Reich are singular. There are some precedents and parallels to the concentration camps and even to the "destruction of the labor movement." But the extermination of several million European Jews—and also of many Slavs, mentally ill, and Gypsies—is, judged by its motivation and its execution, without precedent. It has aroused an unparalleled sense of horror, particularly because of the cold, inhuman, technical precision of the gas chambers. It is true that many Germans repressed or ignored these facts for a long time, but in "published opinion" the facts have appeared with such exclusivity that only the voices of the victims have been audible. Vindications of the Nazi period have never been seriously attempted, and the only attempts to weaken the prevailing view merely suggested that the numbers of people killed by the Nazis were smaller than what had been accepted. Finally, the Third Reich lends itself exceptionally well to caricature. Hitler was made for Chaplin. The "Reichs-drunk" Ley, the vicious pornographer Streicher, the bull-necked Bormann, the vain bungler Göring, the bespectacled *Reichsheini* Himmler, who took himself to be a reincarnation of the first

Saxon king—these men represent a portrait gallery that by its inherent inanity, never ceases parodying itself.

Thus the Third Reich has a vividly negative character. The literature about the Third Reich is both a symptom and a cause of this. In essence, it is a literature of catastrophe and indictment. Titles such as *The German Catastrophe* and *The Road to Catastrophe*, published right after the war, characteristically emphasized catastrophe. A title like *The German Lack of Existence* took indictment to the extreme. In general, however, the indictments were aimed at certain traditions or classes: at the "Junkers" as well as at the Prussian spirit in general—these being blamed for the fateful separation from Western European developments and thus for the German *Sonderweg*—and at the capitalists as the most important promoters, even as the patrons, of the National-Socialist party. Neither tendency was found strictly in the literature. The state of Prussia was dissolved by unanimous resolution of the four occupying powers, and the Nuremberg Trials prosecuted not only the "main war criminals" but also diplomats and business magnates such as Flick and Krupp.

It is true that early on, different versions of events were already being presented. The Americans and British released a large number of the convicted "war criminals," and the literature of indictment was joined by a literature of exculpation in which, to mention two examples, Gerhard Ritter argued that we should understand the Prussian spirit, and Louis P. Lochner fashioned himself as an advocate for the capitalists. But these were always individual corrections, never attempts to promote a fundamental shift in our understanding of the overall picture.

Nor did the literature influenced by the concept of totalitarianism bring about any changes in our view. It merely extended the negative view so that one of the old Allies could also be included. More precisely, the literature used the positive concept of liberal democracy to cast a more encompassing negative light on all totalitarian systems such as National Socialism and communism. Moreover, within this view, in essence limited to comparing the Third Reich and the Stalinist Soviet Union in terms of their social and governmental structures, it was very difficult, for reasons inherent to the discipline and stemming from vague general assumptions, to generalize beyond the immediate object of study, the Third Reich.

As late as 1959, William Shirer's clearly anti-German book was a huge commercial success, and the gradual rise of neo-Marxist scholarship effectively reexamined the Nuremberg Trials, which it refashioned into a comprehensive indictment of the "capitalist system." However, even the so-called bourgeois literature about the Fascist movements and regimes in Europe does not contradict our general impression, despite the fact that it was an attempt to examine European history since 1917 as a whole.

In spite of this, it cannot be denied that the vivid negativity of a historical phenomenon represents a great danger for the discipline of history. A permanent negative or positive image necessarily has the character of a myth, which is an actualized form of a legend. This is true because a myth like this can be made to found or support an ideology of state. As a thought experiment, one only has to imagine what would happen if the PLO, with the help of its allies, were to succeed in destroying the nation of Israel. Suppose the historical portrayals in books, lecture halls, and schoolrooms then focused on the negative traits of Israel. The victory over racist, repressive, even Fascist Zionism would become a historical legend used to provide a foundation for the state. For decades, perhaps even for a century, nobody would venture to accurately portray the rise of Zionism from its spirit of resistance against European anti-Semitism, to describe the extraordinary things it achieved before or after the foundation of the nation of Israel, or even to show what clearly distinguishes it from, say, Italian fascism. In fact, "victory over fascism" has become a historical myth that provides a foundation for the state in the GDR. For Western scholarship, however, "revision" has become an essential characteristic— that is, the constantly renewed critique not just of individual events but also of prevailing assumptions. Each completed revision itself becomes an assertion and thus in the short or long term the object of a new revision. Thus, for example, the history of the American Civil War was initially written only from the perspective of the victors. But soon, a greater comprehension of the motives and the way of life of the defeated Southern states made itself felt in the North. Even if such understanding was never strong enough to prevail, it was sufficiently influential to precipitate a new revisionism. The same can be said about German historiography, which at first prepared and then later portrayed the path that led to the founding of Bismarck's empire. But the spectrum of this historiography was always broad enough to prevent the establishment of an unshakable myth of state.

The fundamental question must then be, Is the history of the Third Reich, thirty-five years after the end of the war, in need of revision? And what could such a revision look like? It certainly could not be a reversal of the negative tendency in historical literature, that is, an apologia. For then it would either deny undeniable facts or implicitly seek to renew the National-Socialist ethos and its chief postulates. An example of such a defense might be a justification for the demand for absolute sovereignty for a unified German nation; or, to take a more extreme example, a resurrection of the thesis about the fateful influence of the Jews in German society. Neither is possible. The innermost core of our negative image of the Third Reich is neither in need of revision nor capable of being revised. Nonetheless, contemporary events might eventually convince us to present the Third Reich from an entirely new perspective and to generalize our negative understanding of it in a different way than did the classical totalitarianism theory of the 1950s. The rise of anarchistic historiography provides an instructive example. For it, everything that is hierarchically organized possesses an essentially negative, repressive character—no matter whether the system is based on the slave state of the Greek polis or on the modern states of "real socialism." Thus it is difficult to assign the Third Reich a unique place in a universal history of oppression.

In the early 1960s, established historical scholarship saw two books as forms of revisionism and thus as a challenge to prevailing views: A. J. P. Taylor's *The Origins of the Second World War* and David Hoggan's *Der erzwungene Krieg*. Both were limited in their revisionist aims. Taylor basically presented one version of the anti-German literature of indictment; Hoggan, by confining himself to the question of why the war broke out, cut himself off from the really decisive questions. Still, one book served to underscore the question of continuity and the other raised questions about the simplistic thesis suggesting that Hitler "unleashed the Second World War." Both books were thus in a sense symptoms for the end of the second phase of the postwar period.

At the beginning of the 1960s, the war in Vietnam created a completely new situation. Granted, the war had a direct and comprehensive effect only on the way the history of the cold war was written, but it indirectly provided substantial support for the neo-Marxist thesis about the demise of capitalism. At the same time, as a result of the détente of the 1970s, our conception of totalitarianism was weakened to the extent that now only the Western, or capitalist, system seemed to remain as an object of indictment.

At the end of the 1970s, the situation was again profoundly shifted. The cessation of U.S. "intervention" in Vietnam had brought no peace. The alleged victims of genocide, the now-unified Vietnamese, proved to be strong enough to wage war against Cambodia. Then the Vietnamese themselves became the victims of a "punitive expedition" by the People's Republic of China. At the same time, an ethnic mass exodus took place, later known as the "holocaust on water," a term that describes the brutal mass death of countless refugees.

The weakness and fragility of so-called Western imperialism became evident as from Africa to Afghanistan the Soviet Union very successfully supported "liberation movements" that were expected to assert themselves against other "liberation movements." Then, to the amazement of the entire world, a new kind of revolution took place in Iran, a revolution that according to established concepts was "progressive" in that it threw off U.S. influence but was also thoroughly "reactionary" in that it established the predominance of a high priest. Doesn't this situation once again force us—and this time in a less partial and isolated way—to consider revising the history of the Third Reich?

Before I attempt to answer this question I would like to sketch the main thoughts and the chief conclusions of three recent books that must be seen as revisionist points of departure—even though they do not treat this "new kind of revolution" described above. Two of these, by Englishmen, are works about aspects and periods of the Third Reich; the other is a comprehensive interpretation of Italian fascism written by an Italian. We can use these books in answering the question about the necessity of revising the history of the Third Reich.

Domenico Settembrini gave his 1978 interpretation a provocative title: *Fascismo Controrivoluzione imperfetta*. He sets out from the thesis, posited by Piero Gobetti in his journal *Rivoluzione liberale*, that the real modern revolution was that of liberal capitalism or economic freedom, which began in England 200 years ago and was completed in the United States. This revolution of individualism was countered early on by so-called revolutionary socialism, which oriented itself toward the notion of a primal community and an archaic transparency of social relationships. Revolutionary socialism was a comprehensive counterrevolution in that it represented the tendency toward totalitarian collectivism. It was no coincidence that this counterrevolution came to power in Russia in 1917. And there it soon unveiled its true nature: the desire to restore the omnipresence of the authoritarian center and to subjugate individualism to the needs of an economic plan that solved the biggest problems of economic development but proved to be completely ineffective in fulfilling the needs of individuals.

The great question in 1918–1919 was whether Russia should become a model for Italy, a country that despite all its backwardness was much more differentiated and much more closely tied to the history of Western civilization. In the struggle against socialist maximalism, Mussolini, then the first man of the PSI, initially stood almost alone. Settembrini sides almost completely with him in his battles against his early comrades.

The fascism that Mussolini founded was a two-sided phenomenon: negative and positive at once, antirevolutionary and revolutionary at the same time. It was negative in that by eliminating political freedom and instituting corporatist regimentation of the economy, it diverged from the Western model. It was positive in that it did not entirely eliminate economic freedom or the market. In this way, Mussolini spared the Italian people the perfected totalitarianism of Stalin.

Mussolini was again correct when he later turned against his party's left wing, which saw in the duce's compromise an early stage on the road to complete collectivism. It is no coincidence that the representatives of this group went over to the Communists after the war. According to Settembrini, however, the decisive question today is whether the Italian Communists see the "historical compromise" they are attempting to achieve by the Fascist model as a merely tactical instrument that will help them to attain their old goals, or whether they are reproducing Mussolini's shift from 1919 on toward the liberal-democratic and capitalist system. In this way, Mussolini and fascism have once again been drawn into Italian national history. They have become a point of orientation for the most pressing of contemporary questions. This has not taken place in an atmosphere of uncritical glorification, but rather from a perspective that is emphatically non-Fascist.

If this interpretation were to find recognition, it would be a prime example of a successful revision. But its extension to Germany would apparently not be possible. German Social Democrats of 1918–1919 were no maximalists. Hitler's decision in favor of war was not merely an "unfortunate one." His totalitarianism, at least after the outbreak of the war, did not take a back seat to Stalin's, and his will to annihilate was not, like Mussolini's, merely political. It was based on biology. Thus even a successful revision of Italian fascism within the framework of Italian history could not be transposed to National Socialism and Germany.

In 1975 Timothy W. Mason's comprehensive study *Arbeiterklasse und Volksgemeinschaft* attempted a completely different kind of revision. Since 1945 it has been more or less assumed that no German social class could be exonerated from collective guilt for the National-Socialist regime. Shortly after the war, even the Communists admitted their guilt. The "petit-bourgeois thesis" of many fascism theories was already shifting its emphasis substantially, but Mason may be the first to see a chief reason for Hitler's defeat in the struggle of the working class, which, he says, prevented the National-Socialist regime from preparing for the war with the energy that was "objectively" possible and that (one has to add) would have led to Hitler's victory over the Allies.

In fact Mason is able to produce many examples where the mood of the working class has to be taken into account. Mason considers himself justified in speaking of the powerlessness of the totalitarian dictatorship in this regard. Speaking skeptically, one could say that Mason's revisionism consisted of proclaiming the German working class to be the actual victor over National Socialism. But when one closely examines the gigantic documentation Mason presents, one discovers more and more discordant notes: for example, the important role played by the organizational infighting of the DAF (German Labor Front), which used internal power struggles to make itself a spokesman for the wishes of the masses; the almost complete absence of acts of resistance; the adroit exploitation of the conditions in the tense labor market; the consequences of the improvement in the standard of living, which Mason does not deny; and the unscrupulous competition of business owners for limited labor.

It is more his material than Mason himself that provides us with a picture of an economy under pressure, an economy that demanded substantial sacrifices from all classes, including the stockholders. The economy was also confronted with the people's deft egoism in exploiting such situations.

What is completely missing here is a consideration of Hitler's "weltanschauung," which, after all, was more responsible than any other element for the fact that the reservoir of female workers was nowhere near as effectively utilized as in England and that in the middle of the war great resources were appropriated for mass murder. Viewed from the perspective of the war effort, this last was totally irrational and even counterproductive. Thus in spite of Mason, we will still have to assume that Hitler's war was waged by "the German people," despite the fact that certain frictions or even individual acts of resistance cannot be denied.

A completely different motive underlies the revisionist book by another Englishman: David Irving's 1975 *Hitler und seine Feldherren*, which appeared two years later in the English original under the title *Hitler's War*. Irving's quite transparent goal is to vindicate Hitler, who, according to Irving's thesis, "no longer was able to speak for himself after 1945," while his colleagues and opponents used one-sided portrayals and downright falsifications to draw an incorrect picture of the war. It was characteristic that the German publisher refused to print the author's exaggerated claim that Hitler had known nothing about the Final Solution. This fact was demonstrated, Irving suggested, by a telegram that forbade the liquidation of the Jews. In truth, however, this was the weakest part of the book. The telegram, when examined more precisely, says just the opposite of what Irving suggested. But not all of Irving's theses and points can be dismissed with such ease. What Irving suggests as an overall impression, namely that Hitler could have won the war if the people surrounding him had better understood his strategic intentions and had implemented them without resistance or attempts at sabotage, is more than dubious. However, it is hard to deny that Hitler had good reason to be convinced of his enemies' will to annihilate long before the first reports about the events in Auschwitz became public. The 1940 brochure "Germany Must Perish" by Theodore N. Kaufman has rarely been mentioned in the literature. But I cannot remember having read in any of the larger German studies of the period about Chaim Weizmann's statement in the first days of September 1939, that in this war the Jews of all the world would fight on England's side. In any case, I have to accept the accusation that I neither knew nor used this statement in 1963—despite the fact that it can be found in the *Archiv der Gegenwart* of 1939 and despite the fact that it provides information that could lay a foundation for the thesis that Hitler would have been justified in treating the German Jews as prisoners of war [or more precisely, as civilian internees like the Germans in England from September 1939, or U.S. citizens of Japanese heritage in the United States from 1941 to 1945]* and thus interning them. Similarly, we cannot simply dismiss Irving's assertion that the bombing of Hamburg in 1943 (an event that cannot have had its origin and cause in Allied knowledge about the Final Solution) was proof of the Allies' desire to destroy the German civilian population. Irving's tendency to place even Auschwitz in a more comprehen-

---

Author's Note: Bracketed material added April 1986.

sive perspective would be remarkable even if the counterthesis—that the president of the Jewish Agency had no legal status that would allow him to declare anything like war and that the attack on Coventry preceded the bombing of Hamburg by three years—had to be recognized as more convincing.

Subjecting the Third Reich to a revisionist treatment from the perspective of 1980 seems to me to be a difficult and pressing task. Such a view should not begin with the Weimar Republic or with the European situation in 1919. It might take its point of departure from the proclamation of the so-called National Unity Front in Cambodia, which was reprinted in December 1978 in *Neues Deutschland* and therefore cannot be described as "anti-Communist propaganda." From there the path might lead backward to the beginnings of the industrial revolution in England and France. The proclamation read:

> The reactionary clique of Pol Pot/Ieng Sary has seized all power. It had done its best to betray the country and to harm the people. It brought endless sorrow and misery upon our fellow citizens and threatened to exterminate our people. The Chinese authorities have encouraged and supported these traitors and tyrants right to the end. Just a few days after liberation these leaders began, using the slogans "radical social revolution in all areas" and "purify society," to wipe out cities and to force whole communities to abandon their houses and their property and to move to the country. There they lived in poverty under a regime of forced labor. They were faced with a slow death. The traitors severed all of the sacrosanct emotional connections of the people, to their parents, of wife from husband, of brother from sister, and even of neighbor from neighbor. And they eradicated villages and rural areas in which our people have lived for centuries and to which the people's feelings are closely tied. They proclaimed "forced collectivization," and the "elimination of money and the market" and compelled people to eat and sleep communally. In reality, however, they locked our fellow citizens away in camouflaged concentration camps, confiscated all means of production, obligated our people to endless toil while giving them only a minimum of food and clothing. That forced all segments of the population to live in poverty, returning the people to a state of slavery. The leaders divided the people into various categories in order to better subjugate them and to have them kill each other. The crimes of the Pol Pot/Ieng Sary clique can no longer be enumerated. (*Frankfurter Allgemeine Zeitung*, December 8, 1978)

This text awakens all kinds of memories. It arouses a memory of the slogan "Steal what has been stolen," to which the beginnings of the Russian Revolution in 1917 and 1918 owed so much of its effectiveness. It leads our thoughts back to the bellicose communism of those years, when it was claimed that money had been banned and that people had been returned to a communal existence.

The proclamation brings to mind the forced collectivization of 1929, a time when millions of kulaks were forced not from cities into villages but from villages into the tundra to "trickle away," as Solzhenitsyn wrote; that is, to die. It revivifies the terrible period of 1936 to 1938, of which Mosche Pijade wrote in 1951: "In 1936, 1937, and 1938, over three million people were killed in the Soviet Union. They were not members of the bourgeoisie, which had been liquidated in this country years before."

The Cambodian text also recalls memories of far older times, times that persisted in thoughts and endeavors. These include well-meaning and partially positive or at least understandable ideas and endeavors that cannot be made to disappear from history and that in more than one sense doubtlessly played a positive role. Thomas Spence, for example, the English "agrarian reformer," considered a parish unhealthy when it was excluded from the commons and the privileges related to it and given over to the control of the landholding class and a distant central authority. He called time and time again, in the last instance in his journal *The Giant Killer*, for the elimination of the class of landlords and for the restitution of a far-reaching sovereignty for the parishes.

Before him there was Morelly, the early French socialist, as he is sometimes called. He was a kind of village collectivist who wanted to restore or, better, to reestablish the village community, which had been altered by the development and differentiation of agriculture.

Then there was John Gray, who in his philanthropically motivated and influential 1825 "Lecture on Human Happiness," examined all social classes for their "usefulness" and completely expelled the "freeholders of the better sort" from the productive realm while recognizing as socially necessary about half of the "lesser freeholders" and "farmers."

Then there was William Benbow, who in 1832 introduced the concept of the "sacred month" in which the poor, the great majority of the people, would reexpropriate the surplus of their labor, which had been taken by the predatory classes, the rich and the civil servants.

Men such as Fourier and Owen are also part of this picture because they were guided by an ideal of a simple human community that was autonomous and that functioned without a set division of labor—a society that was not endangered by crises, that was independent of events in foreign countries and undisturbed by the din of factories. Even Babeuf wanted to lead the population of the big cities back to the country and to found "an agricultural republic without money" and without "artificial needs."

One can characterize all these incipient projects as communalistic, that is, as interpretations of social developments that arose from a utopian perspective rooted in real social relationships. This was the perspective of a small and scarcely differentiated commonwealth that considered the rising economy based on currency and trade, with its accumulations of capital, its uneven and painful replacement of manual labor with machines, its increasingly opaque credit transactions, and its worldwide and yet not fully reciprocal economic dependencies and the crises that arose from them, to be a disease that threatened the social body. Tories such as Robert Southey and Samuel Taylor Coleridge differed only little from those who were thought to be their most vociferous political enemies. But these men made no suggestions for a radical therapy.

Therapies can be divided into two main groups: those that advocated peaceful and evolutionary change and those that demanded annihilation. Thus Fourier and Owen ended up on the one side while Spence, Babeuf, Benbow, and Bronterre O'Brien formed the other.

Because of the widespread misery and extraordinary differences in income in the England of the early nineteenth century and because the new social form—an individualistic money economy—was closely linked to the old corporatist society ruled by the aristocracy, but also because the new poverty legislation was felt to be a "Poor Man's Destruction Bill," all these diagnoses and all these therapeutic suggestions are quite understandable. They had a positive significance as a precondition for new forms of consciousness. Still, expectations were rife that the first attempts at putting annihilation therapies into actual practice would be the acid test for the correctness or incorrectness of the analysis and that such attempts could possibly lead to grave and unexpected consequences.

If the "ruling class" were more than a tiny minority in the society, if its members were filled with the conviction that they did not have to be a leisure class but were intended to fulfill a vital and progressive role, if substantial parts of the oppressed population maintained loyalty to the ruling class—if, in a word, society had become too complex and unsettled to be appropriately described with simple dichotomies such as "rich" and "poor," "rulers" and "ruled," "oppressed" and "oppressors," then annihilation therapies would fail and possibly lead to a backlash against their supporters or at least against those who were thought to be supporters.

In fact, fundamental differences between the nations quickly became evident. The French Revolution had, for the first time in European history, made the concept of annihilating classes and social groups a reality. But this too must be understood as one of the "uncompleted" revolutions such as the American Revolution of 1776, the English Reform Bill of 1832, or the German Revolution of 1918. The Russian Revolution of 1917–1918, however, had an entirely different character. Here, more of a Babeuvist-Spencian than a Marxist annihilation therapy succeeded because of the weakness of the embryonic bourgeoisie and because of the special conditions of the war. This process was so novel, so monstrous, and so bewildering that unusually grave reactions were to be expected.

Still, it would be a crass simplification to see in the National-Socialist will to annihilate nothing but a reaction to the Bolshevist acts of annihilation. The National-Socialist will had independent roots that reached far back into history. Examples:

1. The annihilation theories of early rightists were developed as a reaction to the terror and to the political programs of the French Revolution and published in the books of men like Joseph de Maistre, Abbe Barruel, or the Scottish nature philosopher Robinson. Here, terms such as "vermin" started to play a role on both sides. Until the Dreyfus Affair, these postulates of counterannihilation rarely had an anti-Jewish slant. But even Metternich sought a connection between the liberals and the Jews.

2. The annihilation strategy of the radical wing of Malthusianism grew out of the fear of an unprecedented increase in population and in some cases led to the suggestion that surplus children should be eliminated by using gas.

3. The Prussian variant of Napoleon's military annihilation strategy was apt to lose its Clausewitzian restrictions and, at least during World War II, did lose them.

One could make the following objection: The annihilation of infidels and heretics was accepted practice during the Middle Ages and continued in the early modern age. One only has to recall the Spanish Inquisition or the Revocation of the Edict of Nantes. From the Enlightenment on, so the argument goes, the liberal belief in progress was so predominant that the facts listed above should just be seen as corollaries and the National-Socialist measures of annihilation should be seen as merely an incomprehensible relapse into barbarism.

But it seems to me that a completely new situation arose by virtue of the fact that the Enlightenment and its victorious polemic against the religious wars of the past brought forth a new kind of society based on tolerance—a society in which the unprecedented process of the industrial revolution could take place. Thus a stage was established on which pronouncements could be made, questions asked, threats spoken, and new anxieties experienced—things that were not possible in more closed societies, as powerful and natural as the hate of deviation in these kinds of societies might be. Moreover, the rhetoric about the victory of light over darkness should not be understood to be merely naively optimistic. Only in the light is the light light and the dark dark; only in the light can we do battle; only in the light can we see wounds for what they are. The light, that is, a sharp and inclusive consciousness, is not in itself good. Rather, it is the precondition for goodness as well as evil, and what appears in it are almost exclusively mixtures of both. With this in mind, I would like to summarize and conclude:

The revolutionary and bewildering process of the industrial revolution instigated among the social classes and groups most affected by it an interpretation that explained this process as pathogenic. Among the therapies suggested, the more prominent (although by no means exclusive) ones were those that envisioned a cure by annihilating entire social classes or groups. According to the structure of the society, this therapy has a more or less rational character. The strategy is not necessarily intended to exterminate individuals, and it can be accompanied by very respectable motives. In a developed country with a broad and complex middle class, the archaic nature of such therapies soon become evident. In a backward country, the elimination of a small, parasitic ruling group can be an elementary precondition for "modernization," even if the original motive that leads to this act is the radical-reactionary one of reestablishing a "pure" society. But even in this case this kind of solution can lead to extraordinary suffering for large parts of the population. And if this process has an unusual dimension, it can elicit powerful and possibly quite irrational reactions in neighboring countries. This was just the situation in the relationship between Soviet Russia and Germany after World War I. It is true that the Red terror was hardly worse than the White terror in terms of the number of victims. But it belonged to a fundamentally different dimension. When membership in a social class was declared to be cause for death; when Lenin demanded the purification of the Russian soil from the "dogs and swine of the dying bourgeois class"; when Zinovyev cold-bloodedly calculated the eradication of ten million people; when, according to widespread reports, the sailors of Sevastopol or Odessa shot everybody who had clean fingernails, then a greater sense of horror had to be expected than that caused by the mass executions carried out by the Whites. Despite the fact that there are, to my knowledge, still no thorough studies, one can still say that the terror during the civil war and the annihilation of the kulaks caused no particularly grave reactions in the distant and secure West, that is, in France, in England, and in the United States. But in the much closer Germany, a country that was being shaken by economic and spiritual crises, things were different. This despite the fact that the form the reactions were going to take was not predetermined.

The annihilation of social classes in Soviet-occupied Eastern Europe after 1945 generated for its part the mentality of the cold war in the West, but these events were often—and certainly not without reason—understood as the elimination of corrupt and backward-looking regimes and social conditions. It was Khrushchev's acknowledgment in 1956 of the Stalinist terror and its many millions of victims that marked the beginning of "détente." But the events in Indochina should have made clear what, in terms of annihilating classes, nationalities, and social groups, was the original and what was the copy. Those who do not wish to see Hitler's annihilation of the Jews in this connection are perhaps led by very noble motives, but they are falsifying history. In the legitimate search for direct causes, they overlook the chief preconditions, without which all other causes would have been ineffective. Auschwitz is not primarily a result of traditional anti-Semitism and was not just one more case of "genocide." It was the fear-borne reaction to the acts of annihilation that took place during the Russian Revolution. The German copy was many times more irrational than the original (it was simply a delusion that "the Jews" intended to annihilate the German bourgeoisie or even the German people), and it is difficult to accord such thoughts even a perverted ethos. The destruction of the Jews was more terrible than the original because it carried out the annihilation of humans in a quasi-industrial way. It was more repulsive than the original because it was caused by mere suppositions and was almost entirely free of the kind of mass hatred that would be capable of providing an element that would help us understand these acts. All this provides a foundation for the notion of singularity, but it fails to alter the fact that the so-called annihilation of the Jews by the Third Reich was a reaction or a distorted copy and not a first act or an original.

Seen this way, the following—and concluding—three postulates can be derived for future history-writing about the Third Reich:

1. The Third Reich should be removed from the historical isolation in which it remains even when it is treated within the framework of an epoch of fascism. It must be studied in the context of the disruptions, crises, fears, diagnoses, and therapies that were generated by the industrial revolution. Moreover, this period has to be examined in terms of its historical genesis and not merely by comparing it structurally with other totalitarian systems. The Nazi period must be seen in relation to the Russian Revolution, which was its most important precondition. The Nazi period's future-oriented character should be traced anew from the "liberation movements" to which it belonged; these movements in turn should also be shown to be connected to the peculiar "nationalizations" of the Communist world movement.

2. The instrumentalization to which the Third Reich owes a good part of its continuing fascination should be prevented. Those who criticize the Third Reich in order to strike at the Federal Republic, or even the capitalist system, must be shown to be the fools that they are. It is true that the liberal system is the root of fascism, because without the freedom of the individual and the resulting limitation of the power of the state, fascism cannot arise. But without this freedom and without these limitations there can be no criticism, no protest, no anarchism, and no socialism. Many critical things can be said about the Federal Republic, for example that the artistic and intellectual life of this successful economy consists chiefly of clownishness of an intricate or provocative kind. And one would be even more justified in adding that Western society has become much too complex and incomprehensible for such a thing as a sense of common purpose to be established via social classes. But one should also not overlook the fact that Hitler, in addition to hating the "Bolshevist chaos," hated no form of society as much as that which was being established in the Weimar Republic and which later found its fulfillment in the Federal Republic.

3. The demonization of the Third Reich is unacceptable. We may speak of demonization when the Third Reich is denied all humanity, a word that simply means that all that is human is finite and thus can neither be all good nor all bad, neither all light nor all dark. Thorough observation and penetrating comparisons will not eliminate the singularity of the Third Reich, but they will allow it to appear as a part of human history that not only concentrated traits of the past in an extreme form but that also anticipated aspects of the future. The Third Reich, too, must become an object of scholarship, of a scholarship that is not aloof from politics but that is also not merely a handmaiden of politics.

Without doubt, the Third Reich is cut from the cloth from which legends are made. And thus it becomes an even greater challenge for a society whose nature is incompatible with legends and historical myths because such a society allows scholarship, that is, constant revision.

But revision is not incompatible with lasting insight. From the history of the Third Reich we must achieve the insight that the lack of acts of annihilation aimed at social or biological groups is the greatest distinction of the society that we, despite that society's many weaknesses, call liberal. And revision must not become revisionism in the narrow sense, that is, an attempt, guided by declared or undeclared intentions, to ceaselessly reinterpret. Neither historical legends nor revisionism, but revision proceeding from changed historical situations should be, it seems to me, the postulate of a discipline that when viewing the Third Reich from the perspective of 1980, tries to free itself from the constraints imposed by the time in which we live and tries to become more than just individual or specialized research.

Publisher's Note: This text is based on a lecture the author gave at the Carl-Friedrich-Siemens-Stiftung in Munich. An abridged version appeared in *Frankfurter Allgemeine Zeitung*, July 24, 1980, under the title "Die negative Lebendigkeit des Dritten Reiches. Eine Frage aus dem Blickwinkel des Jahres 1980." A translation that was corrected by the author and revised by the editor appeared in H. W. Koch, ed., *Aspects of the Third Reich* (London, 1985), 17–38.

MICHAEL STÜRMER

History in a Land without History

In a country without memory anything is possible. The pollsters warn that among the industrialized countries the Federal Republic displays the greatest lack of communication between the generations, the smallest sense of self-confidence among its people, and the most thorough shift in values among these people. How will the Germans themselves see their country, the West, themselves tomorrow? One can assume that there will be continuity in the Germans' understanding of their country. But one cannot be certain.

Throughout the country one notes the rediscovery of history and finds that praiseworthy. Museums are booming, flea markets are alive with the nostalgia for olden times. Historical exhibitions have nothing to complain about in regard to interest and attention, and historical literature, peripheral for twenty years, is now being written and read again.

There are two possible explanations for this search for a lost time. One sees in this search a renewal of historical consciousness, a return to our cultural traditions, a promise of normalcy. The other reminds us that if we find no substance in the present we will turn our gaze to the past in order to find direction and assurance. Both explanations are relevant to the recent search for older history. A loss of orientation and a search for identity are closely related. But anyone who believes that this trend will have no effect on politics and the future is ignoring the fact that in a land without history, the future is controlled by those who determine the content of memory, who coin concepts and interpret the past.

It is doubtful whether this insecurity began in 1945. Hitler's rise stemmed from the crises and catastrophes of a secularized civilization that tumbled from new start to new start and whose main characteristic was a loss of orientation and a futile search for identity. "There is nothing that is not questionable," Karl Jaspers said in 1930 in a memorable Heidelberg lecture. From 1914 to 1945, the Germans were exposed to the cataracts of modernity to a degree that destroyed all tradition, making the unthinkable thinkable and barbarism a form of state. This is the reason Hitler was able to triumph; this is the reason he was able to capture and corrupt Prussia and patriotism, the state, and middle-class virtues.

But even before this epoch of wars and civil wars our history was a history of permanent upheaval. To lament the absence of revolution in our

16

history would be to little understand the agrarian revolution, the demographic revolution, the industrial revolution, the semirevolution of 1848, and the revolution from above that triumphed with Bismarck. A horizon of hope has presented itself anew to each generation of the past 200 years. German history can claim to have worn out a great number of constitutions, value systems, and images of the past and future.

For a long time the German dictatorship was the be-all and end-all of German history writing—and how could it have been otherwise? The more the Federal Republic gained distance from its beginnings, the more past epochs presented themselves to our view. Since 1973, when the price of oil shot up and *Tendenzwende* [conservative shift] became the name for a new consciousness, the Germans have been discovering that the Federal Republic and the world system of which it is part are subject to historical movement. Today, studying the history of the postwar system has become a part of political and historical studies.

That, however, has had the result that the achievement of Konrad Adenauer, the man who did everything to overcome our moral and political alienation from the West, has become clearer. At the same time the infamous Stalin note of 1952, which was intended to prevent just this reversal of alienation, is being portrayed as a myth about missed chances for unification, while the Russian tyrant is being portrayed as a Santa Claus who would grant the Germans' every wish: unity, freedom, prosperity, and security. In truth, what the Russians were offering was an early stage of a Soviet Germany. And amidst the ghosts of the past we are again becoming aware of antifascism: the legend of the noble intentions of the Communists, of the failure of the German Social Democrats, and of the blessing of a popular front. The fact that Kurt Schumacher's party recently—it was the fortieth anniversary of the German surrender—assigned itself the task of battling the social foundations of fascism in the Federal Republic betrays concealed thoughts about the future.

Nonetheless, when looking at the Germans and their relationship to their history, our neighbors are bound to pose the question: Where is this all leading? The Federal Republic has political and economic responsibility in the world. It is the centerpiece of European defense within the Atlantic system. But it is becoming evident that each generation living in Germany today has differing, even opposing, views of the past and the future. It is also becoming evident that the technocratic underestimation of history by the political Right and the progressive strangulation of history by the Left is seriously damaging the political culture of the country. The search for a lost past is not an abstract striving for culture and education. It is morally legitimate and politically necessary. We are dealing with the inner continuity of the German republic and its predictability in foreign policy terms. In a country without memory anything is possible.

Source: *Frankfurter Allgemeine Zeitung*, April 25, 1986

ERNST NOLTE

The Past That Will Not Pass: A Speech That Could Be Written but Not Delivered

The "past that will not pass" can only mean the National-Socialist past of the Germans or of Germany. The theme implies the notion that normally the past passes and that thus this nonpassing must be something exceptional. Still, in normally passing, the past cannot be seen as disappearing. The age of Napoleon I, for example, is repeatedly made present in historical studies. The same is true for the age of Augustus. But these pasts have apparently lost the vividness that they had for their contemporaries. For this reason they can be left to the historians. The National-Socialist past, however, appears not to be subject to this process of attenuation, as Hermann Lübbe recently pointed out. It seems to be becoming more vital and more powerful—not as a representative model but as a bugaboo, as a past that is in the process of establishing itself in the present or that is suspended above the present like an executioner's sword.

BLACK AND WHITE IMAGES

There are good reasons for this. The more unequivocally the Federal Republic and Western nations in general develop toward social-welfare societies, the more disturbing becomes the image of the Third Reich with its ideology of warlike self-sacrifice; its maxim of "canons instead of butter"; and the Edda quotations, such as "Our Death Will Be a Festive One," loudly chanted at school celebrations. All people today are pacifists by conviction, but they cannot look back from a safe distance upon the bellicosity of the Third Reich because they know that year in and year out both superpowers spend far more for their arms than Hitler spent from 1933 to 1939. Thus a deep-seated insecurity remains. We prefer to confront our enemies from a position of certainty rather than from the confusion of the present.

Much the same can be said for feminism: In National Socialism, the "mania of masculinity" was still full of provocative self-confidence. In the present, however, this masculinity tends to efface itself and go underground. Thus National Socialism is the present enemy. Hitler's claim of "world domination" appears to us to be all the more horrifying as it becomes the more evident that in world politics today, the Federal Republic can at maximum play a moderately important role. Still, harmlessness is not attributed to this country, and in many places the fear is still alive that while the Federal Republic could not be the cause, it could be the place where a third world war begins. More than anything else, however, memories of the Final Solution have contributed to the inability of the past to pass. The monstrousness of the factory-scale annihilation of several million humans appears to us to be all the more incomprehensible since the Federal Republic has joined the vanguard of humanitarian nations. But doubts have remained even here, and numerous foreigners have been as unlikely as the Germans to believe in the identity of *pays legal* and *pays réel*.

But has it only been the stubbornness of the *pays réel* of normal, everyday Germans who have set themselves against this nonpassing of the past and have wanted a line to be drawn so that the German past might be seen as not essentially different from other pasts?

Is there not a core of truth in many of these questions and arguments that in a sense erect a wall against the desire to ceaselessly deal with National Socialism? I am offering some of these arguments and questions in order to conceptualize this "failing," which, in my opinion, is the decisive one, and to outline this process of "coming to grips with the past," which has little to do with the much-evoked desire to finally draw a line under the German past.

It is especially those people who most frequently and most negatively speak of "interests" who fail to allow the question whether with this nonpassing of the past interests are also at play, for example, the interests of a new generation in the age-old struggle against "the fathers"—or interests of the persecuted and their heirs in having a permanent special status and the privileges that go with it.

The talk about "the guilt of the Germans" all too blithely overlooks the similarity to the talk about "the guilt of the Jews," which was a main argument of the National Socialists. All accusations of guilt that come from Germans are dishonest since the accusers fail to include themselves or the group they represent and in essence simply desire to administer the coup de grace to their old enemies.

All the attention devoted to the Final Solution simply diverts our attention from important facts about the National-Socialist period—such as the euthanasia program and the treatment of Russian prisoners of war. More important, however, it diverts attention away from pressing questions of the present—for example, the question of "unborn life" or the presence of genocide yesterday in Vietnam and today in Afghanistan.

A rash pronouncement by a member of the Bundestag about certain demands by spokesmen of Jewish organizations or the slip into tastelessness of a municipal politician are blown-up symptoms of "anti-Semitism," as if all memory of the genuine and by no means exclusively National-Socialist anti-Semitism of the Weimar period had disappeared. And at the same time the television broadcast *Shoah*, the moving documentary film by a Jewish director, in several places makes it seem plausible that the SS troops in the concentration camps might themselves have been victims of a sort and that among the Polish victims of National Socialism there was virulent anti-Semitism.

The visit of the U.S. president to the military cemetery in Bitburg was the cause of a very emotional discussion. The fear of being accused of settling old scores, and in fact of any comparisons at all, prevented the simple question of what it would have meant if in 1953 the chancellor of the Federal Republic had refused to visit the national cemetery in Arlington, arguing that men were buried there who had participated in terror attacks on the German civilian population.

For the historian the most regrettable result of the nonpassing of the past is that the simplest rules that are in effect for every past appear to be suspended: Every past is knowable in its complexity; the connectedness in which the past is interwoven should be made more visible; black-and-white images of politically involved contemporaries should be correctable; earlier histories should be subject to revision.

But in the case of the Third Reich, this rule seems to be "dangerous for the people": Could it not lead to a vindication of Hitler or at least to exculpation of the Germans? Might it not allow for the possibility that the Germans could again identify with the Third Reich, as the great majority did between 1935 and 1939, and that they might fail to learn the lesson imposed upon them by history?

These questions can be answered briefly and apodictically: No German can desire to justify Hitler, even if only because of his March 1945 order to annihilate the German people. Historians and journalists cannot guarantee that the Germans will learn lessons from history—but that is guaranteed by the total shift in the relationships of power and by the obvious and evident results of two great defeats. The Germans can of course still learn false lessons, but only in one way, a way that would be novel and "anti-Fascist."

It is true that there has been no shortage of efforts to transcend the level of polemic and to draw a more objective picture of the Third Reich and its führer. It will suffice to mention the names of Joachim Fest and Sebastian Haffner. Both focused on the domestic German situation, however. I would like to attempt, using a few questions and key words, to suggest the perspective in which this past should be viewed if it is to be treated with the equality that is a principal postulate of philosophy and of any historical scholarship that desires to highlight differences.

SHEDDING LIGHT WITH KEY CONCEPTS

Max Erwin von Scheubner-Richter, who later was to be one of Hitler's closest associates and who in 1923 during the march to the *Feldherrenhalle* in Munich was felled by a bullet, was a German consul in Erzerum. There he was witness to the deportations of the Armenian population, which represented the beginnings of the first great act of genocide in the twentieth century. He spared no effort to try to hinder the Turkish officials, and in 1938 his biographer concludes his description of these events: "But what were these few people against the Turk's will to annihilate, against people who closed their ears even to the most direct reproaches from Berlin. What could they do against the wolflike savagery of the Kurds who were loosed upon the Armenians, against this horrendous catastrophe in which one people of Asia was settling scores with the other one in an Asiatic way, far from European civilization?"

No one knows what Scheubner-Richter would have done if he, instead of Alfred Rosenberg, had been made minister for the occupied *Ostgebiete* [Nazi-occupied eastern territories]. But little speaks for the idea that there was a fundamental difference between Scheubner-Richter and Rosenberg and Himmler, or even between Scheubner-Richter and Hitler. But then one must ask: What could bring men who had experienced the act of genocide as "Asiatic" to initiate an act of genocide of an even more brutal nature? There are a few concepts that can shed light on this situation. One of them is the following:

When Hitler received news of the capitulation of the 6th Army in Stalingrad on February 1, 1943, he predicted in his briefing that several of the captured officers would become involved in Soviet propaganda: "You have to imagine, he (an officer like this) comes to Moscow, and imagine the 'rat cage.' He'd sign anything. He will make confessions, proclamations."

Commentators offer the explanation that "rat cage" meant Lubjanka. I think that is wrong.

In George Orwell's *1984* there is a description of how the hero, Winston Smith, after long abuse is finally forced by Big Brother's secret police to deny his fiancée and thus to renounce his humanity. They place a cage containing a half-starved rat in front of his head. The interrogator threatens to open the door, and at that point Winston Smith collapses. Orwell did not invent this story. It can be found in numerous places in anti-Bolshevist literature about the Russian Civil War, among other places in the writing of the usually reliable socialist Melgunov. It is attributed to the "Chinese Cheka."

GULAG ARCHIPELAGO AND AUSCHWITZ

It is a notable shortcoming that the literature about National Socialism does not know or does not want to admit to what degree all the deeds—

with the sole exception of the technical process of gassing—that the National Socialists later committed had already been described in the voluminous literature of the 1920s: mass deportations and executions, torture, death camps, the extermination of entire groups using strictly objective selection criteria, and public demands for the annihilation of millions of guiltless people who were thought to be "enemies."

It is likely that many of these reports were exaggerated. It is certain that the "White terror" also committed terrible deeds, even though its program contained no analogy to the "extermination of the bourgeoisie." Nonetheless, the following question must seem permissible, even unavoidable: Did the National Socialists or Hitler perhaps commit an "Asiatic" deed merely because they and their ilk considered themselves to be potential victims of an "Asiatic" deed? Was the Gulag Archipelago not primary to Auschwitz? Was the Bolshevik murder of an entire class not the logical and factual prius of the "racial murder" of National Socialism? Cannot Hitler's most secret deeds be explained by the fact that he had *not* forgotten the rat cage? Did Auschwitz in its root causes not originate in a past that would not pass?

One does not have to have read Melgunov's now-vanished book to ask such questions. But one fears to pose them. I have long feared to pose them. They are seen as bellicose anti-Communist slogans or as products of the cold war. They also do not quite fit into the discipline of history, which is often forced to choose narrower questions. But these questions rest on simple truths. To intentionally ignore truths may have moral reasons, but it also violates the ethos of the discipline.

This ethos would be violated if historians were to stop at such facts and questions and not seek to place them in a greater context—such as the qualitative ruptures in European history that begin with the industrial revolution and that have always inspired an agitated search for the "guilty parties" or for the "originator" of what is seen as a threatening development. Only in this framework can it become clear that despite all similarities the acts of biological annihilation carried out by the National Socialists were qualitatively different than the social annihilation that Bolshevism undertook. No one murder, and especially not a mass murder, can "justify" another, and we will be led astray by an attitude that points only to the *one* murder and to the *one* mass murder and ignores the other, even though a causal nexus is probable.

Those who desire to envision history not as a mythologem but rather in its essential context are forced to a central conclusion: If history, in all its darkness and its horrors, but also in its confusing novelty, is to have a meaning for coming generations, this meaning must be the liberation from collectivist thinking. That should also mean the decisive turn to a liberal and democratic political order that allows and even encourages criticism insofar as it takes aim at acts, ways of thinking, and traditions, and thus also at governments and organizations of all kinds. Organizations and governments, however, are obliged to stigmatize criticism of existing states of affairs as impermissible. Individuals can free themselves from these stigmas only with great difficulty. This means criticism of "the" Jews, "the" Russians, "the" Germans, or "the" petit-bourgeoisie. To the degree that the debate about National Socialism is characterized by this kind of collectivist thinking, one should draw a line. It cannot be denied that if this happens, thoughtlessness and self-satisfaction will have a heyday. But it *does not have to be* that way, and truth does not have to be made dependent upon utility. A more comprehensive debate, one that would have to mostly consist of thinking about the history of the past two centuries, might cause the past about which we are talking here to pass—as is suitable for every past. And this kind of a debate would also appropriate the past, making it our own.

Source: *Frankfurter Allgemeine Zeitung*, June 6, 1986

Author's Note: The title for this speech suggested by the Römerberg Talks (a conference) was "The Past That Will Not Pass: To Debate or to Draw the Line?"

CHRISTIAN MEIER

Condemning and Comprehending

A TURNING POINT IN THE RECOLLECTION OF GERMAN HISTORY

Among the three nations into which Hitler's Reich was divided, only the citizens of the Federal Republic have troubled themselves to any degree about the mass murder of more than five million Jews in the Second World War. There are, I assume, three reasons for that: The Federal Republic accepted the legal succession of the Third Reich. The only way the country could again achieve a respected place among nations included reparations and a lot of hard thinking. Finally, the repudiation of everything that Germany did between 1933 and 1945 provided the foundation for the fledgling democracy. The responsibility that is a part of freedom and that is a special experience when freedom is new was not possible without Germany taking possession of its past. Thus the memory of German crimes is deeply embedded in the foundations of the Federal Republic.

If all that is true, then we must draw a remarkable conclusion: A relatively strong historical consciousness is inherent in the West German identity—an identity that has entered our self-comprehension and our imagination and that expresses itself in grief and shame. It also finds expression in perplexity, obsessions, and compensations, that is, in forms that all can be interpreted as symptoms of one and the same condition: a by-and-large unreflected memory of our history as a part of our shared identity.

It is precisely from the strength and virulence of this memory that all the difficulties in our relationship to our history arise. These twelve years have cut us off from past times. They form a no-man's-land in our history. In 1964 Wolf Jobst Siedler noted a numbed insensitivity in the Germans. He was surprised by the robustness with which people, even after Auschwitz, dared to speak of injustice against Germany while at the same time seeing the Federal Republic, even after Yalta and Potsdam, as a "Weimar reborn under fortunate circumstances"—as if there were not an endless amount to grieve about there, too. Not much changed until 1986—except that this no-man's-land today appears to be much more powerful, and the entire complex is still being mentally processed.

In essence, this has to do with the crimes committed against the Jews. Other people, as much as they had to suffer under us, are of secondary importance compared to what was done to the Jews. And the second

24

problem in our relationship to our history as it applies to the division of Germany is only a problem because in the Federal Republic the years between 1933 and 1945 lie between us and our history. Otherwise, the division of the nation would offer us a challenge to maintain an intense consciousness of history that would be able to support a notion of what we have in common. But that has only been partially successful here—unlike in the GDR, which has increasingly reflected on German history.

Whether and how we can recognize what we caused between 1933 and 1945 continues to be an open question. It is a matter of clearly understanding exactly what happened back then and determining who was responsible for these deeds: Were we, the German people, the ones, or was it only our parents and grandparents (who in the meantime are either dead or on the threshold of death), or was it the German bourgeoisie (or more likely, petit-bourgeoisie), or "fascism"? Or was it only a few criminals among us (in an entire nation that retained its "decency")? Or just Hitler?

WORLD HISTORY IS DIFFERENT TODAY

The question of what happened in those twelve years does not pertain only to this or that accumulation of injustice and crime. Such things have always happened in world history. Nor does it pertain only to recognizing the criminal character of the National-Socialist regime. Rather, the question of singularity is at issue. That a country, a people represented by a government, could arrogate to itself the decision whether an entire people (whose membership it arbitrarily determined) would be permitted to live on earth or not!—a people, incidentally, who have never been hostile to the Germans, who, on the contrary, in many ways established a relationship of love; a people who with few exceptions did not even defend themselves, whose members, in the words of a witness, "went to death like marionettes"; whose annihilation was planned and administrated using methods that are usually reserved for vermin — there are no parallels for this. This was a totally new kind of crime against humanity.

It is apparently incredibly difficult to recognize this singularity of German crimes. Much can be said about it; facts can be isolated and examined. But we tend to sidestep the question of singularity if there is any way to get around it. We like to take refuge in lists of crimes committed against us. But just the fact that such immense crimes were possible (and thus still are possible) has changed world history. Because of this and because of the Second World War, we have dragged our victims, indeed we have dragged the world, into our history. Thus we cannot remember our fallen soldiers in a national memorial cemetery without also dedicating a memorial to those we fought, oppressed, and murdered.

But because forty years have passed since the end of the war, a new set of problems joins the old ones. The great majority of Germans alive today were not involved in the crimes of the Nazi period. This also includes people whose children are today coming of age. Moreover, we are re-spected, we live in a fairly stable democracy, and we endeavor (with some success) to be a normal people.

Then should we not, must we not, put an end to the accusations and "self-indictment" (as it is often put) because of the years 1933 to 1945? Do we have to say such things about ourselves, do we have to listen to them time and time again? And should we have to take that from countries that have since done things that were called war crimes when we did them? Should we allow ourselves to be restricted to the extent that, for example, plays with a strong anti-Semitic content cannot be played in our theaters? Should we not—and especially the young ones among us—be permitted to "be proud of our country"? The SPD introduced this slogan, accompanied by a portrait of Willy Brandt, to the election campaign of 1972. The question becomes all the more pressing the longer it takes to answer. In 1983 the parliamentary leader of the CDU declared that the Germans should finally "step out of Hitler's shadow."

Much speaks for this new way of seeing things. But we will not be released from our responsibility. Time and time again there will be occasions when recollections of the Holocaust come up. Time and time again we will experience a deep sense of horror in young people who can scarcely comprehend the crimes of the Nazi regime. What happened back then must never be forgotten, at least not in the time spans that people alive today can think in. Thus we are constantly faced with the presence of these memories and with a sense of horror about them. Responsibility requires us to accept this history as our own. But our consciousness of the crimes blocks our access to our history.

That is the lesson of our many attempts to escape this memory. At first we experienced a sense of resistance and denial when the victors blamed our own government, our own nation, for those atrocities. At that point the rapidly spreading doubts about the Nazi regime did not extend to the atrocities committed by the regime; instead one focused on the regime's mistakes. The doubts failed to challenge the roles that most of the people actually played in the system, exempting the government, the *Wehrmacht*, the nation, the church, the economy, middle-class decency, German vir-tues. People made incredible sacrifices for these institutions, and so it was unthinkable that they were just wrong. People who were neither partici-pants in the Nazi regime nor victims of the regime and who in the early postwar days took over many political functions were able to spread a sense of good conscience.

Later, all that had existed until 1945, minus anything that could be split off as National Socialist, was carried over into the new democracy. Then began a remarkable and, as Hermann Lübbe has convincingly shown, necessary process of integration during which few questions were asked about what one had been, thought, or done before 1945. Soon the nation had a new unity in anticommunism. That was quickly transformed to the antitotalitarianism that allowed people to understand communism and the Nazi regime as being equally reprehensible.

The first disturbance of this widespread process of psychological repression of the past took place around 1960. It was caused by the publication of Hochhuth's [play] *The Deputy* and other related works. Soon after the Eichmann trial in Jerusalem, a series of court cases captured public attention. In 1964–1965 the Frankfurt trial against "Mulka and others," the Auschwitz trial, took place. It had a powerful effect on the population. This caused the first widespread expressions of shock. At the same time people began to have a closer look at the Nazi past of judges, professors, economists, and others.

The student movement of 1968 followed. Its German variant was especially motivated by a sense of shock about National Socialism, which, however, was soon instrumentalized to cast doubt on German and middle-class ways of thinking and life-styles and on the social order in general. And thus the student movement set off on another escape from this past—only this time it was an escape into wishes for a better future or into the moral rigorism that later set such a precedent. It became common practice to use the secure footing of the present to criticize the deeds of one's parents and grandparents. In this situation every soldier found himself forced to justify why he did what he did. If the totalitarianism thesis ducked the singularity of Nazi crimes by equating Nazi Germany with the Stalinist Soviet Union, then fascism theory had a quite similar effect in that it allowed people to understand Nazism as one in a series of other Fascist or even capitalist states to which it was opposed. A remarkable trivialization!

Still, it is notable that there is much grief, sorrow, and shame about the crimes we committed between 1933 and 1945. Nonetheless, repression in the form of generalization or of escape mechanisms continue to assist us in our efforts to deny the singularity of the crimes. A well-developed consciousness of the atrocities committed by the regime has in many cases served to assign these deeds to groups to which one does not belong. We have not yet really taken ownership of our history.

We are still experiencing the psychological repression of our history. The only difference is that today we achieve this same effect under a different banner. This is an attempt to normalize our relationship to our own history. There is no doubt: We should have a more conscious, orderly relationship to our history. That would make it possible for us to see this history with the eyes of identity. Seeing history this way is important for a number of reasons, not the least of which is that the link of a society to its reality depends upon it. There are, roughly, two ways to measure actions: historical experience or a role model and the demands of a general, or in extreme cases, rigorous, morality. Compromises are a part of everyday life. But compromises are regularly achieved in a field of tension between the demands of morality and of ethical conviction. In these cases it is important that one learn about life from what is closest and most intimate, that is, from one's own parents and grandparents—not by ignoring general morality but in a way that makes it possible for us to navigate through life.

But if we condemn the life-style of entire generations, such as has been happening to a great extent in the Federal Republic, then demands for rigorous morality in politics are able to gain ground. And disappointment is often the result. One can judge this in various ways, but there is good reason to believe that this process is accompanied by a loss of reality, which also has its political consequences.

All reflection on history should begin by our determining that no attempt is made to deny or ignore what has really happened. Knowledge of the singularity of the crimes we committed in those twelve years must be an important part of the historical consciousness of the Germans—if for no other reason than the fact that otherwise we would never be able to understand why the crimes of the Nazi period are measured with a different yardstick than is used to judge the unpleasant parts of the history of other peoples, whose crimes at some point are expiated so that tact prevents us from publicly reminding them about these deeds.

We will thus never again have an unbiased relationship with our past. It does not help when a chancellor, referring to the "blessing of a late birth," again plays fast and loose with our history—for which conservatives should have a strong consciousness. The long discussions about the question of how we should treat May 8, 1985, but also the Faßbinder debate and the debate about the change in the penal code (which again advanced the notion that we can draw a line through the recent past) have shown all too clearly that we are far from being out of Hitler's shadow. And the Bitburg affair has clearly demonstrated that everything will just get worse if we simply steer a course toward historical normalcy.

LEARNING TO BEAR THE TRUTH

The less there is such a thing as collective guilt, the more we have to accept responsibility for all that we caused and that was done in our name if we are to take possession of German history. Because that is so, even the younger people among us must keep the memory of these crimes alive. We owe the victims that much. Guilt will begin at the point where we fail to do that. And if we in any way seek to relativize the Nazi period or fail to clearly condemn all that happened, then every attempt to establish a new relationship to our history will be built on sand.

This clarity is, incidentally, particularly necessary because there is a close connection between the way we deal with this part of our history and the way we are received in various parts of the world. If we remember better, we make it easier for others to treat us with indulgence. Those who resent certain accusations, such as could be heard on the occasion of

Bitburg in the U.S. media, should not attempt to provoke such accusations by attempting to demonstrate how historically healthy they are.

We are about to attempt to place ourselves in a better relationship with our history, in a certain sense relying on the hope that that will not be made too difficult for us. But it is reasonable that we expect to live with this history. Without wanting to compare incomparable things, we should also be able to say that it is difficult to be one of the descendants of the perpetrators of the Holocaust. Thus it should be easy to develop an understanding of the problems that we have with our history. But that will only happen if we spare no effort. This process of understanding and communication, especially with the younger generations of Jews, seems to me to be extraordinarily important. If it does not succeed, then there is danger of positions being hardened anew. But there is also the danger that too many accusations might cause powerful defensive reactions that are not far from anti-Semitism.

One has to keep in mind that with the decades since 1945 a deep transformation has taken place in the temporal perspective with which we view the Nazi crimes. The rigor of some verdicts may have been reduced over this time. At the same time the occurrences that took place in those years tend to appear greater and more incomprehensible. In other words, they tend to increasingly appear to us as aspects of potentiality rather than aspects of reality. At first, right after the war when the generations of those directly involved set the tone for public life, one was almost directly confronted with the original sense of outrage. There were accusations and defensive reactions, there was a sense of shock and attempts to repress the reality of what happened. The entire horror and cruelty of war and persecution were present. It was clear to those who knew, not to mention those who hated, how unique *Einsatzkommandos*, concentration camps, and gassings were. But many things that today seem monstrous to us in peaceful Europe were not so unusual back then.

Today we live in a world that all in all is only a little better than that world. It is a world in which peace prevails, at least in Europe; and in the West, at least, we have the rule of law and a minimum of state encroachment upon our personal freedoms—not to mention the fact that there is little material want. Now, looking back from a distance of forty years, we are perplexed by how war could have been possible, the shooting, the threats, the swift condemnation of people. Today, we are deeply troubled by the possibility of totalitarianism. Not only the crimes themselves but all the surrounding circumstances appear to us to be barely comprehensible: the secrecy, the precise obedience of orders, the eagerness to serve, the open inhumanity, the manifestations of violence, and the readiness to accept them.

At the same time democracy, with its demands of responsibility from all people, has a much stronger effect. Knowing this, we are tempted to supplant the old view, according to which a small number of people gave the orders while others obeyed, by trying to find out about the large number of people who created the conditions of Nazism and who patiently went along with it, the people who actually committed such acts.

Thus it is a pressing need today to leave no stone unturned in trying to understand what can be understood in the acts of our parents and grandparents. We have to confront our past not only with condemnation but also with understanding. If the younger people, the future generations, are to achieve access to the German history between 1933 and 1945 and to German history in general, then we cannot simply blanket-condemn everything. But it is important not only to get closer to the truth of what happened; the process of recognizing the facts must be made bearable for generations who will soon have grandparents that were not involved in these deeds.

Today we know—or at least we could and should know—that participation in these crimes was widespread. Behind those in power and the administrators of the machinery of murder, not to mention the concentration camp guards, were the police that rounded up the victims, the railroaders who transported them. In front of them was the *Wehrmacht* that was defending the fronts behind which the machinery of destruction was able to function. There were soldiers, many of whom became witnesses of mass executions and of deportations, without resisting, without drawing practical conclusions. "If that is true" (what he had heard about the mass shootings of Jews), a young officer said back then, "then we should not win the war." But he continued to fight, as he considered it his duty, for his country, with his comrades in arms whom he did not want to betray. And how many went along and in that way built up a broader circle of accomplices in the criminal acts, people who allowed and passively watched the shooting of prisoners, to take one example. Doubtless, a perfected apparatus of oppression. But how much readiness to go along or at least human weakness was needed to facilitate the work of this apparatus! In the process of reciprocal encouragement of injustice, teachers and parents, supporters as well as opponents of the regime, were able to contribute some part—even little boys who were members of the Hitler Youth and who in 1945 were no older than the present chancellor. Even publicly singing bloody anti-Semitic songs, as was not unusual back then, meant contributing to the system. And so it really was the Germans (and German Jews among them as well as numerous non-Germans) who kept the regime running and who were directly or indirectly involved in its crimes.

Because this is true, the regime had a different character than the people who lived under it. The acts of the majority of Germans of that time, people who did not incur guilt by participating in crimes, can only be understood within a framework of a whole they were a part of and to which they contributed.

BETRAYING ONE'S COUNTRY BECAUSE OF THE REGIME?

Germans were able to discern all kinds of injustice caused by the Nazi regime, but that was no proof that they knew about the gigantic, unique crimes their country was in the process of committing. If one could have predicted the Holocaust to them, they would hardly have considered it possible—and not only because they were mostly unpolitical and had been raised with great respect for the state.

Many were caught up in the successes of and were seduced by a fascination with the regime—all this against a backdrop of the unemployment and hopelessness of the years before. People who were of the right age tried to climb socially, to take advantage of their opportunities. No doubt, that was accompanied by the need to conform. And this brought the need to make concessions and to ignore the facts, a process that was voluntary but that also came about under pressure or because of the opinion, shared by most people of that time, that one was defenseless against the regime. Certainly there are questions to be asked in retrospect. Certainly we can criticize or condemn many weaknesses and acts of shabbiness. We can also criticize the many cases where people acted as if they were committed to the regime so that they would not lose their positions. The same applies to examples of people failing to offer assistance. But does this justify us in considering the actions of most Germans—with the exception of those who committed crimes—to be something unusual?

Harmless statements could have deadly consequences; anger at parents or colleagues, if given free reign in the wrong circumstances, could lead to denunciation. The borders between permissible and damnable were, even in light of the possible consequences, often not recognizable. Ambition, eagerness, pomposity were subject to great temptations in a people so oriented toward orderliness and duty. Thus extreme demands were placed upon reason, self-control, self-denial, and upon the ability to make independent decisions.

One can hardly hold it against the Germans that they carried out their duties punctually, properly, and competently, or that they risked their lives. How and why should they leave their country in the lurch because of the regime? In this sense they acted no differently—and thus presumably no worse—than their opponents. It is just that the number of people who were prepared to command others or to be commanded to perform obviously unjust deeds was much greater on the German side than in other armies. And that the regime, motivated by its racial dogmas, encouraged not only grand crimes but also smaller acts of unlawfulness, which were possible because ethical norms had been shaken or weaked.

If one considers the still very large number of people who were not involved in greater or smaller crimes and who in their own realm lived and let live, one must conclude time and time again that they participated in the events in the Germany of the time in a way that really does not demand reproach but often even demands our respect. This despite the fact that at times it was completely inappropriate to the situation and in sum contributed to crimes of incomprehensible measure.

ORDINARY MORALS IN AN EXTRAORDINARY TIME

It is just this fact that makes the period incomprehensible—the point at which the older people, by today's standards, failed. Normal actions by normal people were suddenly thrust into a greater context, of which the people were hardly aware. This was a context that they could not comprehend as a totality and in which there was little they could do to change things. Totalitarian regimes are characterized by the fact that they demand and utilize actions and intentions to an incredible extent.

It is probably only possible to withdraw from this process by joining the opposition or at least by engaging in sabotage or resistance. Even then it is difficult to determine whether one, by taking the measures necessary to seem normal, does not contribute more to the regime than one can harm it through resistance. And how can we require such dangerous behavior from the majority?

Because under a regime such as this one, correct and even exemplary actions in one's limited circle are completely inappropriate in a larger context. When must a locomotive engineer seriously ask himself what freight he is carrying and why? At what point does a soldier have to ask himself what kind of a regime he is serving? At what point can one person or another incur culpability by doing more or less what all people are prepared to do? At what point does a symphony conductor deserve reproach for practicing his art wonderfully and providing pleasure for many people in a dark age—but also by lending an unjust regime an aura of cultural glamor? At what point can one say of an entire generation that they should not have availed themselves of their professional and occupational opportunities since that necessarily caused them to come into close contact with the ruling elite?

What would we who are alive today have done in similar situations? Only if we were certain that under the conditions existing in the Nazi period and with the knowledge people had then (of course excluding those who committed the crimes), we would have done better—only then could we condemn the Germans of the period. We presumably do not have to be ashamed of our parents and grandparents. But we can probably also not use them as role models. We all also have cause to ask if we could have done it better—especially because we know today what a totalitarian regime is and how one comes to power. Still, there is no reason for us, in our much more fortunate situation, to play ourselves up as pharisees.

How is it possible to understand the majority of parents and grandparents and not condemn them but also make sure that people remain conscious of the nation's responsibility? How is it possible to be like others—a problem that is all the more acute the younger one is—and yet also to be the children of the perpetrators of the Holocaust? We still have a lot of work to do on this. And this task cannot be delegated to scholarship. We will need new categories—not only for reason but also for the heart. Perhaps the events of that time should be told in more and finer detail and in direct reference to this or that event, as Vassily Grossman did for the Soviet Union of the time of Stalingrad in his *Leben und Schicksal* [Life and Fate]. But if we do not take these events upon ourselves, if we think we can simply draw a line under them, then they will come back to haunt us in a worse way. And then we also will fail to gain the steadfastness that we might need to face exacting demands that may some day be placed upon us.

Source: *Frankfurter Allgemeine Zeitung*, June 28, 1986

Author's Note: This is an abbreviated version of a speech given on January 8, 1986, at the University of Tel Aviv.

JÜRGEN HABERMAS

A Kind of Settlement of Damages: The Apologetic Tendencies in German History Writing

> It is a notable shortcoming that the literature about National Socialism does not know or does not want to admit to what degree all the deeds—with the sole exception of the technical process of gassing—that the National Socialists later committed had already been described in the voluminous literature of the 1920s. . . . Did the National Socialists or Hitler perhaps commit an "Asiatic" deed merely because they and their ilk considered themselves to be potential victims of an "Asiatic" deed?
>
> Ernst Nolte, in the
> *Frankfurter Allgemeine Zeitung*, June 6, 1986

I

The Erlangen historian Michael Stürmer argues for a functional interpretation of historical consciousness: "In a land without history, the future is controlled by those who determine the content of memory, who coin concepts and interpret the past." In keeping with Joachim Ritter's neoconservative image of the world, which was updated by his students in the 1970s, Stürmer envisions the processes of modernization as a kind of unavoidable settlement of damages. This settlement occurs because the individual must be compensated for the inevitable alienation that as a "social molecule" he experiences in material industrial society. In keeping with the molecule metaphor, Stürmer is less interested in the identity of the individual than in the integration of the community. Pluralism in values and interests leads, "when it can no longer find common ground, sooner or later to civil war." What is needed, according to Stürmer, is "a social mechanism for endowing higher meaning, something that, after religion, only nation and patriotism have been capable of." A politically responsible discipline of history will heed the call to activate such a mechanism and produce and disseminate a historical image that can foster a national consensus. The discipline of history is "propelled by collective, for the most part unconscious, drives toward the inner endowment of higher

34

meaning, but it must"—and this is what Stürmer sees as a real dilemma— "work this out according to scholarly methods." In this view, the discipline sets out to "find the balance between endowing higher meaning and demythologizing."

Let us first observe the Cologne historian Andreas Hillgruber as he walks this tightrope. I feel confident in approaching the most recent study of this renowned historian, even though I have no special competence in the field, since the investigation evidently is addressed to laymen. Hillgruber's study was recently released in a deluxe edition by Siedler Verlag with the title *Zweierlei Untergang* [Twofold Fall]. I will record the observations of a patient subjected to a revisionist operation on his historical consciousness.

In the first part of his study Hillgruber describes the collapse of the German eastern front during the last year of the war, 1944–1945. In the first pages he mentions the "problem of identification." With which side in the conflict should the author identify? Four possible perspectives suggest themselves. He dismisses the position taken by the would-be assassins of Hitler on July 20, 1944, as merely "preferentially ethical" and therefore inferior to the "responsibly ethical" position of the local commanders, state officials, and mayors. This leaves three perspectives for consideration. Hillgruber dismisses Hitler's perspective of perseverance and survival as social Darwinism. Nor does an identification with the victors seem possible; such a perspective of liberation would only be appropriate for the victims of the concentration camps, he claims, and not for the German nation as a whole. The historian has just one choice: "He must identify with the concrete fate of the German population in the East and with the desperate and sacrificial efforts of the German army in the eastern theater and of the German navy in the Baltic. The military forces in the East were trying to protect the German population in the East from the orgies of revenge by the Red Army, the mass rapes, the random murders, and the forced deportation, and . . . to hold open the escape route to the West."

Perplexed, one wonders why a historian in 1986 has to block out a retrospective point of view from the distance of forty years, in other words, his own perspective, a standpoint from which he cannot remove himself anyway. Additionally, his own real-time perspective offers hermeneutical advantages. It sets in relation the selective perceptions of the parties involved; it weighs them against one another and completes them from the perspective of knowledge acquired since then. Hillgruber does not want to write his presentation from this, dare one say "normal" standpoint, because, as he claims, then questions of "morality in wars of annihilation" would come into play. And they are to be ruled out. Here Hillgruber brings to mind the remark by Norbert Blüm. Blüm argued that the actions of annihilation in the camps could in fact continue only as long as the German eastern front held. This fact ought to cast a long shadow on the "picture of horror of raped and murdered women and children" that presented itself to the German soldiers who retook Nemmersdorf, for example. Hillgruber wants to present what happened in eastern Germany from the view of the brave soldiers, the desperate civilian population, also the "tried and true" higher-ups of the Nazi party (NSDAP); he wants to set himself inside the experiences of the fighters of yesteryear, at a point when they are not yet compromised and depreciated by our retrospective knowledge. This intention explains the principle behind his dividing the study into two parts: "Collapse in the East" and "Annihilation of the Jews." These are two processes that Hillgruber precisely does *not*, despite the announcement on the dust jacket, want to show "in their gloomy interweaving."

II

After completing this operation in the first part of his study, which evidently is the kind of history that Stürmer would call the endowing of higher meaning, Hillgruber does not hesitate in the second part of his study to make use of the knowledge of the latter-day historians in order to prove a different thesis. In the foreword he introduces the notion that the expulsion of the Germans from the East is in no way to be understood as a "response" by the Allies to the crimes in the concentration camps. By reference to the Allied war aims he argues that "at no point was there ever a prospect, once Germany was defeated, of preserving the greater part of the Prussian-German eastern provinces." He explains the lack of interest on the part of the Western powers in preserving the eastern provinces by referring to a "cliché-image of Prussia" that conditioned the thinking of Allied policymakers. It does not occur to Hillgruber that the structure of power in the Reich could actually have had something to do, as the Allies assumed, with the social structure especially well preserved in Prussia. He makes no use of social-scientific information. Otherwise he could hardly have attributed the transgressions of the Red Army, for example, which occurred not only in Germany but also before that in Poland, Rumania, and Hungary, to the barbaric "notions of war" of the Stalinist period. Be that as it may, the Western powers were blinded by their illusorily perceived war aim, the destruction of Prussia. Only too late did they recognize how "all Europe," through the march forward of the Russians, would become "the loser of the catastrophe of 1945."

By setting the stage in this way, then, Hillgruber can push the "struggle" of the German Army of the East into what he sees as the proper light—the "desperate defensive battle for the preservation of the great power status of the German Reich, which, according to the will of the Allies, had to be destroyed. The German Army of the East provided an umbrella of protection for a centuries-old settlement area, the homeland of millions, who . . . lived in the heartland of the German Reich." The dramatic presentation closes then with a wishful interpretation of the surrender on May 8, 1945: Forty years later the question of the "reconstruction of the destroyed European Center (is) . . . as open as it was then. Those living at that time, whether as actors or as victims, became witnesses of the catastrophe of eastern Germany." The moral of the story is obvious (to him): Today at least the alliance of forces is correct.

In the second part, Hillgruber takes twenty-two pages to treat the aspect of the war that he had so-far kept separate from the "tragic" acts of heroism on the eastern front. The subtitle of the book already signals a changed perspective. The "Destruction of the German Reich," something that had been pledged in the rhetoric of the war pamphlets (and that evidently happened only on the eastern front), stands in contrast to the soberly registered "End of the European Jewry." Now, "destruction" requires an aggressive opponent; an "end" seems to some extent to appear on its own. In the first part of the book "the destruction of whole armies" stands "beside the sacrifice of individuals"; in the second part of the book, the topic is "stationary successor organizations" of the *Einsatzgruppen*. While in the first section "many anonymous people reached beyond themselves in the imminent catastrophe," in the second section the gas chambers are euphemized as a "more effective means" of liquidation. In the first section, we read the unrevised, unpurified clichés of a jargon retained since childhood; in the second section, we experience the frozen language of bureaucracy. However, the historian does not simply switch the perspective of presentation. In the second section he sets out to prove that "the murder of the Jews" was "exclusively a consequence of the radical doctrine of race."

Stürmer was interested in the question, To what extent had it been Hitler's war and to what extent the war of the Germans? Hillgruber poses the analogous question with regard to the annihilation of the Jews. He poses hypothetical considerations about how life would have looked for the Jews if a right-wing coalition like the nationalists and the *Stahlhelmer* [veterans' group] instead of the Nazis had come into power in 1933. The Nuremberg laws would still have been introduced, just as would all other measures up through 1938 that forced on the Jews a "separate consciousness." This would have been so since these measures found "accord with the sensibilities of a large part of the society." Hillgruber doubts, however, that *all* decisionmakers between 1938 and 1941 saw a policy of forced emigration as the best solution to the Jewish question. Still, by that time, two-thirds of the German Jews had "ended up abroad." Finally, regarding the implementation after 1941 of the Final Solution, it was Hitler alone, according to Hillgruber, who had his mind set on it from the beginning. Hitler wanted the physical annihilation of all Jews "because only such a 'racial revolution' could lend permanence to the world-power status of his

Reich." Since Hillgruber does not use the verb in the subjunctive, one does not know whether the historian has adopted the perspective of the participants this time too.

At any rate, Hillgruber makes a sharp distinction between the euthanasia programs, to which 100,000 mentally ill fell victim, and the annihilation of the Jews proper. Against the backdrop of the social Darwinism of human genetics, the killing of "life unworthy of living" is supposed to have found support in the populace. However, Hitler in his idea of the Final Solution is supposed to have been isolated even in the narrowest leadership circles, "including Göring, Himmler and Heydrich." After Hitler has been identified as the sole responsible author for the idea and decision, only its execution needs an explanation. But this explanation ignores the frightening fact that the mass of the population—as Hillgruber certainly assumes—was silent throughout all of it.

To be sure, the goal of the difficult neoconservative revision would be endangered if this phenomenon of silence had, after all, to be delivered up to a moral judgment. At this point, therefore, the historian, who has been writing in the narrative mode, switches over to an anthropological-general tone. In his opinion, "the acceptance by the mass of the populace of the gruesome events, events that were at least darkly suspected, points out the historical singularity of the event." Standing firmly in the tradition of the German mandarin, Hillgruber is most deeply appalled by the high proportion of university-trained men who participated—as if there were not a completely plausible explanation for that. In short, the phenomenon that a civilized populace let these horrible things happen is one that Hillgruber removes from the technical competence of the overburdened historian and blithely pushes off into the dimension of the generally human.

III

In the *Historische Zeitschrift* (vol. 242, 1986, pp. 465ff.) Hillgruber's colleague from Bonn, Klaus Hildebrand, commends a work by Ernst Nolte as "showing the way" because the work does the service of removing the "seemingly unique" quality of the history of the Third Reich. As part of the process of historicizing, he categorizes "the destructive capacity of the worldview and of the regime" as part of the global development of totalitarianism. Nolte, who with his book *Faschismus in seiner Epoche* [Fascism in Its Epoch] (1963) had already found wide acclaim, is in fact cut from a different cloth than is Hillgruber.

In his contribution "Zwischen Mythos und Revisionismus" [Between Myth and Revisionism], he based the necessity for a revision on the observation that the history of the Third Reich had predominantly been written by the victors, who then made it into a "negative myth." To illustrate, Nolte invites us to take part in a tasteful thought experiment. He sketches for us the image of Israel that would be held by a victorious PLO after the destruction of Israel: "For decades, perhaps even for a century, no one would venture . . . to attribute the rise of Zionism to its spirit of resistance against European anti-Semitism." Even the theory of totalitarianism, which predominated in German historical scholarship of the 1950s, offered no change in perspective from the negative myth initiated by the historians of the victorious nations; instead, the totalitarianism theory had only led to the Soviet Union also being pulled into the negative image. A concept that lives to that extent off the contrast with the democratic constitutional state is not enough for Nolte; he attributes much to mutual threats of destruction. Long before Auschwitz, Hitler, so he claims, had good grounds to believe that his opponents wanted to destroy him— "annihilate" is the word in the English original. As proof he cites the "declaration of war" that Chaim Weizmann in September 1939 delivered on behalf of the Jewish World Congress and that then was supposed to *justify* Hitler in treating German Jews as prisoners of war—and in deporting them. A few weeks ago one could have read in *Die Zeit* (although without names being named) that Nolte served up this argument to a Jewish dinner guest, his colleague, historian Saul Friedländer of Tel Aviv.

Nolte is the officious-conservative narrator who tackles the "identity problem." He solves Stürmer's dilemma between the endowment of higher meaning and scholarship through an energetic decision and chooses as a point of connection for his presentation the terror of the Pol Pot regime in Cambodia. He reconstructs a background history for mass terror. As it reaches back in time it includes the "Gulag," Stalin's expulsion of the kulaks, and the Bolshevik revolution; he sees antecedents to mass terror in Babeuf, the early socialists, and the agrarian reformers of the early nineteenth century. In all these figures he perceives a line of revolt against cultural and social modernization, a revolt driven by the illusionary and passionate longing for the reestablishment of an understandable, autarchic world. In this context of terror stretching across the globe and over the centuries, the annihilation of the Jews appears as a regrettable, but perfectly understandable, result. It is seen as a reaction by Hitler to what he is assumed to have sensed as a threat of destruction: "The so-called annihilation of the Jews during the Third Reich was a reaction or a distorted copy, but not a first act or an original."

Nolte attempts in another essay to explain the philosophical background of his "trilogy on the history of modern ideologies." This essay will not be discussed here. In what Nolte, the student of Heidegger, calls his "philosophical writing of history," I am interested only in the "philosophical."

In the early 1950s there was a debate in philosophical anthropology about whether human beings were "open to the world" or "captives of the environment." The discussion involved A. Gehlen, H. Plessner, K. Lorenz, and E. Rothacker. Nolte's rather odd use of the Hedeggerian concept of "transcendence" reminds me of this discussion. He has been using "transcendence," actually since 1963, to explain the great shift, the historical process of the breakup of a traditional way of life in the transition to modernity; his explanation invokes the timeless category of the anthropological-original. At this depth of abstraction, in which all cats are gray, he pleads for understanding for the anti-modernist impulses. These impulses are directed against an "unconditional affirmation of practical transcendence." By this category of practical transcendence Nolte refers to the putatively ontologically grounded "unity of world economy, technology, science and emancipation." All this fits neatly with attitudes that dominate today—and with the circle dance of Californian worldviews that sprout from it. The leveling of differences required by this abstraction, however, is rather more annoying; from this perspective it makes "Marx and Maurras, Engels and Hitler, despite all the emphasis on their contrasts, nevertheless related figures." Not until Marxism and fascism are acknowledged to be attempts to answer "the frightening realities of modernity" can the true intention of National Socialism be neatly and cleanly separated from its unhappy practice. "The 'atrocity' was not concluded with the final intention, but rather with the ascribing of guilt, a process that directed itself against a human group that itself was already so severely affected by the process of emancipation in liberal society that it declared itself, in the words of some of its prominent representatives, to be mortally endangered."

Now, one could let the scurrilous background philosophy of this prominent, eccentric mind rest on its own merits, if the neoconservative historians did not feel obliged to play the game of revisionism in precisely this way.

As a contribution to this year's Römerberg Talks, a conference that also treated the topic of the "past that will not pass" in presentations by Hans and Wolfgang Mommsen, the culture section of *Frankfurter Allgemeine Zeitung*, June 6, 1986, included a militant article by Ernst Nolte. It was published, by the way, under a hypocritical pretext with the heading "the talk that could not be delivered." (I say this with knowledge of the exchange of letters between the presumably disinvited Nolte and the organizers of the conference.) When the Nolte article was published Stürmer also expressed solidarity. In it Nolte reduces the singularity of the annihilation of the Jews to "the technical process of gassing." He supports his thesis that the Gulag Archipelago is "primary" to Auschwitz with the rather abstruse example of the Russian civil war. The author gets little more from the film *Shoah* by Lanzmann than the idea that "the SS troops in the concentration camps might themselves have been victims of a sort and that among the Polish victims of National Socialism there was virulent anti-Semitism." These unsavory samples show that Nolte puts someone like Fassbinder in the shade by a wide margin. If the *Frankfurter Allgemeine Zeitung* was justifiably drawn to oppose the planned performance of Fassbinder's play, then why did it choose to publish Nolte's letter?

I can only explain it to myself by thinking that Nolte not only navigates around the conflict between the endowing of higher meaning and scholarship in a more elegant way than others but also has a solution ready for another dilemma. This other dilemma is described by Stürmer with the sentence: "In the reality of a divided Germany, the Germans must find their identity, which is no longer to be grounded in the nation state, but which is also not without nation." The planners of ideology want to create a consensus about the revivification of a national consciousness, and at the same time, they must banish the negative images of the German nation-state from the domain of NATO. Nolte's theory offers a great advantage for this manipulation. He hits two flies with one swat: The Nazi crimes lose their singularity in that they are at least made comprehensible as an answer to the (still extant) Bolshevist threats of annihilation. The magnitude of Auschwitz shrinks to the format of technical innovation and is explained on the basis of the "Asiatic" threat from an enemy that still stands at our door.

IV

If one has a look at the composition of the commissions that have designed the plan for the German Historical Museum in Berlin and the House of the History of the Federal Republic in Bonn, one cannot help but get the impression that the new revisionism is to be realized in these museums in the form of displays and pedagogically effective exhibits. It is true that the expert reports submitted so far have a pluralistic face. But things will be no different with the new museums than they were with the Max Plank Institutes: The programs and memos that regularly precede the founding of a new institution have little to do with what the newly appointed directors actually make of it. That has also dawned on Jürgen Kocka, the token liberal on the Berlin expert commission: "In the end the decisive matter is what person takes charge. . . . Here, too, the devil resides in the details."

No one desires to oppose seriously meant attempts to strengthen the historical consciousness of the population of the Federal Republic. There are also good reasons for a historicizing portrayal that seeks to gain distance from a past that will not pass. Martin Broszat has written convincingly on this. Those complex connections between the criminality and the dubious normality of everyday life under Nazism, between destruction and vital productivity, between a devastating systematic perspective and an intimate, local perspective, could certainly stand being objectified and brought up to date. Then this pedantic co-optation of a short-circuited, moralized past might give way to a more objectified understanding. The careful differentiation between understanding and condemning a shocking past could also help put an end to our hypnotic paralysis. But this kind of historicization would not be guided by impulses such as the ones that provided impulses to the revision recommended by Hildebrand and Stürmer and conducted by Hillgruber or Nolte, who set out to shake off the mortgages of a past now happily made morally neutral. I do not want to impute negative intentions to anyone. There is a simple criterion that distinguishes the people involved in this dispute. The one side assumes that working on a more objectified understanding releases energy for self-reflective remembering and thus expands the space available for autonomously dealing with ambivalent traditions. The other side would like to place revisionist history in the service of a nationalist renovation of conventional identity.

Perhaps this formulation is not unequivocal enough. Those who seek to do more than revivify a sense of identity naively rooted in national consciousness, those who allow themselves to be guided by functional imperatives of predictability, consensus-formation, social integration via endowing meaning, are bound to avoid the enlightening effect of history writing and reject a broad pluralism of historical interpretations. One will hardly misrepresent Michael Stürmer if one is to understand his editorializing in the following way: "When looking at the Germans and their relationship to their history, our neighbors are bound to pose the question: Where is this all leading? . . . The Federal Republic is the centerpiece of European defense within the Atlantic system. But it is becoming evident that each generation living in Germany today has differing, even opposing, views of the past and the future. . . . The search for a lost past is not an abstract striving for culture and education. It is [an undertaking that is] morally legitimate and politically necessary. We are dealing with the inner continuity of the German republic and its predictability in foreign policy terms." In reality, Stürmer is making a plea for a *unified* understanding of history that might replace the increasing privatization of religious values with identity and social integration.

Historical consciousness as vicarious religion—isn't this overtaxing the old dream of historicism? To be sure, German historians can look back on a truly national tradition in their discipline. Hans-Ulrich Wehler recently reminded us of its ideological contribution toward stabilizing the *kleindeutsches Reich* and excluding "enemies of the Reich." Until the late 1950s the discipline had been dominated by an attitude that had been in the process of being shaped ever since the failure of the revolutions of 1848–1849 and the defeat of liberal history writing such as that of Gervinus: "For almost 100 years, liberal, enlightened historians could only be found either isolated or in small fringe groups. The majority in the discipline thought and argued in a way that was conscious and affirmative of nationalism and influenced by the state and the power of the state."

The fact that since 1945, at least among younger historians educated after 1945, not only a new spirit but also a pluralism of modes of understanding [*Lesarten*] and of methodologies has made itself felt is not a mishap that can simply be undone. The old attitude was really just an expression of mandarin consciousness, rampant in the discipline. And this attitude has fortunately not survived the Nazi period. By its impotence against or even complicity with the Nazi regime, the discipline showed itself to be without real substance. The resultant self-reflection by the discipline influenced more than just the ideological premises of German historiography; it also intensified the methodological consciousness of the contextual dependence of *all* history writing.

However, it would be a misunderstanding of this hermeneutic insight if the revisionists of today assume that they can illuminate the present with the spotlights of arbitrarily constructed prehistories and choose from these options a particularly suitable notion of history. The intensified methodological consciousness also means the end of a closed understanding of history and precludes any conception of history that might be prescribed by government historians. The unavoidable pluralism of modes of understanding [*Lesarten*] is a reflection of the structure of open societies. This pluralism provides us with the opportunity to more clearly understand our own identity-forming traditions and their ambivalences. Precisely this is necessary for a critical appropriation of ambivalent traditions and to shape a historical consciousness that is as incompatible with closed and organic images of history as it is with all forms of conventional identity.

What is today being lamented as a "loss of history" is not just an aspect of deliberately repressing and ignoring; it is not only an aspect of being overly focused on an encumbered history that seems to have come to a standstill. If the traditional national symbols have lost their power for younger people, if a naive sense of identification with one's own history has given way to a more tentative way of dealing with history, if the discontinuities are felt more strongly and continuities are not celebrated at every turn, if national pride and a collective sense of self-worth are forced through the filter of a universalist orientation of values—to the degree that these things are true we can speak of evidence for the formation of a postconventional identity. In Allensbach this evidence is described with forecasts of doom. But this evidence seems to reveal one thing: that we have not gambled away the opportunity that the moral catastrophe could also mean for us.

The unconditional opening of the Federal Republic to the political culture of the West is the greatest intellectual achievement of our postwar period; my generation should be especially proud of this. This event cannot and should not be stabilized by a kind of NATO philosophy colored with German nationalism. The opening of the Federal Republic has been achieved precisely by overcoming the ideology of Central Europe that our revisionists are trying to warm up for us with their geopolitical drumbeat about "the old geographically central position of the Germans in Europe" (Stürmer) and "the reconstruction of the destroyed European Center" (Hillgruber). The only patriotism that will not estrange us from the West is a constitutional patriotism. Unfortunately, it took Auschwitz to make possible to the old culture nation of the Germans binding universalist constitutional principles anchored in conviction. Those who want to drive the shame about this fact out of us with phrases such as "obsession with guilt" (Stürmer and Oppenheimer), those who desire to call the Germans back to conventional forms of their national identity, are destroying the only reliable foundation for our ties to the West.

Source: *Die Zeit*, July 11, 1986

MICHA BRUMLIK

New Myth of State: The Eastern Front. The Most Recent Development in the Discipline of History in the Federal Republic of Germany

This is a report on the decline of the German discipline of contemporary history to the level of the *Landserheft* [the cultural equivalent of Combat Comics]. In Siedler Verlag's fancy and much-too-expensive gift editions, which were shamelessly christened "elegantly appointed," two lectures and essays of Hillgruber's that had recently been presented elsewhere have appeared under the title *Zweierlei Untergang* [Twofold Fall]. This little volume contains a long essay with the title "Der Zusammenbruch im Osten 1944/45 als Problem der deutschen Nationalgeschichte und der europäischen Geschichte" [The Collapse in the East 1944–45 as a Problem of German National History and European History] (59 pages) and a much shorter effort, "Der geschichtliche Ort der Judenvernichtung" [The Historical Locus of the Annihilation of the Jews] (22 pages).

A NEW LEVEL

In terms of shamelessness and cynicism, the first essay puts everything in the shade that has appeared as "serious" scholarship with a pro-Nazi position; the second essay disposes of its subject with rather less enthusiasm.

The appearance of Hillgruber's book with Siedler Verlag marks German conservatives' turn to aggressive nationalism. The framework of this turn is the nationalists' insight into the paradox of their attempt in Bitburg and then on the Rhine to force a reconciliation between victims and executioners. It is as though those who planned the collective commemorative cermonies in the patriotic, nationalistic mode were aware of this paradox. The awareness led them to avoid the useless attempt to be reconciled with the murdered Jews, Gypsies, and Slavs. They concentrated totally on the Germans who died in the war and during the deportations.

Examples of this are the statements of Dr. Alfred Dregger, the CDU majority leader. In the discussion about the planned national memorial, he let it be known unambiguously that he and many of his political friends wanted above all to commemorate the German dead of the Second World War.

At this point a schism opens up; a consensus will hardly be achieved in the Federal Republic, or elsewhere. Specifically, there is a difference of opinion about the absolute incommensurability of the industrial mass annihilation carried out by the National Socialists, that is, about its inconceivability and its incomparability to all other forms of organized death, including the Stalinist work camps, the bombing of Dresden, and the crimes of the resettlement of the German populace of the East. The political culture of psychological repression becomes most evident when people cannot resist the understandable temptation to assimilate the incomprehensible, historically unique event of the mass annihilation called the Holocaust, to other, familiar, imaginable actions of killing.

AUSCHWITZ THE LESSER EVIL, IN ORDER TO PREVENT THE GREATER ONE, THE SOVIET MASSACRE

When this assimilation is accomplished, the Shoah is redefined as a kind of comprehensible massacre that had to be tolerated in order to prevent further massacres. In this way the German defensive battle in the East becomes in the last analysis a tragic occurrence. The soldiers, in this view, had to protect the slaughter in the concentration camps in order to save their own countrymen from the Soviet massacre. The otherwise respected conspirators of July 20, 1944, turn out to be, in this perspective, supporters of a preferential ethic who were not acquainted with the seriousness of the situation.

Such theses are put forward not by the *Deutsche National- und Soldatenzeitung* [a right-wing newspaper], which has always taken this position, but instead by a serious academic historian, Andreas Hillgruber. I quote extensively below:

> The complexity of the problems one surveys from here makes itself plain with the few examples that continually become the focus of public discussions. Norbert Blüm touched one such neuralgic point a few years ago when he brought the thesis to a disconcerted yet polarized public that the gruesome crimes in the death camps and concentration camps could continue only as long as the German fronts held.
>
> This thesis allows the conclusion that in order to put an end to the terrors of the concentration camps, it would have been desirable to let the fronts collapse as quickly as possible, including also the German eastern front. Until the winter of 1944–45 the eastern front had protected the populace in the east of the Reich from the inundation of the homeland by the Red Army.
>
> In reality the mass murder of the European Jews in the camp at Auschwitz-Birkenau was continued after July 24, 1944, the day when the camp at Majdanek near Lublin was so quickly occupied by the Red Army that it was impossible for the withdrawing SS units to disassemble the places of horror (so that for the first time the world learned of the

conditions in such a camp). The murders at Auschwitz-Birkenau continued up to the beginning of November 1944, when Himmler issued his order for discontinuance.

The murders continue at the point—mid-October 1944—when the German front had already withdrawn under the pressure of the Red Army into eastern East Prussia, where it was able only with great effort to bring the Soviet attack to a standstill.

In the village of Nemmersdorf, south of Gumbinnen, which had been retaken by German troops, the soldiers were presented with the horror of raped and murdered women and children. "Nemmersdorf" became the slogan for what the German populace had to expect if the "dams were to break."

Of course we are still left with the structural or functional problematic discussed by Blüm: Holding the fronts made possible the continuation of the crimes in the concentration camps. The contemporary observer is also confronted with the dilemma of those who had to act then. On the one hand we have the preferentially ethical men of July 20, 1944, who decided to assassinate Hitler because of a long-hopeless foreign policy situation. They wanted to give the world a sign from the "other Germany." And they wanted to do this at a time when the *Heeresgruppe Mitte* [Central Army Group], which until then had been the bulwark protecting East Prussia, was smashed in the course of the Soviet summer offensive begun on July 22, 1944. Then the way to eastern Prussia seemed fairly free.

On the other side was the responsibly ethical position of the commanders, district magistrates, and mayors, in whose views everything depended on building up at least a weak veil of defenses on the eastern Prussian border in order to avoid the worst: the threatened orgy of revenge on the German population for crimes committed in the parts of the Soviet Union occupied by German troops—regardless of which Germans in which line of duty had committed the crimes. (Hillgruber 1986, pp. 18–21)

WORDS OF TRAGEDY TO HIDE THE HORROR

I have quoted this section so extensively because in my view it—along with Bitburg—represents an incision into the historical consciousness of the Federal Republic of Germany.

For the first time a conservative, well-known, and respected historian states publicly for the record that the extermination of the Jews and Gypsies under certain circumstances, while not quite sanctioned, may nevertheless legitimately be taken into account!

Despite what Kohl and Dregger say, it should no longer be a matter simply of commemorating the *Wehrmacht*, that is, the protector of the murderers. Instead it should be a matter of expressly acknowledging the protection by the *Wehrmacht* of an act of industrial mass murder.

The reconstruction of national history inevitably leads to a view of the

Shoah as one of two equally important catastrophes: The title of Hillgruber's little volume of two essays reads *Zweierlei Untergang: Die Zerschlagung des deutschen Reiches und das Ende des europäischen Judentums* [Twofold Fall: The Destruction of the German Reich and the End of European Jewry].

The euphemistic title already announces the program: While the German Reich was destroyed, European Jewry ended—a process presented in such a way that the instigator is not to be seen. Raul Hilberg's standard work on the Shoah carries the precise title *Die Vernichtung der europäischen Juden* [The Annihilation of the European Jews]. Hillgruber writes of a theatrical-tragic fall in the East. The annihilation becomes an end; the murdered Jews become the Jewry. The abstraction into tragedy, which is not really so well maintained in the book, only has the function of letting the horror of the actual events disappear under the veil of words, of writing it off, of closing it off—of repressing it.

It was possible to let millions of people be murdered by redefining them as abstract numbers. Attempting to understand their horrible fate by means of equally abstract concepts represents something in the same vein: treating the memory of the victims just as the murdered ones themselves were treated.

ANTICOMMUNISM AS A NECESSARY COMPONENT OF THE PSYCHOLOGICAL REPRESSION OF THE ANNIHILATION OF THE JEWS

Even if we do not look into Stalinist totalitarianism and its murderous work camps, the expansionism of the Soviet Union since 1945, the irresponsible foreign-policy adventures of the Soviet Union and its thoroughly repressive regime, it now is becoming clear what role anticommunism played and plays in the political culture of psychological repression.

The culture of repression depends on equating, contrary to fact and against all historical experience, two evils. One evil is the Stalinist despotism and the pent-up rage of the East European peoples against German atrocities. The second is the cold-blooded, planned, administratively and industrially driven mass annihilation. Only if this equation is made; only if it is further insinuated that the Soviet Union wanted to exterminate the Germans; only then does it seem legitimate that the nation conducting the war protected the annihilation camps. In this regard anticommunism is a necessary component of psychological repression of the Holocaust—both depend on each other.

THE THOUGHT OF HEINRICH HIMMLER AS THE FEDERAL REPUBLIC OF GERMANY'S NEW MYTH OF STATE

If in these days the conservative *Frankfurter Allgemeine Zeitung* lets a Jewish-German emigrant comment extensively on Bitburg, National Socialism, and German anti-Semitism, if in the same newspaper the French Jew André Glucksmann recommends that the West Germans arm themselves with atomic weapons, then it only shows that even many Jews are not in a position to grasp the singularity of the Shoah. In the contemporary dispute of Western Jews with the Soviet Union, they want to attempt a form of resistance today that was impossible in those days.

When Franz Oppenheimer, who himself lost relatives at Auschwitz, writes in the *Frankfurter Allgemeine Zeitung* that the great majority of Germans have in general no larger guilt for Hitler's crimes, just as others have none for the crimes of Stalin and Gorbachev today, he knows he is laying himself open to vigorous complaints. "One will say that I am downplaying the Holocaust, that I am absolving its perpetrators, and only making a display of 'insensitivity' to the torture of the victims. . . . Only the devil can have amused himself with the recent Bitburg-circus in the American media. It is the devil who wants the murdered victims of the past to let us forget the murdered and tortured slaves of an empire that lasts into the present" (*Frankfurter Allgemeine Zeitung*, May 14, 1986, p. 11).

Psychological repression only recedes for those who view reality. In this respect anticommunism presents a challenge—at least with respect to overcoming the National-Socialist past and repressing the Shoah. Anticommunism leaves us with just one question: Were there or are there gas chambers in the Soviet Union? And if not, can the Soviet Union nevertheless be compared to National Socialism? Are then the gas chambers, railroad operations, and bureaucracies of mass annihilation of the Third Reich in a moral and political sense the incidental by-product of just any totalitarianism? Or are they not the expression, no, the essence, of a crime singular in world history, a crime whose dimensions elude our moral capacity for understanding again and again, so that we are always tempted to comprehend the crime by assigning it to familiar and trusted categories?

Hillgruber's attempt at any rate to weigh the mass annihilation of the Jews against the collapse of the eastern front represents nothing other than the program of Himmler in the last months of the war. (Separate peace in the West; keep on "fighting" and murdering in the East.) Should the program of Heinrich Himmler become the myth of state of the Federal Republic?

Source: *Die Tageszeitung*, July 12, 1986

Author's Note: This article is based on a lecture delivered by the author on May 28, 1986, in Augsburg to a specialist conference of the Bundeszentrale für politische Bildung [Federal Agency for Political Education] with the theme "Two Generations after the Holocaust . . ." The lecture "Die Spätfolgen des Menschheitsverbrechens: Über die politische Kultur in der Bundesrepublik Deutschland" [The Late Consequences of Crimes against Humanity: On Political Culture in the Federal Republic] can be found in the conference documentation of the Bundeszentrale, Bonn 1986.

KLAUS HILDEBRAND

The Age of Tyrants: History and Politics: The Administrators of the Enlightenment, the Risk of Scholarship, and the Preservation of a Worldview. A Reply to Jürgen Habermas

Jürgen Habermas's article "A Kind of Settlement of Damages," July 11, 1986, in *Die Zeit* about the putative "apologetic tendencies in German history-writing" is a dark brew of politics and scholarship, of weltanschauung and historical perspective, of prejudices and facts. That the Hamburg weekly [*Die Zeit*] characterizes his so-called call to arms as in the "best Enlightenment tradition" does not alter the facts. Precisely under the rubric of Enlightenment, antienlightenment is being conducted. And, as always in cases of a mixture of politics and scholarship, the one betrays the other; scholarship gets completely lost along the way.

Even the obligatory reference to the value-ladenness of all scholarship hardly helps. It seems threadbare when one strays from the search for the truth into politicizing. The author of an article wrapped in the veil of the philosophical, an article that really has nothing to do with the essence of scholarship, namely, to set oneself above desire and aversion and to be committed to objectivity, renders a bad service to politics and denies scholarship outright.

FALSE QUOTATIONS

It is not the intention of this reply to take issue with the judgments of worldview and politics that dominate in Habermas's article. Detailing the error-filled quotations of his essay will also be avoided. Habermas's ridiculous mischaracterizations (for example that Jürgen Kocka is a liberal) will be skipped over with a grin, along with the enraged roundhouses against Michael Stürmer's views on history and politics. One quotation that virtually falsified the sense of the text must, however, be mentioned.

Habermas claims that the Cologne historian Andreas Hillgruber wanted

50

to present "The Destruction of the German Reich and the End of European Jewry" (*Zweierlei Untergang* [Twofold Fall], Bibliophile Edition, Siedler, Berlin, 1986) "from the perspectives of the brave and obedient soldiers, the desperate civilian population, and also the 'tried and true' higher-ups of the NSDAP." This is supposed to be posthumous whitewashing for Hitler's "Golden Pheasants" by an acclaimed representative of West German historical scholarship—or so suggests Habermas, the "practitioner of the Enlightenment." A glance at Hillgruber's study reveals, however, something substantially different.

Hillgruber's elaborations attempt to make precisely those distinctions that must remain foreign to Habermas, lest his "call to arms," which had been thrown together in the first place by blurring distinctions, collapse on itself. At any rate Hillgruber writes: "Of the higher-ups in the NSDAP, many proved themselves in the crisis of the final, confused defense, of collapse and flight; others failed, in part in a miserable fashion." And then for the next sixteen lines the conclusion about the failures of the others is illustrated with examples. But this so obviously interferes with Habermas's black-and-white rendering of progress and reaction in the German writing of history that he blithely skips over the sixteen lines and foists on Hillgruber an appreciation for the "tried and true higher-ups of the NSDAP."

The content speaks for itself and is rounded off by the snide accusation that Hillgruber's essay recalls in its first part the "rhetoric of the war pamphlets." One can well imagine what the reactions of the "critical" social scientists would be if their works were to be certified using the jargon of a once-fashionable, but now radically antiquated, adolescent Marxism. Such a polemic would have led yet again to the deepest "concern" for those who, ignoring the truth, deal in morality and "sensitivity": fascism *ante portas*! Therefore, with this one example we will let the matter rest so we can make the transition to the central problems with Habermas's "call to arms." These problems concern his disturbed relation to scholarship and research.

Along this line, Andreas Hillgruber, in his study referred to above, with the subtitle "The Destruction of the German Reich and the End of European Jewry," is supposed by Habermas to have undertaken a project to partition, so to speak, the "German catastrophe" (Friedrich Meinecke) and to segregate the presentation of the annihilation of European Jewry from the glorification of the final struggle of the German soldiers on the eastern front during 1944–1945. The suggestion is misleading. Ignoring for a moment the second part of the bibliophile volume, in which Hillgruber presents in extenso the positions of the research in the field and his interpretation of the National-Socialist politics of race, the consciousness of this moral outrage, consistently referred to in plain language, permeates his book (see, for example, pages 45 and 64).

It is crucial that only against such a backdrop of moral outrage does

Hillgruber's interpretation of German and European history of these years become comprehensible at all. He understands this period as a tragedy. The historical situation for the Germans in the East was reduced to an alternative that had been falsely proclaimed from the beginning by the National Socialists in their propaganda but that in the last months of the war had ironically become reality for the Germans. They were boxed in between the archevils of the century, between Hitler and Stalin, between an annihilation under the banner of race or the banner of class.

In stating the alternative in this way, Hillgruber is not trying, as Habermas's "call to arms" asserts, to balance the atrocities of the Russians with those of the Germans. But this fact escaped Habermas, perhaps due to a lack of expertise, perhaps also due to an unfamiliarity with historical research. In Solzhenitsyn's *August 14* the medievalist Olda Orestovna once correctly observed that one should remember from time to time that history is not politics, where one repeats or refutes what another has said: "The stuff of history is not views, but the sources."

HISTORY AS UTOPIA

In this vein, above all as a result of his study of British files that have become accessible only in recent years, Hillgruber came to the insight that the wide-ranging war aims that entailed frightening displacements of territory and population had been drawn up not only by Stalin, who was of Hitler's ilk and so resembled him, but also by the British leadership, and all before the National-Socialist atrocity of genocide was well known. Thus the plans to break up the German East were not a reaction to the West's knowledge of the Holocaust. It is obvious that in this connection there needs to be a lot of research into backgrounds, motives, and aims. Time and again on the English side in this connection the record reveals an antipathy toward Prussia, whose history and existence were viewed as the cause responsible for Hitler's violent politics.

The reasons for Habermas's sneering at these facts about the war aims do not really become plausible. It is his right to demand a social-scientific explanation. What he tries then, admittedly in another connection, to conclude about the atrocities of the Red Army as social-scientific interpretation remains obscure. "He [Hillgruber—K. H.] makes no use of social-scientific information. Otherwise he could hardly have attributed the transgressions of the Red Army, for example, which occurred not only in Germany but also before that in Poland, Rumania, and Hungary, to the barbaric 'notions of war' of the Stalinist period." One should differentiate between spontaneous atrocities and isolated war crimes, on the one hand, and long-term programs of war aims and a programmatically executed murder of populations, on the other. The latter was followed and realized by Hitler's Germany under the banner of racial dominance and by Stalin's Russia under the banner of class dominance.

By evaluating the preferentially ethical resistance and mentioning Hitler's "halt commands," Hillgruber investigates the destiny and sensitivities of the German soldiers fighting in 1944–1945 in the East, the soldiers who dueled for Hitler against Stalin. In complete contradiction to Habermas's suspicions about a putative glorification and false justification of such deeds, this approach appears legitimate and necessary, not least of all against the backdrop of Hillgruber's presentation of the state of research. The tragedy of these soldiers, whose battle against the Red Army prevented untold harm and nevertheless extended the existence of the National-Socialist regime of injustice, becomes more evident in this volume, page by page.

To take up this issue in the effort to understand is, without a doubt, among the highest tasks of the historian. If he abandons this effort too soon, perhaps through an all too optimistic faith in social-scientific explanation, then he will certainly miss a central dimension of human and historical existence. All that remains then are the one-sidedly demanding gestures of the prophet and the deceiving belief in secular salvation. "If one counts on the revolution to remove his own tragedy from the world, one is simply thinking wrongly." Clearly this statement is as valid now as when André Malraux formulated it in 1937.

Consistent with this perspective, Hillgruber formulates the judgment according to which it is not appropriate "in relation to the fate of the German nation as a whole" to think of the end of the war in 1945 simply as a liberation: "Liberation does not circumscribe the reality of spring 1945." To work further in this field and to come upon differentiating results is a task that does not fit for Habermas into the simplistic image of history with which he has become familiar. He wants steadfastly to hold on to his image without regard to new sources, new realizations, and new questions—the very things that constitute the progress of scholarship. According to his image, however, history and the writing of history would be converted to a final situation resembling a utopia. Dangerous, and in many respects even totalitarian, traits would be connected to this utopia, as to every utopia. History, as the declared enemy of stasis, is the opposite of utopia: The writing of history, properly understood, is accordingly the constant defense against totalitarianism.

Even pertinent scholarly questions, which always contain a certain measure of opinion, seem unsympathetic and suspicious to Habermas. Those who set up such obstructions to scholarship in the service of what they believe to have been established once and for all hinder research. They pay homage to a dogma. Thus, in contrast to Nolte's questions and theses posed independently of political tides and turns, Habermas's unabashed politicizing on the problem of the singularity and comparability of the National-Socialist genocide yields nothing productive. Habermas is struggling against a growing insight that historical facts could just possibly be stronger than uncritical philosophy.

To be sure, historicizing the National-Socialist genocide is a project that cannot yet be comprehensibly completed. It still requires research and debate. If completed, it would not automatically lead to the political consequences that many on the Right would like to connect to it. They must be disappointed just as others on the Left must be who want automatically to derive political action from the singularity of the phenomenon. For the political consequences cannot simply be logically postulated out of the scientific findings. Since there are no liberal or reactionary research findings, however, it is not evident why we should stand with our feet in the cement of any particular image of history and prohibit the posing of questions. Such prohibitions in particular would prevent our inquiring about parallels between the quality of annihilation of communism and that of National Socialism or for that matter prohibit our pursuing the forerunners and traces of the "murder of the Jews" in history.

Certainly one is not obliged to agree with all of Ernst Nolte's interpretive suggestions about the "plurality of the Hitler epoch." At the same time, the obligation is unavoidable to take up intensively the issues he raises and not simply deny them. The racial atrocity of the Third Reich has widely and justifiably been seen for some time as unique. The atrocity explains— or serves as an explanation for—the consequences of the war that affected Germany and that were also often seen as incomparable. With continued research we now see at any rate that the Reich was not conquered solely in order to liberate, tame, and civilize the Germans. The reality of the Soviet war aims, and in part of the Britons and Americans, was much more extensive than that.

THE EVIL AND THE GOOD

Independently of what the Germans did, Stalin primarily followed his wide-ranging foreign policy goals and—tolerated by the United States— shaped postwar developments substantially to his benefit. That the former Allies nevertheless acted as they did and always set their mutual differences aside in the face of the presumed unique "brown" past of the Germans is decisively related to Hitler's previous politics. His policies had starkly broken with all standards of the practical and the principled.

The Germans are still burdened with the legacy of Hitler. The comparison with the quality of annihilation under Soviet communism and the realization of the antagonistic relationship between National Socialism and communism clearly lead, however, to the following insight. Completely differently from what Ranke formulated, a compelling, violent force lay in the ideas that came to power in both countries. This violence must be taken into account in explaining the phenomenon of the "unsuspected baseness of human beings" (Wilhelm Röpke) that became evident in the dictatorships of race and class. Totalitarianism, genocide, and mass displacements belong to the signature of the twentieth century, even if they also, thank god, do not describe its normal state of affairs.

Such a conclusion about the familiar quality of annihilation in no way speaks for trivializing the National-Socialist past. On the contrary. Even the totalitarianism of the twentieth century, which portrays so gruesomely the absurdity of human existence, does not have to be blindly accepted as destiny. Liberation from totalitarianism is accomplished not least of all by the work of the historian to understand the past and tell about it. His search for truthfulness works against the rule of terror, just as his scholarly work, even in the certainty of error, endows the past with both a particular and a general meaning. This is all the more so since today, unlike in antiquity, we can conceive of "Sisyphus as a happy man" (Albert Camus). Or less "existentially" speaking and more "Enlightenment-like," less "philosophically," and more "practically": Successful therapy assumes a *comprehensive* diagnosis.

With regard to the pressure for therapy, Jürgen Habermas has been reproached in another connection for the fact that his diagnosis fell short. Therefore he should not, out of falsely understood concern, advise historians to do something for which he himself could be criticized. To be specific, he should not—under the spell of a fixed image of history—mistrust research and use in its place bloated concepts like "postconventional identity" without saying whether the "undiscoverable socialism" (Raymond Aron), or whatever, is concealed behind them, and without acknowledging historical facts that do not translate concisely into political terms but instead only require freedom of thought and expand freedom of action. But this is just what Habermas seems to fear, just as he is afraid of a comprehensive revelation of the terror and outrages of a century that early on was characterized as an "Age of the Tyrants" (Elie Halévy). The territory of these terrors is not limited to Germany.

As always, he who wants to preserve his image of history and its power at the expense of the discovery of truth must take refuge in simplifications and distance himself from research. The consequences articulate themselves as the loss of reality and Manichaeanism. Then the German world is once again divided, characteristically for the land of the Reformation, into evil and good, into black and white, into, if simplicity so desires, so-called government historians and Jürgen Habermas. The maxim of Boethius fits his "call to arms" quite well, that he would have been better silent—*philosophus mansisses.*

Source: *Frankfurter Allgemeine Zeitung*, July 31, 1986

ERNST NOLTE

Letter to the Editor of *Die Zeit*, August 1, 1986

A letter to the editor is not the right place to take up a battle to which the "neoconservative historians" have been "ordered" by Mr. Habermas. A few sentences are not enough to say anything of substance about taste and tastelessness, the permissibility of certain comparisons, legitimate criticism, and malignant imputations. I will limit myself to correcting two statements by Mr. Habermas and will derive a few conclusions from them.

Mr. Habermas refers to the interview with Saul Friedländer, which was published in *Die Zeit* of May 16, 1986. Here, Friedländer reports statements by his host at a little evening gathering. These statements supposedly caused him to demonstratively leave the party. Mr. Habermas now thinks it in good taste to lift the last veil that in the interview concealed the private realm. And he names the name—mine. But in the interview there is word of a second incident that is supposed to have disturbed Mr. Friedländer no less than the first. One could thus search for additional names. If Mr. Habermas had inquired of certain Berlin friends, he would have immediately known how fogged the glasses were through which at least the second incident—and thus perhaps also the first—was viewed. Mr. Habermas speaks a lot about the Enlightenment (too much, as I see it), but this movement's most basic element, the endeavor to throw light on facts and circumstances in order to gain critical distance from one-sided portrayals, seems foreign to him, at least in this case.

Based on his knowledge of sources, Mr. Habermas is also convinced he can assure his readers that my undelivered Frankfurt speech was published under a "hypocritical pretext." It is true that the invitation to the Römerberg Talks was not withdrawn by an official letter. But it is equally true that the invitation to speak on this topic was withdrawn in a Sunday phone call from the organization's secretary. I have no idea whether Mr. Habermas, as a member of the board of directors, was responsible. But I can remember very well a far more grave incident of several years ago that involved me, despite the fact that I was not the initiator. This incident cannot be reconstructed from "files." For this reason I am all the more convinced that my old assumption that the same man who in theory is a protagonist of "dominance-free discussion" in practice skillfully and energetically employs the formal and informal positions of power that he holds on committees and in publishing houses to exercise the function of a special kind of censor.

Source: *Die Zeit*, August 1, 1986

JÜRGEN HABERMAS

Letter to the Editor of the *Frankfurter Allgemeine Zeitung*, August 11, 1986

Regarding Klaus Hildebrand's "Das Zeitalter der Tyrannen" [The Age of Tyrants] (*Frankfurter Allgemeine Zeitung*, July 31), Klaus Hildebrand slips tellingly under the wings of the *Frankfurter Allgemeine Zeitung* and does not answer my article where it appeared and could have been read—in *Die Zeit* (July 11). In order to give the substance of his "reply" its due, the reader of the *Frankfurter Allgemeine Zeitung* would have to have informed himself somewhere else about its object. The bad situation is not made any better by the fact that Hildebrand feels hurt and reacts diffusely. The contours of the dispute are blurred through the translucent window. It is a murky polemic.

1. First, the dispute concerns the putative "loss of historical consciousness" and the public educational mission of the discipline of history. In accord with Stürmer's concept, this discipline ought to, by reaching back to the history of the nation, help produce a German identity. A way of writing history that is narrative, geopolitically sober, and oriented to the national question ought, under the motto of "the search for identity," to boldly go about "assigning and endowing higher meaning." In this regard I had objected that history writing—historical consciousness as vicarious religion—might be overtaxed by this program.

2. Next, the dispute concerns a methodological question. In what sense can—and should—the Nazi period be historicized in the public consciousness? A distanced understanding requires, of course, a critical attitude toward ambivalent traditions. Objectifying a problem in this way, however, would work against the process of identification desired in the neo-conservative view. For this reason the variants of the contemporary writing of Nazi history that tend to trivialize the crimes take on importance for another form of historicizing that works out of empathy, through relativizing, to bridge interrupted continuities.

In this connection I discuss the odd consideration with which Andreas

58

Hillgruber prefaces his presentation of the events on the eastern front in 1944–1945 (*Zweierlei Untergang* [Twofold Fall], Berlin 1986). He does not want to identify himself with Hitler, or the resistance fighters, or the inmates of the concentration camps; instead he sides with the "concrete fate of the population in the East." That would perhaps be a legitimate point of view for the memoirs of a veteran—but not for a historian writing from the distance of four decades. Among those actors with which Hillgruber identifies himself are found, besides soldiers and civilians, also the "tried and true" higher-ups of the NSDAP—the quotation marks I have used for this one cited expression do not exclude the possibility that Hillgruber finds harsh words for the not-so-tried-and-true "Golden Pheasants."

3. Finally, the dispute concerns examples of apologetic tendencies. I am convinced that Hillgruber feels the same abhorrence of the Nazi atrocities as most of us do—and he says so, too. His little book nevertheless has an apologetic effect, which begins with the subtitle. A German reader would have to bring along a healthy portion of linguistic insensitivity in order not to let himself be influenced by the juxtaposition of an aggressive "destruction of the German Reich" by its external enemies and an almost automatically following "end of European Jewry." This first impression justifies itself above all through the compilation of two parts so unlike in their style of presentation and declared partisanship. And the thesis of the last part fits seamlessly in the familiar pattern: "The greater the role of Hitler and his system of domination, the more the German society can be exonerated" (K. E. Jeismann).

The second example of neoconservative apologetic tendencies is of another caliber. In his essay "Between Myth and Revisionism" Ernst Nolte treats the "so-called" annihilation of the Jews (in H. W. Koch, ed., *Aspects of the Third Reich*, London 1985). Chaim Weizmann's declaration in the beginning of September 1939 that the Jews of the world would fight on the side of England, "justified"—so opined Nolte—Hitler to treat the Jews as prisoners of war and to intern them. Other objections aside, I cannot distinguish between the insinuation that world Jewry is a subject of international law and the usual anti-Semitic projections. And if it had at least stopped with deportation. All this does not stop Klaus Hildebrand in the *Historische Zeitschrift* from commending Hillgruber's "pathfinding essay," because it "attempts to project exactly the seemingly unique aspects of the history of the Third Reich onto the backdrop of the European and global development." Hildebrand is pleased that Nolte denies the singularity of the Nazi atrocities.

Hildebrand does not seriously address these three complexes. His explanations illustrate perhaps how extremely he is still caught up in the suggestive imagery of an enemy characteristic of the Bund Freiheit der

Wissenschaft [an association of conservative scholars founded following the unrest of 1968]. One wonders, by the way, which standard of measure Hildebrand was using if he can only characterize my estimation of his liberal colleague Kocka as "ridiculous mischaracterization."

Source: *Frankfurter Allgemeine Zeitung*, August 11, 1986

Publisher's Note: The letter to the editor appeared under the title "The Writing of History and Historical Consciousness."

MICHAEL STÜRMER

Letter to the Editor of the *Frankfurter Allgemeine Zeitung*, August 16, 1986

Concerning Professor Jürgen Habermas's letter to the editor titled "The Writing of History and Historical Consciousness" (*Frankfurter Allgemeine Zeitung*, August 11, 1986), Habermas can either be taken seriously or he can continue to combine sloppy research with patched-together quotes in an attempt to place historians on his blacklist. He cannot do both. Concerning his statements:

1. National question? He confuses that with the German question, which I did not invent and which without doubt is frequently posed today. That has nothing to do with geopolitics, but it has a lot to do with the economic, intellectual, and strategic preconditions of Europe in history and in the present. My answer lies not in the socialist nostalgia of Jürgen Habermas but in the affirmation and development of the Atlantic and European ties of our country.

2. Endowing meaning? Whatever identity is, somebody seems to be in search of it. To what degree history as a discipline has contributed to this is a matter of controversy. Endowing meaning should be left to others. Jürgen Habermas has attempted to endow meaning—fortunately without success—long enough.

3. Endowment of higher meaning? Not long ago I asked whether history was called upon to provide such a thing (*Dissonanzen des Fortschritts*, Piper Verlag, 1986). I did not leave the readers in the dark regarding the answer: "From its very beginning history has had to counter legend, myth, and partisan distortion. That remains its dilemma: It is spurred on by collective, largely unconscious needs for the endowment of higher meaning, but it must rid itself of such notions in its scholarly methods."

What should one think of an indictment that even fabricates its own sources? Habermas will not be able to duck the accusation of, say, imaginative invention. He stakes an exclusive claim on the Enlightenment

61

and has the ends justify the means. It's a shame about this man who once had something to say.

Source: *Frankfurter Allgemeine Zeitung*, August 16, 1986

Publisher's Note: This letter to the editor appeared under the title "An Indictment That Fabricates Even Its Sources."

JOACHIM FEST

Encumbered Remembrance: The Controversy about the Incomparability of National-Socialist Mass Crimes

A U.S. historian recently lamented the lack of freedom in the style of academic debate in the Federal Republic. Whenever the discussion moves to the Hitler period and its moral evaluation, he said, the tone of voice suddenly changes. One either places himself on the side of compact morality with formulaic invocations and professions of guilt that are as empty of meaning as they are of credibility, or, he continued, the discussion ends with moral denunciation.

There is, as everyone knows, a lot of truth to that. But it is no less true that the public sphere, despite all encouragement from the political side, has still not stepped out of the shadow cast by Hitler and the crimes committed under him. This shadow still unavoidably falls over all serious attempts at historical debate and analysis. To the scholarly integrity of the historian belongs the awareness that his actions do not take place in a vacuum but in front of a public and with, in many ways, unpredictable amplification and fading. He cannot ignore these effects and must still attempt to make progress by asking questions and suggesting answers. In a recent article for this paper, Christian Meier movingly showed how hard that could be. It takes responsibility and inner independence. What it does not take are rituals of fake obsequiousness.

These rituals are decreed by a conformism that places under moral suspicion every position maintaining the freedom to ask questions. At least since the end of the 1960s it has become customary to accuse of clandestine complicity with "fascism" every historical perception that does not adhere to the prevailing view. It does not depend upon the scholarly finding or the presented results, no matter how experimental they might be. What really counts are the presumed motives of the person who presents them.

For this impoverished practice of history there is now a new variant. It comes from Jürgen Habermas. In an article in *Die Zeit*, which has been publishing a variety of historical articles of a neoconservative trend, he placed several famous historians of the Federal Republic under suspicion of being tools of NATO. From articles and other publications that appeared in this newspaper, he discerned in all seriousness a strategy that attempted "to use a revivification of (German) national consciousness to banish the negative images of the German nation state from the domain of NATO" and to replace them with new hostile national images from the East. It was an article by Ernst Nolte (*Frankfurter Allgemeine Zeitung*, June 6, 1986) that served as evidence. In it, Nolte denied, as Habermas sees it, the singularity of the Nazi crimes by at least making them "comprehensible as an answer to the (still extant) Bolshevist threat of annihilation." He also attempted, as Habermas views it, to reduce Auschwitz to "the format of technical innovation."

In fact, Nolte does not deny the singularity of the National-Socialist acts of annihilation. He expressly notes that they are, "despite all comparability, qualitatively different than the social annihilation that Bolshevism undertook." Nonetheless, he continues, one should not simply look at the one mass murder while ignoring the other, especially where there is probably a causal connection between the two.

It is questionable how Habermas could have overlooked this central thought upon which Nolte's entire argumentation rests. If it is not a case of academic dyslexia, then one can only assume that an ideological form of prejudgement is setting up a straw man here in order to be able to attack it. The second assumption seems likely since Habermas supports his thesis with fragments of quotations. He falsely attributes utterances of third parties or even his own ideas to the authors he attacks, and he distorts things with a carelessness the likes of which have not been seen for a long time. The accused have since responded briefly.

I am not concerned here with this attempt at scholarly, and perhaps personal, character assassination. The dispute, however, conceals a core that reveals all the difficulties of the questions posed about the Hitler period. Of particular interest is the thesis of the singularity of the Nazi crimes. It is worth having a closer look at the reasons that are brought forth to support this notion.

At first it is claimed that the monstrous and unheard-of aspect of the so-called Final Solution is that the perpetrators were not concerned with guilt or innocence. Instead, they made membership in a race the exclusive cause for decisions about life and death. But at the end of 1918, in a speech before the commissars, one of the first heads of the Cheka, the Latvian Martyn Latsis, declared that in the course of the Bolshevist revolution not guilt but membership in a social group would determine punishment and liquidation: "We are in the process of exterminating the bourgeoisie as a class. You do not have to prove that this or that person acted against the interests of Soviet power. The first thing you have to ask of a prisoner is, What class do you belong to, where do you come from, what education have you had, what is your occupation? These questions are to decide the fate of the accused. That is the quintessence of the Red Terror." And one can read in Alexander Solzhenitsyn how literally this was taken—at least to the extent that proof was considered and people were not shot simply "by lists." Unlike the famous expression implies, one could not choose his social class. One was, at least in this time, irrevocably bound to it by birth and origin.

But was the same view not behind "guilty verdicts" of the *Reichs-sicherheitshauptamt*, only that here not social but biological existence was considered reason for death? In the one case as in the other, there was no possibility of defending oneself or of proving one's innocence because there was never a question of guilt or innocence but only of membership, here to a class, there to a race.

To support the singularity of Auschwitz and all it stood for, one often cites the administrative and mechanical form in which mass murders were carried out. The indeed monstrous image of the bureaucratic executioner who, unmoved, far from the sufferings of his victims, pursues his annihilation with stamps and files, to a large extent caused the shock that has continued to affect us today. Bound up in the concept of the *Schreibtisch-mörder*, the man who commits mass murder from his desk, is the horror of our halting ability to understand that so much coldness and so much pedantry can only with great difficulty be linked to the fear and the death struggle of the victims.

But can we believe that Stalin's exterminations were achieved in a substantially different, less administrative way? Habermas accuses Andreas Hillgruber of using palliative vocabulary because in the title of a book he speaks of the "destruction" of the Reich on the one hand and of the "end" of European Jewry on the other. But what he himself, in hardly surpassable trivialization, calls "the expulsion of the kulaks by Stalin," means in reality the death of millions. Can we, inasmuch as there are no accessible sources, seriously assume that there was no far-flung bureaucracy with files and stamps and *Schreibtischmörder*? The gas chambers with which the executors of the annihilation of the Jews went to work without a doubt signal a particularly repulsive form of mass murder, and they have justifiably become a symbol for the technicized barbarism of the Hitler regime. But can it really be said that the mass liquidations by a bullet to the back of the neck, as was common practice during the years of the Red Terror, are qualitatively different? Isn't, despite all differences, the comparable element stronger?

We know the horrifying images of piles of bodies, the shoes, eyeglasses, suitcases, and other valuables of the victims that were brought together into greater and smaller mountains. But what justifies us in thinking that that sort of thing did not happen in the murder factories of the Stalin period? We did not see it. There are no photos or films about it. But is it not a shortcoming of human imagination that not even the mind's eye has an image of it? Are the events here and there, all in all, not comparable in their decisive characteristics? In both cases there are mechanical and abstract killing practices that can be massively reproduced. They are planned administratively and carried out by executioners who, unmoved, perform their duties in the name of a greater cause. What they did took place without inner participation, without any affect, which even in the most extreme perversion would manifest in at least a shimmer of what could be considered "human nature" in its mean and repulsive traits.

The third argument, finally, with which the singularity of the Nazi crimes is supported, rests upon the claim that it is so much more horrifying when this kind of relapse into dehumanized behavior takes place in a cultured people. Indeed, this is nearly impossible to comprehend. The persistent shock about this is accompanied by the silent and recurring questions about how it was possible. It is also met with speechlessness by many people who cannot comprehend what happened. All this is related to the fact that Germans thought up, planned, and carried out these mass murders and that this took place against a background of century-old German-Jewish symbiosis, a process that belongs among the greatest cultural achievements of history.

The shock about what happened can be the origin of very personal shame, but also of an embarrassment about the things that have been done to the name of the nation. But does this attitude really make sense, even when such events happen again and again? Strictly speaking, this argument presumes the old Nazi distinction according to which there are higher peoples and more primitive peoples who do not even know about the commandment against killing. Those who are more sensitive will recognize the arrogance in this, the master race attitude, even if it is concealed beneath a gesture of humility.

The thesis of the singularity of Nazi crimes is finally also placed in question by the consideration that Hitler himself frequently referred to the practices of his revolutionary opponents of the Left as lessons and models. But he did more than just copy them. Determined to be more radical than his most bitter enemy, he also outdid them. That can be demonstrated at all levels and was by no means limited to the public appearances and rituals by which the NSDAP represented itself as a party of a new kind. Far more important was the tone and style of civil war that Hitler gave to the political disputes of the time. He was prepared, as he said, "to counter every act of terror by Marxism with a response ten times greater."

One does not have to be of the opinion that Hitler's desire to annihilate was predominantly inspired by the threat of annihilation posed by the Russian Revolution. It came, judging by its origin, from the German-Austrian's earlier fears and phantasies of being overwhelmed. But that he was entirely uneffected by the Russian Revolution is hard to imagine. In any case the resonance created by his insane ideas, which for a long time had no public following, cannot be understood without understanding the sense of panic that spread from Russia and affected Munich in 1919. The reports about deporting, murdering, and exterminating entire ethnic groups were doubtless exaggerated. But they also contained a core of truth that gained in credibility through the pathos of the approaching world revolution. Despite their distortions, they gave Hitler's extermination complexes a real background. And the fact that among the people who had led the Munich Soviet Republic, which was now going down in chaos and terror, there were more than a few Jews, provided his anti-Semitic obsessions with what seemed to be a confirmation that could later be used in political agitation. He as well as the insecure masses may well have believed that salvation was only possible through the decision to act with equal force in resistance, even if that meant being "ten times" more terroristic. It must be possible to represent this thought process and to establish a connection between the horrifying reports coming from the East and Hitler's readiness to engage in excesses. But then one is at loss to explain the indignation caused by Nolte's remark that the events in Russia were "the logical and factual prius" to Auschwitz and that between both a "causal nexus is probable."

These thoughts have been countered by widespread objections. They point out the fundamental, scarcely measurable difference between the two ideologies. Communism, as is claimed or at least tacitly presumed, goes back, even in its Russian variant, to a set of great humanitarian ideas. An unconsumed remainder still lies at the heart of this ideology, as the argument would have it. Neither the sufferings that it caused nor the countless deaths that it demanded can extinguish this heritage. In contrast to that, National Socialism stems from inferior thoughts of folkish sectarians— thoughts that were distributed among the people around the turn of the century in treatises and cheap pamphlets.

This argument is not without merit. And when in the vehement challenges of the one or the other side the word "annihilation" comes up, one cannot ignore the fact that the radical Left generally did not have physical but apparently social and historical elimination of their opponents in mind. But the parareligious claim with which they charged their slogans, the Manichaean implacability with which they harshly subdivided the world into good and evil and the people into the just and abject, this by necessity blurred the borders that would have guaranteed their sworn enemies the right to live. The memory of the religious wars and the fanaticism they had cast aside did not lie so far back in time that one could be assured that such postulates could not be taken literally and that "social annihilation" could not be transformed into the expressly physical kind.

In all kinds of rhetoric there is an automatism that sees deeds emerging from words and robs thoughts of the innocence to which they appeal to justify themselves. When Lenin demanded that the Russian soil be liberated from the "dogs and swine of the dying bourgeoisie" and Zinovyev glibly spoke about the extermination of ten million people, that was no longer a purely metaphorical extreme but already the consequence of it. It can hardly be demonstrated that this was different with National Socialism. And who is to decide whether this movement, too, did not become caught up in a net of verbal excesses with its crimes?

In any case, Martin Broszat and Hans Mommsen, in a piece about the murder of the Jews, applied just this consideration to the Nazi regime and claimed that the Nazi leadership did not from the beginning systematically work toward the so-called Final Solution. Rather, so the argument goes, they became prisoners of a process that they themselves, by their phraseology, their legislation, and a complex of self-generating and self-intensifying activities, set in motion.

This doubtless does not debunk the idea that these ideologies had very different origins. But why then, one must ask, especially if one takes this background seriously, has so little been preserved of Marxism's grand view of history, as rudimentary as it may have been? And why are the disputes in the leadership circles, no matter who happens to be in power, basically never about humanitarian principles? And why has all resistance based on this idealist motivation always remained the lost cause of nameless individuals (not to mention individuals who were made nameless)? And what difference does it make on the part of the perpetrators whether they believe that they are justified by a corrupted humane ideal or by a weltanschaung that was degenerate from the very beginning? Does it amount to a different thing that the one side pursued its murderous activities with a good conscience while the other side did the same with a less good one?

This idealized difference evaporates even more when viewed from the side of the victims. Strangely, the supporters of this modern view of history make things easy for themselves when they assert that they pay less attention to those in power and their passage through history than to the suffering individual. But what difference can it make to those who have been murdered whether they fell victim to a historical principle that once had intellectual and humanitarian dignity or "only" to a delusion permeated by phantom fears? In his book *Faschismus in seiner Epoche* [Fascism in Its Epoch], Ernst Nolte also made this distinction in the final sentence of his chapter about National Socialism. Beginning with this thought, he sought solace in the fact that the millions murdered by Hitler "did not die as unlucky objects of a repulsive crime but rather as representatives in the most desperate attack ever made on the human being." But is that more than a thought, and what desperation could it ward off?

There are questions upon questions, but no answer can be offered here. Rather, it is a matter of rousing doubt in the monumental simplicity and one-sidedness of the prevailing ideas about the particularity of the Nazi crimes that supposedly had no model and followed no example. All in all, this thesis stands on weak ground. And it is less surprising that, as Habermas incorrectly suggests in reference to Nolte, it is being questioned. It is far more astonishing that this has not seriously taken place until now. For that also means that the countless other victims, in particular but not exclusively those of communism, are no longer part of our memory. Arno Borst once declared in a different context that no group in today's society has been as ruthlessly oppressed as the dead. That is especially true for millions of the dead of this century, from the Armenians all the way to the victims of the Gulag Archipelago or the Cambodians who were and are being murdered before all of our eyes—but who have still been dropped from the world's memory.

Perhaps these dead have been dropped not so much from the world's memory as from the memory of the Germans. Have we asked ourselves why the revelations by Solzhenitsyn, unlike their effect in France or Italy, caused so little change among intellectuals in the Federal Republic? Here, his book caused suspicion to be placed on the author himself. It would be a mistake to explain why Solzhenitsyn's revelations have had less impact here than elsewhere simply by suggesting that the sons and grandsons of executioners are too full of shame to speak of the nooses they might see hanging in the houses of others. In the face of French massacres in Algeria, later in the face of Vietnam and then of Chile or Argentina, there was no timidity—and this for good reason. The assumption is not farfetched that moral irritation follows political intentions. And with an insensitivity that recalls our worst memories, people are busy at some professorial desks "selecting" the victims.

Anyone who wants to question the thesis that the National-Socialist mass crimes had a unique character also has to deal with the objection that referring to similar crimes committed by others reduces one's own blame. The "tu quoque," it is said, is always nothing more than an attempt to seek exoneration for one's own crimes in the crimes committed elsewhere. In a comprehensive reckoning, so the argument goes, genocide would fall to the side of historical normalcy, a situation in which each nation is involved with its own crimes; thus also in the last analysis—and rather late at that—the Germans are too.

There is no doubt that this kind of rationalizing happens. But no thought is safe from being falsified in this or that direction. The cause of this article is an example of that. One cannot ignore the facts, and sometimes they rub open wounds. But as long as we desire to be concerned with historical perception and not with ever-changing opinions, these facts are not a mass of discretionary material that can be used as we see fit. Habermas calls Nolte's reference to "virulent anti-Semitism" among the Polish victims of National Socialism "unsavory"—as if facts were a matter of taste. Marc Hillel's book *Le Massacre des Survivants en Pologne 1945–1947*, informs us, as can be read in a review in *Merkur*, that in July 1946, one-and-a-half years after the liberation of Auschwitz, a pogrom was carried out in Kielce by the Polish army. The perpetrators, according to eye-witnesses, went to work with the call: "We are completing Hitler's work." If we are to search for knowledge, then we must also be able to refer to events like this. Perhaps the current dispute has to do with the fact that historians, unlike social scientists, feel they are bound to demonstrable facts. These are the foundations on which historians stand.

It must also be said concerning the dispute about the incomparability of the Nazi crimes that one crime cannot simply balance another. No one else's crimes diminish one's own, and no murderer has ever been able to exculpate himself by referring to another murderer. These are insights of such a simple and obvious character that one is hesitant to remind people of them. And still, behind many reflections on the singularity thesis, there is a concern that this kind of general rule might be suspended and all historical guilt would then dissipate in a frenzied round of compensation.

Beyond all the noise and shouts of accusation that stand in the fore-ground, the current dispute is possibly dominated by quite different oppositions. Jürgen Habermas, deeply rooted in the intellectual battles of yesterday and yesteryear, still sees the boundary separating the opponents as one between conservative and progressive, between German-national and liberal historians. He sees strategies of moral relativization as doing the dirty work for a view of history that exonerates the guilty and thus in its own way contributes to the chimerical *Wende* [conservative shift] whose helpers he sees at work everywhere—Nolte, Hildebrand, Stürmer, and Hillgruber—all under a common, conservative denominator. This amounts to the most absurd kind of conspiracy theory, which here, as is usually the case, is no more than an expression of uncomprehended contexts. Maybe the discussion would be furthered if one could coax these people out of this dispute about directions and out of such fossilized categories.

One could ask whether another kind of differentiation would be prefer-able: On the one side there is the pessimistic view that is incapable of perceiving much more in history than the murder and mayhem that always existed. This view sees history as dominated by hate, fear, and extermination, without meaning and goal. But due to the technical innovations available today, history lives on with an unheard-of passionlessness while demanding an endlessly greater number of victims than in the past. In this view, Auschwitz does indeed shrink to the status of a "technical innovation."

Opposing the pessimists are those who have salvaged from the moral catastrophes of the century the hopes of the past in the "perfectibility" of man as well as in his educability. These people see in the Holocaust a singular aberration, in the wake of which the march to a better world can continue. On the horizon, in some distant future, rises—battered but not surrendering—the image of the "new man." For the other side, man remains his old self, with evil as part of the *"condition humaine."* No utopia can ever shake this belief. The one side is convinced that Hitler was a terrible mistake in the historical process and must never be forgotten. The other side bows to the insight that the act of genocide that Hitler set in motion was not the first and will not be the last. This side is convinced that we owe remembrance to the victims here as well as there and have to live with all that happened in mind.

Both sides have their reasons, and it is not even clear that the individual has a real choice about where he stands. If participants would concede their opponents this, the dispute would presumably surrender its cantankerous, derogatory character and gain in seriousness and substance. Habermas credits himself and his generation with unconditionally opening the Federal Republic to the political culture of the West. Thus he likes to see himself as the advocate of a "pluralism of modes of understanding [*Lesarten*]." Inasmuch as that means anything at all, it can and should not exclude the possibility of debate. It should, however, exclude personal defamation. No achievement of thought, no historical-literary life's work that demonstrates as much scholarly seriousness as it does moral uneasiness and that in the meantime has gained a worldwide reputation, was able to protect men like Ernst Nolte or Andreas Hillgruber from the accusation that they are lackeys of reactionary and amoral interests. They see themselves as "revisionists" who have been dragged into discredit; as if scholarship, just like thinking in general, could exist without permanent revision. It is again evident that the keepers of the seal of the new enlightenment, if circumstances and interests warrant it, are willing to become the "mandarins" of myths. For Hitler and National Socialism, despite years of study and reflection about them, have remained more myth than history. And public discussion still aims more at incantation than at knowledge. It is not inconceivable that the increasing academization of this process could weaken the moral impulse to honestly examine the past. But it is more likely that new considerations as well as more differentiated and more broadly based insights will open new moral access to this subject, which is frequently treated only in ritualized ways.

Source: *Frankfurter Allgemeine Zeitung*, August 29, 1986

KARL DIETRICH BRACHER

Letter to the Editor of the
Frankfurter Allgemeine Zeitung,
September 6, 1986

The recent great discussion (see the *Frankfurter Allgemeine Zeitung* of August 29) about the comparability of the National-Socialist and Communist policy of mass murder contains nothing new in the way of scholarship. Virtually all essential facts and arguments were published in books of the 1940s and 1950s. Not the least of these arguments was that the "totalitarian" force of these two ideologies seized the whole human and seduced and enslaved him. These insights have been fatally and widely repressed in the past two decades by tabooing the concept of totalitarianism and inflating the formula for fascism (of which by the way neither Ernst Nolte nor Jürgen Habermas are innocent). Debasing the concept of totalitarianism shielded from view the systematic elements of repression that dictatorships of the Left and Right have in common. Furthermore, the use of the word "totalitarian" aroused suspicion of anticommunism. For these reasons contemporary theories of fascism underestimate the central meaning of the National-Socialist ideology and politics of race.

We have attempted to work against this bending and obscuring of the questions with, however, only limited success (see also my book, *Zeit der Ideologien* [Age of Ideologies]). It is regrettable that discussion about the comparability of systems is being carried out in such politically polarized controversies. It is as if there has not already existed, for some time, a body of serious research into the totalitarian movements and regimes of our century. While it is certainly in need of being expanded, it is a body of research that, naturally, constantly considers national differences. But the essential point remains that those ideologies and dictatorships, which made the terrible possible, lose nothing of their respective "singular" inhumanity by comparisons. Neither a national nor a socialist apologetic can be supported on that basis. The shame about the failure of a cultured civilization, one that believes itself formed by the values of Christianity, humanism, and the Enlightenment, can help us to recognize the dangers of totalitarian manipulation. References to similar phenomena in other civilizations should not relativize this experience; rather it should broaden it and make it general. That means not only a remembrance of the past but also a warning for the present and the future.

Source: *Frankfurter Allgemeine Zeitung*, September 6, 1986

Author's Note: I have treated the whole problematic in two larger articles:
1. "Das Modewort Identität und die deutsche Frage" [The Fashion-word Identity and the German Question], in *Frankfurter Allgemeine Zeitung*, August 9, 1986, supplement *Bilder und Zeiten* [Pictures and Times].
2. "Zeitgeschichtliche Erfahrungen als aktuelles Problem" [Historical Experiences as a Contemporary Problem], in *Aus Politik und Zeitgeschichte* [From Politics and Recent History] supplement to *Das Parlament*, March 14, 1987.

Publisher's Note: The letter appeared under the title "The Common Elements Are Shielded from View."

EBERHARD JÄCKEL

The Impoverished Practice of Insinuation: The Singular Aspect of National-Socialist Crimes Cannot Be Denied

There are discussions that attain their charm by the fact that it is not always clear what is meant. Instead of asking questions and giving answers, which are then examined, statements are presented in the form of questions with the intention of suggesting what cannot and should not be proven. And the people who are caught in this game respond with outrage and a look of innocence and ask, One can ask, can't one? In reality, however, the question is not a question at all but a concealed statement. In this way the apparent questioner manages to sidestep the trouble of having to provide reasons. Instead, he has left the job of convincing people to a few innuendos. This is the kind of perplexing game that is being played in this country.

It began with the *Frankfurter Allgemeine Zeitung* article of June 6, 1986, in which Ernst Nolte pleaded that we should look "not only at the one murder," that is, the one committed by the National Socialists, but recognize the other, that is, the Bolshevist one. It is characteristic of the rules of the game that Nolte, if taken quite literally, did not plead but rather only stated (and even then qualified by a secondary clause) that *an attitude* that examined only the one murder would lead us completely astray. Nolte did not betray the name of the person who is supposed to have taken this attitude. But he imputed that someone had.

Should that be true, it would be obviously nonsensical. What would history be if it were so one-sided? But instead of using a few words to make this simple insight even more obvious, he intimated in another secondary clause that between the two murders "a causal nexus was likely." That was news, especially coming from the mouth of a respected historian. One would be justified in expecting Nolte to support his thesis and in this way bring the discussion to a head.

But nothing of the kind occurred. Instead, Jürgen Habermas responded in *Die Zeit* of July 11 by accusing Nolte and several other German historians of apologetic tendencies. Indeed, Nolte's argumentation (we will

74

discuss this later) gave reason for this suspicion, and Habermas backed up his claim by objecting to the choice of words used by some historians. But he said nothing about the topic itself or about Nolte's thesis. Klaus Hildebrand also failed to do so when he, in the *Frankfurter Allgemeine Zeitung* of June 31, responded to Habermas by coming to the aid of his colleague Andreas Hillgruber, whom Habermas, as I see it, treated unjustly. Hildebrand said little more about Nolte than that he could not understand why we should impose "prohibitions on the questions we ask." He did not betray who was trying to impose such prohibitions. He continued the game by insinuating that someone had done so.

And thus the situation continued with a few letters to the editor and a number of articles—until on August 29 Joachim Fest intervened in the discussion by, in the same newspaper, expressing his opinion in detail in "The Controversy about the Singularity of National-Socialist Mass Crimes." He started out by calling Habermas's comments "a new variant" of an "impoverished practice" that had become customary since the end of the 1960s. By this he meant the tendency not to discuss the findings of the historians but their motives. Fest provided no reason to support his assertion that this had been common practice since that ominous date. Nor could he have provided a reason. For it is undeniable that since time immemorial both the motives and the findings of historians have been discussed. It is really old hat that Tacitus claimed to write *sine ira et studio* but in fact did not do so since he, too, had motives. This kind of study is called an ideology critique, and it is both legitimate and an integral part of the discipline. Fest, however, terms it an "impoverished practice" and, using a chronological insinuation, blames it on the Left on top of it all.

But just as one began to fear that the discussion would again end up out of bounds, Fest, this must be said to his credit, got to the point. Of course he took up a topic that had not been discussed to that point. He claimed that Nolte had "not denied the singularity of the National-Socialist acts of annihilation." Indeed, Nolte did no such thing. Only Habermas used the concept, and then only once. But that too is part of the game: One picks up what has not been said because one anticipates what was meant and speaks of a controversy where none exists. Next, Fest produced three arguments that allegedly speak against singularity and then declared himself in Nolte's camp by saying that we must be permitted "to establish a connection between the horrifying reports from the East and Hitler's readiness to act in an extreme way." One also wonders, he continued, about "the real reasons" for the irritation caused by Nolte's comments that the events in Russia were "the logical and factual prius" to Auschwitz and that between both a "causal nexus" was probable.

In this way Fest brought the game to a new climax. He did not say there was no causal nexus. He merely said that it would not be impermissible to establish one. And if the comment caused irritation, then he was not interested whether that could be explained by the fact that the comment contradicts the historical sources. No, he uses the "impoverished practices" he has just castigated and asks about motives.

But now it is time to stop the game. I for one do not want to play any longer. I also do not want to ask for the motives of the participants, even though that would be permissible. I want to talk about the subject. Two clearly phrased claims can be precipitated out of the tangle of legalese and Latinisms such as *prius*, *nexus*, *logical*, *factual*, and *causal*. The first, which, as Fest correctly notes, not Nolte, but Fest himself stated, is: The National-Socialist mass murder of the Jews was not unique. And the second, which Nolte considers probable and Fest calls not impermissible: There is an originary connection between this act of mass murder and that of the Bolsheviks.

Regarding the first claim, Fest cites three arguments that he says he is using to support the singularity thesis—and then he contests them with counterarguments. First, the perpetrators did not care about the guilt or innocence of their victims—but neither did the Bolsheviks. Second, the murders were carried out in an administrative and mechanical way. Third, the murders were carried out by a "cultured people." But this argument, he went on, could not be accepted because in it is "the old master race attitude."

Fest does not say who used these arguments. And I find not one of them valid. Innocent people have time and time again been killed administratively and mechanically. Where the killings took place seems of little importance in determining whether the killings were unique. I, however, claim (and not for the first time) that the National-Socialist murder of the Jews was unique because never before had a nation with the authority of its leader decided and announced that it would kill off as completely as possible a particular group of humans, including old people, women, children, and infants, and actually put this decision into practice, using all the means of governmental power at its disposal. This idea is so apparent and so well known that it is quite astonishing that it could have escaped Fest's attention (the massacres of the Armenians in the Osmanian Empire during the First World War were, according to all we know, more like murderous deportations than planned genocide).

Regarding the Bolshevik murders, Fest quotes the head of the Cheka, who declared at the end of 1918: "We are in the process of exterminating the bourgeoisie as a class." But that in no way proves that he meant that every individual bourgeois was to be killed—not to mention women and children. Fest endeavors to produce proof that such extermination was common practice. The head of the SS, Heinrich Himmler, was much clearer in this respect when he declared on October 6, 1943 (and anyone who so desires can verify that he was speaking the truth): "The question was posed to us: What about the women and children? I have decided to find a clear solution here, too. I just did not feel justified in exterminating the men (that is, in killing them or having them killed)—and allowing avengers in the form of little children to grow up for our sons and grandsons. We had to come to the grave decision to make this people disappear from the face of the earth."

The question of uniqueness is, by the way, not all that decisive. Should the Federal Republic then pay no more reparations? Or should the chancellor no longer bow in Yad Vashem? Or should the citizens feel better? It is really not that this society is languishing, bowed by grief and in need of solace. It lives well and should continue to do so, as far as I am concerned. But the problem is that the society knows little about these murders. When the federal president, in an honorable speech on May 8, 1985, spoke of six million Jews murdered in concentration camps, historians can recognize how small the effect of their research is. According to our latest, quite precise estimates, 150,000 Jews were killed in concentration camps. Another five million were killed in death camps, in the ghettos, and by shooting.

Much more important and stimulating is the second claim that Nolte declares probable and that Fest takes up—that is, the causal relationship between the Bolshevist and the National-Socialist murders. Of course a rational discourse about this is extraordinarily important. The discipline of history knows no more difficult task than linking two historical causes. Historical causes do not exist anywhere such that one can seek and find them. Moreover, two different things are meant by the concept: On the one side are motives that cause someone to engage in an act; on the other are the conditions without which no actions can be imagined. Historians are constantly involved in trying to understand this process.

Nolte does not make these efforts easy. He only provides, as he terms them, "illuminating key concepts." These begin with a statement by Hitler on February 1, 1943, which suggested that in Moscow the German officers captured in Stalingrad would be put in the "rat cage," where they would sign anything. Nolte also noted that the commentators (in reality it was the editor of the stenographic transcript) suggested that "rat cage" meant Lubyanka prison. He continues: "I consider that to be wrong." He has either missed the point or is not bothered by the fact that in this meeting Hitler himself twice said that he meant Lubyanka. Nolte thus knows better; then he speaks about Orwell's novel *1984*, which did not appear until 1949. Here, too, a rat cage appears. Orwell was not inventing history, Nolte says. This rat cage can be found in anti-Bolshevist literature about the Russian civil war, "among other places in the writing of the usually reliable socialist Melgunov" and is attributed to the "Chinese Cheka."

Nolte still needs to explain what that has to do with the killing of the Jews that began in June 1941. It is characteristic that he derives few of his conclusions from this abstruse chain of associations. After a few self-constructed objections he writes: "The following question must seem permissible, even unavoidable: Did the National Socialists or Hitler perhaps commit an 'Asiatic' deed merely because they and their ilk considered themselves to be potential victims of an 'Asiatic' deed? Was the Gulag Archipelago not primary to Auschwitz? Was the Bolshevik murder of an entire class not the logical and factual prius of the 'racial murder' of National Socialism? Cannot Hitler's most secret deeds be explained by the fact that he had *not* forgotten the rat cage?" Then Nolte concludes with the already quoted sentence that "a causal nexus is probable."

This is not what could be called a logical reason. *Post hoc, ergo propter hoc*. The thesis of the logical nexus seems to be based on this most dubious of logical inferences—unless of course Nolte can prove that Hitler's decision to kill the Jews was driven by such fears. In fact Nolte and Fest argue just that. But their arguments are not only unconvincing—they can be disproven with some certainty.

Hitler often said why he wished to remove and to kill the Jews. His explanation is a complicated and structurally logical construct that can be reproduced in great detail. A rat cage, the murders committed by the Bolsheviks, or a special fear of these are not mentioned. On the contrary, Hitler was always convinced that Soviet Russia, precisely because it was ruled by Jews, was a defenseless colossus standing on clay feet. Arians had no fear of Slavic or Jewish subhumans. The Jew, Hitler wrote in 1926 in *Mein Kampf*, "is not an element of an organization but a ferment of decomposition. The gigantic empire in the East is rife for collapse." Hitler still believed this in 1941 when he had his soldiers invade Russia without winter equipment.

In contrast, he knew very well how to mobilize for his own uses the fears of the bourgeoisie. In public he liked to speak of the Asiatic hordes that threatened Europe, and he justified his lebensraum war as a war of prevention. But one should not confuse these tactical statements with his true motives. This kind of confusion seems to be behind the thesis of the "causal nexus." What is being suggested to us is the thesis of preemptive murder. But that is as false as the one about preemptive war. Even though this thesis has been refuted hundreds of times, it is repeatedly dragged out of Hitler's arsenal.

Source: *Die Zeit*, September 12, 1986

Author's Note: The text was originally titled "Factual Prius and Causal Nexus. Murky Game of Bewilderment Concerning the Murder of the Jews."

HELMUT FLEISCHER

The Morality of History: On the Dispute about the Past That Will Not Pass

A "great discussion" is what the historian K. D. Bracher has called the newly enlivened dispute about the Nazi past. The Frankfurt Römerberg Talks in June gave a new impetus to this debate by putting on the agenda this very past that after more than forty years "will not pass." The dispute picked up trenchancy right away, when the talk by Ernst Nolte, which "could not be delivered there," was printed as an essay in the *Frankfurter Allgemeine Zeitung*. At the same time there appeared in Siedler Verlag a little volume of essays by Andreas Hillgruber on the "twofold fall." It treats the military collapse of the German Reich in 1944–1945 and the murder of the European Jews. These and a few other publications challenged the social philosopher Jürgen Habermas to issue in *Die Zeit* a pointed "call to arms" against "revisionist tendencies" in the German writing of history. Habermas is suspicious of such "revisionisms." He suspects they seek to provide West Germans with a peaceful historical conscience by removing from their shoulders the moral burden of that frightful past. In this way they can again speak with continuity on German history and see it as really not so fundamentally different than the histories of other nations. In Habermas's view this is actually a final "settlement of accounts." It has the desired result of allowing Germans to say, now we are even, we can draw a line under it, and now, with a new sense of freedom, let us get on to the tasks that the Western world has set for us in the face of the tangible threats of today and tomorrow. Is that the tenor of the revision of history currently drawing so much attention? "A Kind of Settlement of Damages"—this was how Habermas characterized it in his essay of July 11, and on the same date a sharp reply also appeared in the *Frankfurter Allgemeine Zeitung*. The controversy took its course.

What is the controversy about? First, it is evidently about the fact that some things have taken up too much space in the debate already. One of these is the question of whether the atrocities of the Nazi-SS regime are "singular," that is, whether they are incomparable to all other horrors of ancient and modern history. Whenever the discussion focuses on singularity, then all glances are directed toward the mass murder of the Jews, for which the word "Auschwitz" often stands. Auschwitz stands indeed for the quintessence of the Nazi epoch as a whole. However, the moral earnestness of this memorial can become dubious if for many of us Auschwitz is all that sticks in our memory. (And does not the soothing notion that something comparable cannot happen again inadvertently cling to the word "singularity"?) Should one not believe that our century's history of violence was already terrible enough without Auschwitz? The Soviet Union, after all, lost twenty million people. E. Nolte at any rate presses the point that we should discuss not just the singularity but also the whole politics of annihilation in our time. If someone is convinced of the singularity and incomparability of this the most unambiguous of war crimes, does a higher morality in relation to the Nazi past somehow inhere in his position?

This brings us to the core of the controversy. It is the question about the *moral* judgment of the Nazi past and about the moral "mortgage" that burdens the heirs of Hitler and Himmler.

J. Habermas makes himself solicitor general of the kingdom of morality in the province of history. He seems concerned that the local provincial governors could do damage to the high law of morality. One of his main criticisms takes aim at the historian Hillgruber. Hillgruber labors with the ethical antimonies of the "hopeless situation" of 1944–1945 on the eastern front near East Prussia. Hillgruber makes the case for ethically justifying those who tried to hold the eastern front a little longer for the sake of the survival of the civilian population behind them. Habermas's other critique takes aim at Nolte's attempt to make a plausible genealogical connection between the earlier policy of annihilation on the part of the Bolshevik revolution and the later, biologically defined, mass extermination carried out by the National Socialists, explicitly by Hitler. Nolte's contention of a genealogical connection, according to Habermas, has the effect that the Nazi crimes lose their singularity and appear as a reaction to previous atrocities of the same kind. "Auschwitz shrinks to the format of technical innovation and can be explained as a response to the 'Asiatic' threat from an enemy that still stands before our gates." For Habermas this is the quintessence of the "revisionism" of Nolte and Hillgruber "who set out to shake off the mortgages of a past now happily made morally neutral."

I do not want to treat further who "is right" in this matter of person against person. A bit later in the *Frankfurter Allgemeine Zeitung* Joachim Fest tried to decide the argument about the ominous question of "singularity" with an offering of facts. Recently, in the person of K. D. Bracher, the all-but-defunct theory of "totalitarianism," which always had been a common term for communism and fascism, has weighed in. Indeed, all the scholarship that takes aim at a "systematic historical comparison" of human contempt has not yet, in my judgment, reached a level on which new conclusions for our historical consciousness would be evident. This level would be achieved by a real "historicizing" of National Socialism and Soviet communism, of their proper place in the general history of their respective historical moments, and of their reciprocal penetrations and the collisions between them. More on that later. Habermas's unjust exaggerations certainly account for the dispute's so quickly having become a feud of matadors. Habermas may indeed hit the bull's-eye with regard to some resentments on the part of old veterans; however, he missed the mark with Nolte and Hillgruber.

Next, from his more lofty perspective, a far wider format than that of a personal feud was set up for the "great discussion" by Martin Broszat. The Munich historian's piece of May 8, 1985, in *Merkur* (vol. 435), "Plädoyer für die Historisierung des Nationalsozialismus" [Plea for Historicizing National Socialism], is a plea that every interested person is supposed to hear. We will evidently have to summon Broszat as the leading expert if we want to make any progress in the matter. Habermas picks up directly where the article by Broszat left off, although the positions are again a bit blurred.

"The distinctness of our situation," writes Broszat, "is the necessity and at the same time the difficulty of the proper placement of National Socialism in German history." (This is what is meant by "historicizing,"not filing it away in a historical archive.) The other difficulty, however, was supposed to be even greater: finding a new framework for the moral judgment of National Socialism. "The dictum, flattened to stereotype, of the 'National-Socialist regime of terror' can indeed again be made morally accessible only if we develop a more sharply differentiating insight." Thus, with regard to this morality, Broszat verifies a state of affairs that has arisen in the course of four decades. National Socialism always had figured as a negative standard for political education, as the opposite of the model of rights, freedom, and the peaceful order. However, "working against that is the fact that, over time, this morality based on shock about the Nazi past has largely exhausted itself. This shock-based morality has had to give up some of its singularity because of new historical experiences of violence and catastrophe. Over time it has widely become an established set of risk-free and vague confessions of consciousness without moral force." The name "Auschwitz" does not come up a single time in Broszat's essay, but certainly not because it would not be essential. Auschwitz is not the pivot for the historical-ethical discussion of the phenomenon of National Socialism. It represents the peak of contempt for humanity that national egocentrism achieved in a narrowly circumscribed circle of leadership (and that this circle carefully blocked off from the rest of the population). This peak of contempt was achieved just at the time when the leadership plunged into the uncertain horror of the attack on Soviet Russia. The annihilation of the European Jews is something like an icy peak that sticks up out of a mountainous formation, which itself rises above a broad, high plateau. The ethical discussion about National Socialism will genuinely demand our most earnest reflection. In our reflection we must find or determine the central categories for something like an ethical construction of judgment about the Nazi epoch.

National Socialism is a component part of our modern history. It is a part that cannot be determined "from the top down," that is, by starting from a leadership ideology and proceeding to its real or intended consequences. Instead it must be determined "from the bottom up." This determination begins by tracing the enormous social forces arising out of the First World War. These forces took on a highly nervous political form as they swept through the postwar period. They then reached an extremely high degree of mobilization during the Great Depression. Broszat indicates "how different the political-social profile of the NSDAP was from case to case . . . and how the will of the führer could only set in motion that which had already been very concretely motivated below. The long-dammed-up social fears and demands for change had become more manipulatable because of the depression." He describes the "vague populist attraction of National Socialism" and then the "thousands of small and large leadership positions" that the Third Reich had to award. These positions amounted to arenas "in which young dynamic forces from the middle class were able to prove themselves in competition with other leaders and successfully train their energy by using the ability to improvise." The core of the movement was clearly made up of the hard types of a warrior society who had been turned out of the "firestorms" into a vacuum. The determination to again take up the broken-off war was much more the soul of the Nazi movement than was ideological anti-Semitism. Nolte suggested that anti-Semitism could be a branch of anticommunism.

National Socialism is easier to understand as a movement than as the ideologically cemented regime of violence, as it would be seen from the perspective of social history.

In his essay J. Habermas refers in passing to the fact that his opponent, Michael Stürmer, was interested in the question to what extent World War II was Hitler's war and to what extent a war of the German people. He does not concern himself with this question any further; instead he turns immediately to A. Hillgruber's test of responsibilities for the Final Solution. Here also the question is posed to what extent the murder of the Jews was made possible by segments of the nation. Hillgruber talks of the command decision for the murder of more than five million Jews. He refers to those who stood ready to carry out the crime and of the "acceptance by the mass of the populace of the horrible goings on that were at least vaguely sensed." Hillgruber finds it most unsettling that given the civilizing conditions of the twentieth century, so many people could be won to the purpose of killing other people so indifferently. Hillgruber finds the role played in the machine of annihilation by humanistically trained university graduates like Dr. Mengele the "most deeply frightening" aspect of all. At this point, however, Habermas's discourse takes an unbelievable turn. On a secondary line of argumentation he criticizes Hillgruber for looking for anthropological instead of social-scientific explanations. The main moral line of the debate goes like this for Habermas: He begins with the fact that the mass of the German people were silent. And then he goes on to what Hillgruber does with that. "To be sure, the goal of the difficult neoconservative revision would be endangered if this phenomenon of silence had, after all, to be delivered up to a moral judgment. At this point, therefore, the historian, who has been writing in the narrative mode, switches over to the anthropological-general tone." This means clearly and concisely that Hillgruber has to avoid taking a moral position for the sake of his revisionist intention. The reason for that, as Habermas says further on, is that Hillgruber (like Nolte) is led by the impulse "to shake off the mortgages of a past, now happily made morally neutral."

MORAL *SONDERGERICHT* [SPECIAL COURT]*

Here a kind of forced presentation of historical moralism becomes evident. For Habermas the moral can only be a matter for a *Sondergericht*, or special court, to which the accused must be extradited or "delivered up." It is "a priori" an adventurous assumption that the amoral callousness of the historian could become evident precisely in the most unambiguous of all conceivable cases, in the case of the annihilation of the Jews. And then especially in the person of A. Hillgruber. Hillgruber writes of murder, of crime; he says he is distressed and deeply shocked. One must then ask oneself where the moral evaluation actually is. A lively historical presentation, if it does not follow a sociologically "restricted code," has the potential of throwing into bold relief, together with action and sorrow, the high, mediocre, or common ethos of the participating figures and formations. History can do this so poignantly that morality and humanity do not need their own special court of justice with the special process of extradition. Humanity has its appropriate place unobtrusively "between the lines" of a historical text that in turn owes its life to the ethos of the historian. (Hillgruber's essay is, by the way, a report to a history convention.)

What is Habermas really aiming at with his moralistic censuring? He understands (in accord with Broszat) very well that a "pedantic co-optation of a short-circuited moralized past" (the superficial pedagogy of the fathers and grandfathers) cannot be the genuine article. There would therefore be only a narrow zone to be occupied between the superficial moralizing of previous generations and that other "moral neutrality," which Habermas attributes to his opponents. We find out nothing helpful in his essay about

---

*[This term is not semantically neutral. Between 1933 and 1945 special courts (*Sondergerichte*) were established to take away jobs from politically undesirable persons—Trans.]

this distinction. Is it perhaps really not about an intermediate zone of moral jurisdiction at all but instead about something quite different?

M. Broszat asked for a new moral accessibility by means of a differentiating historical insight. (Insight is, as is well known, not merely knowledge and rationality.) And Broszat imagines a "turn to authenticity and concreteness of the moral in history as well." The temptation to superficially moralize history would then run counter to a long-term historicizing of morality. Morality and history, morality and politics, have always been a rather painful conjunction. Traditional morality originates in the confines of family, of neighborhood, of friendship; its space extends as far as a legally regulated national community or a community of nations in times of peace. The *factum brutum* of war was and remains traditional morality's frontier, at which it had to stand by and mourn powerlessly. In our history we arrived at the outer reaches of our traditional morality. The educating forces of civil society in the twentieth century suffered once again a terrible setback. These forces are not by any means already "over the hump." But there is in the meantime a broad basis, perhaps a viable majority basis for a civil ethos. This new civil ethos might not have to be defeated at the outset by the ethos of the archaic-modern warrior society.

This lively and practical new ethos, and not some abstract metahistorical moral principle for the judgment of past histories, would provide us with the framework for renouncing the violence of a past that in fact is not really past, but present.

At this point one must agree with Habermas that those Germans have come further along the road to a civil society who have achieved a broken, depotentialized relation to their inherited national identity, to their "German-ness." I take it though for a quite unusual paraphrase when Habermas says that here the national pride and collective feeling of self-worth are forced "through a filter of a universalist orientation of values." Is this modest gain in world citizenship thereby correctly classified historically if one sees in it (with Habermas) a sign that "we" therefore "have not gambled away the opportunity that the moral catastrophe could also mean for us"? Only after—*and through*—Auschwitz, according to Habermas, could one forge in the cultural nation of the Germans a connection to "universalist constitutional principles anchored in conviction." The moral catastrophe as moral catharsis? Nonetheless, it would be proper to doubt that Auschwitz could have made it possible for postwar Germans to become more honorable than the wartime Germans were. It could be the case that the incessant moral shock will no longer be sufficient for continued progress if it is not overtaken by an *historical understanding* of what has happened in our century, particularly through an understanding of the ubiquitous driving social forces that have been in effect through the Nazi period up to our present.

Source: *Nürnberger Zeitung*, September 20, 1986

JÜRGEN KOCKA

Hitler Should Not Be Repressed by Stalin and Pol Pot: On the Attempts of German Historians to Relativize the Enormity of the Nazi Crimes

Today, in contrast to the 1960s and 1970s, the relevance of history does not have to be demonstrated; today there is no lack of interest in history. Historical exhibitions enjoy great popularity. Governments have money for historical museums. "Historical Libraries" flourish as well-known paperback series. Cultural history is good business. The demand for sociology has declined. Alternative movements attempt to solidify their critical identity by associating themselves with history—as they understand it. Prominent historians write lead articles in high-circulation newspapers. Controversies about historical topics stand at the center of fundamental intellectual discourses by social scientists (like Habermas), journalists (like Fest), and historians (like Nolte). It would be wrong to complain that history has sunk into oblivion.

The reasons for this contemporary interest in history have shifted. The public discussion and preoccupation with history is motivated not so much by a desire for enlightenment, for a critique of unquestioned assumptions and for contributions to emancipation. Instead it is a search for aids to establishing national identity; it is a search for contributions to the endowment of a higher meaning for the past. "A consensual past" is sought. In this view history is seen as tradition and employed for the purpose of strengthening a collective identity and building a consensus. The search for a consensual past and the cultivation of an identity-promoting memory are taking very different public forms. Three of these will be briefly discussed.

THE PLACE OF NATIONAL SOCIALISM

We must consider the attempt not to actually deny the enormity of the National-Socialist crimes but to relativize and to define anew their place in history. Indeed it is hardly astonishing and not in itself worthy of criticism that we direct different questions to the darkest period of our history now, out of the temporal separation of half a century, than we did immediately

85

after the war because we can now survey the short- and long-term consequences (one of which is also the stability of the Federal Republic) in better and different ways than was possible immediately following the catastrophe.

Hermann Lübbe praises the psychological repression of that past and the avoidance after 1945 of fundamental discussion about the responsibility for the catastrophe. He sees the repression and avoidances as the preconditions for a reconciliation the Federal Republic needed for its survival and stability. One should not, however, deny the true core of this thesis, namely the assertion that the strategy of psychological repression simultaneously had deep-seated political and moral costs. Along with the new credibility arising from the repression of the past, moral deficits were established. Without understanding these deficits we cannot understand the acuteness of the protest movements of the late 1960s and early 1970s. And these deficits still burden the commonwealth today. One should—in contrast to Lübbe—be able to combine a sober insight into the partially healing consequences of this repression with an outrage about the injustice that the avoidance of reckoning with the crimes meant to their victims—and not only on moral grounds, which do not have to be missing entirely from the historicizing discourse of a philosopher, but also in the interest of a view of history that in the short run may well be less "easy to agree upon" but ultimately more viable.

Ernst Nolte took the relativizing of the National-Socialist period a giant step further in his controversial essay "Die Vergangenheit, die nicht vergehen will" [The Past That Will Not Pass] (*Frankfurter Allgemeine Zeitung* of June 6, 1986). One should keep distinct two strands of argumentation in his essay:

1. First Nolte wants to disrobe of its seeming singularity the "so-called annihilation of the Jews in the Third Reich": other genocides both preceded it (the Turkish persecution of Armenians, Stalinist mass terror) and followed it (Pol Pot, for example). Now no objections can be made to historical comparison, quite to the contrary. Such objections are also not new. With the concept of totalitarianism undeniable similarities between National Socialism and Stalinism have been worked out, specifically their common enmity for the liberal democratic constitutional state, their similar forms of repression, and even their mass annihilations.

To recognize these similarities does not mean trivializing the "German catastrophe," nor does it mean discrediting the concept of fascism, which allows for the likewise undeniably deep differences between National Socialism and Stalinism: important differences of ideology and of respective projections of the future, of social causes and consequences, of their place and value in the historical process of development.

The pan-European dimension of the National-Socialist annihilation of the Jews, in contrast to the internal Soviet dimension of the Stalinist annihilation of the kulaks, has also been discussed. And there remains a qualitative difference between the bureaucratized, passionless, perfected system of mass murder in the industrialized, fairly highly organized Reich of Hitler and the brutal mix of excesses of civil war, mass "liquidations," slave labor, and forced starvation in the backward Reich of Stalin. As mentioned previously, historians will always be in favor of comparisons that must always ask about similarities and differences, however much the feeling, the tact, the respect for the millions of dead may run counter to balancing one atrocity against another. But at the same time it is natural to make the comparison with the societies of the Western world with which we otherwise gladly compare ourselves, societies that are more closely related and similar to us in stage of development, in societal structure, and in political ambitions. These are societies that did not pervert themselves through fascism and totalitarianism. The singularity of the German development arising from this frame of comparison should not be repressed by the comparison with Stalin and Pol Pot. The singularity of the German developments remains important, threatening, and shaming.

Why do Nolte and Joachim Fest, who radically defends Nolte against Habermas (*Frankfurter Allgemeine Zeitung*, August 29, 1986), say so little about this? What are the intentions and the functions of this selection? Doubtless, in the search for the cause, character, and consequences of German National Socialism, it is more productive, more appropriate, and more just to compare Weimar Germany and Hitler Germany with contemporary France or England than with Pol Pot's Cambodia or Idi Amin's Uganda. That has nothing to do with "pride" and "master race mentality," as Fest insinuates; rather it has to do with historical knowledge about the connection between economic development and the possibilities of sociopolitical organization, and also with taking seriously the European tradition, in consideration of which the Enlightenment, human rights, and the constitutional state cannot simply be ignored. How could one justify not categorizing the National-Socialist politics of annihilation against this background of once achieved, then more deeply wounded ambitions? In the basic decisions of historical argumentation, scholarship, morality, and politics are always bound together. This accounts for the intensity of many controversies and warns at the same time of their intensification.

2. Secondly Nolte suggests that the National-Socialist "Asiatic" policy of annihilation can be understood as a not altogether incomprehensible reaction to the prior threat of annihilation, as whose potential or real victims Hitler and the National Socialists allegedly were justified in seeing themselves. "Was the Gulag Archipelago not primary to Auschwitz? Was the Bolshevik murder of an entire class not the logical and factual prius of the 'racial murder' of National Socialism?" And in another place he refers to the earlier "declaration of war" made against Germany by the Jewish World Congress in 1939.[1] Now these comments by Nolte, which Fest defends, have nothing at all to do with sober historical analysis of motivations

and causes. The real causes of anti-Semitism in Germany are to be found neither in Russia nor at the Jewish World Congress. And how can one, in light of the facts, interpret the National-Socialist annihilation of the Jews as a somewhat logical, if premature, means of defense against the threats of annihilation coming from the Soviet Union, with which Germany had made a pact in 1941 and which it then subsequently attacked? Here the sober scholarly historical inquiry into real historical connections, into causes and consequences, and about real motives and their conditions would suffice to protect the writer and the reader from abstruse speculative interpretations. Nolte fails to ask such questions. If a past "that is capable of being agreed on" can be gained by intellectual gymnastics of this sort, then we should renounce it.

HISTORIES INSTEAD OF HISTORY

Our "historians of everyday life" in the "history workshops" have little to do as a rule with such revisions of our national image of history, no matter how various the currents in the "new history movement" (to use the language of the media). Politically, morally, and intellectually the work of these less professional local historians, who are hardly protected institutionally, must be understood differently. This work is more likely to be critical of the national historical tradition, more likely to be politically on the Left in many respects.

Nevertheless, these historians also often write history for the purposes of identification. Dig where you are (why?—in order to find your own roots). They are also interested in reconstructing the shocking experiences and the ways of life of the little people in their own area, in order to "locate oneself again" in history. This is microhistory relating to everyday life as a means of founding and assuring identity in the small, surveyable space of a neighborhood, of the movement which it supports, perhaps also of the landscape.

This should not be fundamentally attacked here since this is not at all the place to weigh comprehensively the unarguable advantages and accomplishments of the history of everyday life and the history workshops against their incalculable deficits, illusions, and one-sidedness. Here reference will be made to only one price that normally has to be paid for this form of microhistory: failing to recognize the connections, ignoring the "big questions" about the formation of states and classes, about religion and churches, about industrialization and capitalism, about nation and revolutions, about the fundamental causes and consequences of National Socialism, about the German particularities in international comparison.

Such questions cannot be properly settled by personal and oral history. To answer them one needs complicated concepts and broad reading, theories, and a very long breath—precisely the things that the professional discipline of history is most likely to offer. The discipline has at its disposal to that end the free spaces and means of the universities; it can reach back to its tedious process of education and take advantage of the division of labor. There is unfortunately no direct, quick, unprofessional way to understand the long-term connections of economy, society, culture, and politics.

But in the perspective of the historians of everyday life, it must likewise be a pressing need not to ignore the knowledge of connections that cannot be gained with one's own methods. The changing structures and experiences even in the smallest space are to a great extent the result of those greater connections and processes, and therefore cannot be understood without recourse to them. Also, a great part of our politics and our political agenda-setting, which affect individuals and small groups, plays itself out necessarily in a supralocal, supraregional space. Avoiding the "big questions" of history can mean the loss of the ability to be politically active (this in accord with Richard Löwenthal).

Finally, there is no objection to the existence of several mutually incompatible images of history. But in the interest of their validity or truth and in the interest of the consensus that always has to be worked out anew in important questions, the consensus that in fact is part of the democratic-liberal political culture, these images should not mutually ignore each other. By shutting out the big questions, historians of everyday life make things easier. They work the puzzle in front of them. They value questioning other images of history for this reason just as little as they let themselves be put in question by these other images. A partialization of the understanding of history must be recognized. They create identity in small spaces by blocking off connections—this is intellectually not satisfying and, in the end, politically problematic.

THE MIDDLE OF EUROPE[2]

Finally, a third—national—attempt to answer the problem of identity should be discussed. It is politically ambivalent, intellectually stimulating, but in the last analysis unsatisfying. I refer to the modified resumption of the old thesis of the German *Sonderweg* in the middle of Europe.

"The measure of freedom that can reasonably take place in a nation is inversely proportional to the military-political pressure which is exerted on its borders." This conviction of the Englishman J. R. Seeley was shared by many German historians up to 1918. They supported and justified this argument with the fact that Germany could hardly achieve parliamentary government given its vulnerable geopolitical situation in the middle of Europe—and that its specific traditions could not tolerate a parliamentary system but instead would remain an authoritarian state characterized by the military and bureaucracy. To this extent (in comparison to the rest of Europe) Germany would have to go a "separate way."

Clever historians like Otto Hintze gave up this view after 1918; after the Second World War it found hardly a single defender. Not until the end of the 1970s were critical variants taken up again, and by the American D. P. Calleo, who—quite unconvincingly—attempted to explain the historical difficulties and, in his view, the still extant, incalculable factors based on the Germans' situation in the middle of Europe. Then Michael Stürmer and Hagen Schulze made use of the new geo-historical hypothesis in their weighty books that appeared with Siedler Verlag, *Das ruhelose Reich: Deutschland 1866–1918* [The Restless Reich: Germany 1866–1918], and *Weimar*. Since then this view has had a definite career, continuing into the early speeches of the current Federal president, von Weizsäcker. The view fits quite well with the desire for equidistance between East and West (a desire that Stürmer, Schulze, and von Weizsäcker do not espouse but in fact reject). This view would lend itself well to the establishment of new German separate ways, in who-knows-which areas. Therein lies its explosive power.

"The great constant of German history is its situation in the middle of Europe; Germany's destiny is its geography" (H. Schulze). This assertion conceals the conviction that the European balance of power has assumed a weak middle; thus the particularist organization of the Holy Roman Empire and the German Federation would in principle be a more appropriate solution. The founding in 1871 of the German Reich in the heart of Europe had by this account meant a fundamental disruption of the balance. This was then only temporarily made acceptable to the European powers by the measured foreign policy of Bismarck, which could however only succeed as long as it was combined with an authoritarian policy of repression regarding the constitution, thus holding the internal dynamic of the Kaiserreich in limits. "Germany will only be tolerated by its neighbors for as long as the lid sits securely on its seething internal stew. For this reason the world war will sooner or later become unavoidable, as Bismarck's successors reject his policy of strict limitations . . . and the power of the old Prussian gentry . . . increasingly is subverted. The arrival of organized union interests, nationalistic and imperialistic mass organizations, the gradual rise of a parliamentary process and the creeping loss of power by the Prussian Ministry of State . . . All that combines to destroy unavoidably the boundaries that the European system sets for the existence of the German national state. The conflict is under these circumstances just as predictable as the German defeat, and probably the dissolution of the German Reich as well."

It is clear that this way of seeing things goes against the long-dominant liberal interpretation of the Kaiserreich as it is espoused, among others, by Hans Rosenberg, Ernst Fraenkel, Fritz Fischer, Gerhard A. Ritter, Hans-Ulrich Wehler, Hans-Jürgen Puhle, Heinrich August Winkler, Wolfgang Mommsen, Gordon Craig, and earlier also by Karl-Dietrich Bracher—in differing variants. According to the liberal view, the authoritarian, preparliamentary structure of the Kaiserreich was understood as a burden that made conflicts more acute and as a long-term obstacle of democratization in Germany, the preparliamentary authoritarian character of the Reich seems in Stürmer and Schulze to be a justified consequence of the geographic situation and a guarantor of freedom, a guarantor that in the long run unfortunately did not measure up to the forces of the Nazi movement.

The retarded rise of a parliament and the continuing dominance of traditional elites of nobility, military, and bureaucracy were seen at most as a structural deficit of the Kaiserreich, but according to Stürmer and Schulze, an earlier rise of a parliament and more fundamental democratization would have only made the Reich more immoderate. According to their view, the Reich suffered from a surfeit of democratization, mobilization, and dynamic and less from its authoritarian rigidity. The Reich did not represent a special danger because it was more expansive and aggressive than its western neighbors but because the "normal" expansiveness of the Reich was incompatible with its geographical situation.

But this view is not convincing. With it one cannot explain why and with what necessity this "Reich in the Middle" developed its internal dynamic and ultimately turned to the outside. And this explanation overlooks that it was precisely the authoritarian preparliamentary immobility of the Reich's constitution that forced aside the social and political forces pressing for participation and thus helped to bring forth the irrational, destructive currents that then had a destabilizing effect, internally and externally.

More fundamentally, geography as such explains little. Switzerland and Poland also are "in the middle" and have nevertheless a completely different history. Completely different constitutional structures and constellations of alliances have coexisted with the geographic situation of Germany in the course of this century. The definition of "middle" is itself a historical phenomenon and changes with time. At the Congress of Vienna, for example, France, which had been defeated and was seen as dangerous, was the state in the middle between England, on the one hand, and the beginnings of the German Federation and the empire of the czars, on the other. Geography is not destiny, nor does it explain much. In this way, then, the question of German identity cannot be answered, even if it is useful to mutter momentously about the situation in the heart of Europe and the heritage of destiny bound up with it.

CRITICISM AS IDENTITY

Neither by relativizing and leveling the National-Socialist period and other dark points of our past, nor by affectionately painting miniatures of the history of everyday life, nor through short-circuited geographism should historians react to the challenge to endow identity. Their task is to describe, explain, and present past reality with scholarly means within the context of the changing and never unitary future-oriented problems of the present. In doing that they help set the present in as enlightened a relationship as possible to the past—and that means an appropriate, comprehensive, common, and critical relationship; they fulfill important societal needs and contribute in a fundamental and indirect sense to finding identity, provided one employs a concept of identity that includes self-distancing and reflection, as well as constant change and always renewed criticism.

Source: *Frankfurter Rundschau*, September 23, 1986

Author's Note: The title and subtitle were added by the editors of *Frankfurter Rundschau*. A long version of the article appeared with the title "Criticism and Identity: National Socialism, Everyday Life and Geography," in *Die Neue Gesellschaft/Frankfurter Hefte*, October, 1986, pp. 890–897.

NOTES

1. This formulation has been justifiably criticized as inexact. The reference is to Nolte, "Between Myth and Revisionism? The Third Reich in the Perspective of the 1980s," in H. W. Koch, ed., *Aspects of the Third Reich*, London 1985, pp. 17–38, 27ff. (Compare with the first article in this volume.) Nolte mentions "Chaim Weizmann's statement in the first days of September 1939, that in this war the Jews of all the world would fight on England's side." Nolte cites this in the imprecise reprint in the *Archiv der Gegenwart*, 1939. The actual wording of this letter from Weizmann of August 29, 1939, to the British prime minister, Neville Chamberlain, can be found in *Letters and Papers of Chaim Weizmann. Series A*. Letters, vol. 19, January 1935–June 1940, Jerusalem 1977, p. 145. Weizmann offered in the letter the participation of Jews in military efforts under British leadership on behalf of the Jewish Agency (at that time a recognized public entity and part of the World Zionist Organization for Palestine, which among other things advised the British Mandate Government in Palestine). "In this hour of supreme crisis . . . the Jews 'stand by Great Britain and will fight on the side of the democracies.'" Nolte interprets Weizmann's position as "something like a declaration of war" and concludes indefensibly: "It might justify the consequential thesis that Hitler was allowed to treat German Jews as prisoners of war and by this means to intern them." Weizmann was in 1929–1931 and again in 1935–1946 the president of the World Zionist Organization (WZO), which regularly held Zionist world congresses. The letter may have been written in the context of the Twenty-first Zionist World Congress 1939 in Geneva. There were close ties between the WZO and the Jewish Agency. The letter is to be seen in the context of the connections between the British Mandate Government in Palestine and the Jewish Agency. That is clear in the wording of the letter.
2. The section under the heading "Middle of Europe" can be found, in part word for word, in part just the sense, in my review of the books *Das ruhelose Reich: Deutschland 1866–1918*, by Michael Stürmer and *Weimar* by H. Schulze in *Geschichtsdidaktik* 9 (1984) pp. 79–83.

HAGEN SCHULZE

Questions We Have to Face: No Historical Stance without National Identity

Enlightenment has to do with clarity, and what Jürgen Habermas communicates in his *Zeit* article of July 11, 1986, about recent tendencies in German history writing seems to be clear. The problems are easy to survey: On the one side is the community of enlightened liberals who have learned from the errors of German history and pay homage to a "pluralism of modes of understanding." On the other side is a small clique of questionable historians benevolently supported by ruling conservative circles. These historians, rooted in unsavory older traditions of nationalist and affirmative German historiography, are, in the interest of shoring up the stability of the federal government and the NATO alliance, in the process of designing a statist image of history with the intention of endowing a sense of national identity. To do this they make use of a trick by which they deny the singularity of the decisive point of reference of our constitutional order, National Socialism. They also compare Nazism with other totalitarian systems such as those of Stalin or Pol Pot, and in this way "sanitize" German history.

That is nice and lucid; the moral is obvious, and the *ecrase l'infame* is visible between all the lines. Once again, Habermas demonstrates himself to be a virtuoso simplifier, which in some cases can be useful in explaining complex matters. But this clarity is blurred on closer inspection. The argumentation changes in an irritating way. Habermas is in essence interested in politics, even in morality. His attack takes aim at the theoretical and practical positions of the discipline. But a question on one of these levels can be represented as being on another. For this discipline has to do with the world of being, of morality, of politics—and with the world of ethical obligation. One cannot support moral statements with scholarship, nor can one support scholarly statements with political ones. But that is just what Habermas constantly does.

Anyone who believes he will gain clarity about new historical problems and their difficulties will be disappointed reading Habermas, because the problems at hand are not at all compatible with Habermas's approach. The

93

singularity of National-Socialist crimes, the call of historical scholarship to promote "the endowment of higher meaning," the question about the national identity of Germans, the tension between national and constitutional patriotism—these are problems that are too important to be used as slogans for doing ideological battle.

Are the National-Socialist crimes singular? On the level of historical scholarship the question answers itself: Every historical event is singular or must at least appear to us that way. Every individual historical event stands at the crossroads of undeterminable causal chains, which themselves result from an indeterminate number of related events and can neither be described nor analyzed in their entirety. Which does not mean that a particular historical event might not be comparable to another.

Historians by no means seek to claim the identity of two historical events. They seek a formal process by which two or more individual events can be referred to a transcendent point of view that is constructed from shared aspects. In this way, similarities as well as differences become evident. In the case of the National-Socialist mass murder of the Jews, there are aspects in common with other historical events. Examples would be the extermination of the kulaks in the Soviet Union and the mass annihilations carried out by the Pol Pot regime. Common to these acts are the mechanical massivity of the killing, the membership of those killed in a particular group, and the primarily ideological motivation of the murderers.

When the historian discovers similarities such as these, he can formulate theories with the help of which he can analyze the causes and circumstances of political mass crime in a way that goes beyond the individual case. These analyses can help to prevent comparable acts in the futue. On the other side, the peculiarity of an individual event can be made visible by historical comparison. The rationality and the technicity of the National-Socialist mass murder of the Jews find no correspondence in Stalin's Russia or in Pol Pot's Cambodia—the industrialization of mass murder is a German invention.

For the discipline of history, singularity and comparability of historical events are thus not mutually exclusive alternatives. They are complementary concepts. A claim that historians such as Ernst Nolte or Andreas Hillgruber deny the uniqueness of Auschwitz because they are looking for comparisons stems from incorrect presuppositions. Of course, Nolte and Hillgruber can be refuted if their comparison rests on empirically or logically false assumptions. But Habermas never provided such proof.

But even on the moral-political level the question about the uniqueness of National-Socialist crimes is not without complications. Does the special responsibility of the Germans for the crimes committed in their name depend upon singularity? If the mass murders were only a trace less abhorrent or if comparable crimes had been committed in other places and at other times, is the obligation of the Germans to learn lessons from the crimes of the National-Socialist period reduced? An odd sense of insecurity is at play here. For if the historical question about comparability cannot be answered morally, then historians' answer to this question is morally without consequence. Anyone who tries to connect the one thing with the other is also stepping on politically and pedagogically slippery ground. One just has to recall the initial years of our republic when historians like Friedrich Meinecke, Michael Freund, or Gerhard Ritter tried to explain National Socialism as an incursion of demonic forces, as a withdrawal of Germans from history—that is, as singular.

In recent years one has been able to observe the interesting process by which extensive thematic areas and paradigms of interpretation have shifted from the conservative to the leftist camp. The fact that Jürgen Habermas until now has decisively opposed this process speaks for him, so he in particular should be careful about using concepts like the singularity of National Socialism. Such concepts promote neither the rationality of historical knowledge nor our understanding of the necessity of the Federal Republic of Germany's bond with the West. That which is singular is unhistorical and for that reason can teach us nothing about the future.

And what about another of Habermas's provocative phrases, "the endowment of higher meaning," to which the historians under attack, particularly Michael Stürmer, are said to be obligated? This strikes dread into the heart of the theoretical side of the philosopher Habermas. He invokes the "dilemma between endowing meaning and conducting scholarship" and accuses his opponents of wanting to place the discipline of history in the service of "NATO philosophy colored with German nationalism." That would indeed be bad—not because it would be a NATO philosophy but because scholarship has in principle no normative competence and quickly degenerates into being a producer of ideological slogans if it arrogates this kind of thing to itself. But who is actually trying to do this? It is interesting how Habermas supports his claim. He mixes direct and indirect quotations with virtuosity. Incriminating statements about the alleged intentions of the four "government historians" can exclusively be found in the indirect quotations. The people attacked have since stated that the indirect quotations are not from them but rather represent the interpretation of Jürgen Habermas. If we examine only the direct quotations, a different problem arises: the fact, known all too well by historians, that increasingly, expectations of a political-legitimatory kind are being put onto the discipline of history—and not only by governments and the opposition but also by numerous people ranging all the way to students in history seminars.

What should the historian do in a case like this? On the one hand, since Max Weber's speech "Scholarship as an Occupation," everyone has known the dangers connected with being a "prophet of the lectern." On the other hand, history always has to do with politics. Politics is its object, political interests affect the questions history deals with. Historical research can have political consequences. And thus the question of the political responsibility of the historian arises. That is what Michael Stürmer calls a "tightrope walk between endowing meaning and demythologization"—a tightrope walk with which Jürgen Habermas is very familiar.

Here we have entered realms that are a part of the ethics of scholarship. The question of how far a person on the tightrope is allowed to lean to one or the other side cannot be readily answered. How far can the scholar go in advising politicians? To what degree can he bring his results to market without betraying scholarly standards? What political consequences arise from the historian's constructions and interpretations, and which consequences can one desire? These are questions that must be asked and discussed. And it is to the credit of Michael Stürmer that he asks them.

It is obvious when compared to the previous questions that historians possess their own notions of history and use every available opportunity to propagate them. In a country like ours, in which opinions supportive of the government have no privileged access to the public but are in open competition, a unified progovernment image of history is not possible—as the discussion precipitated by Habermas shows best. The pluralism of interpretations is guaranteed, not only for Stürmer but also for Habermas. For in spite of Habermas's moralizing verdict, historians in the future will also not allow themselves to be deprived of the right "to illuminate the present with the spotlights of arbitrarily constructed prehistories and to choose from these options a suitable notion of history"—inasmuch as "arbitrarily" solely refers to positing questions.

Also Habermas has allowed himself to be deceived by the "conventional forms of national identity" that are allegedly the goal of revisionist historians. He believes that concealed behind this notion lies the attempt to reduce National Socialism to an insignificant episode in German history that will be irrelevant for constructing the self-definition and the memory of Germans today. Here, too, scholarly and political problems diverge.

In this context, "national identity" simply means that the present for the Federal Republic is not sufficient to explain why this nation is the way it is and why the "German question" poses itself in this specific form not only for the Germans but for other Europeans as well. The reason Germans are the way they are, or to put it more simply, the identity of the Germans, can only be sufficiently explained if one understands the conditions of their historical development. For that reason it is important for historians to make the national identity of the Germans an object of their research. The political effect of this kind of description of identity is, incidentally, quite different than Habermas thinks. The necessary linkage of National Socialism and the present cuts across the collective assurance of national identity. For only as participants in the shared historical identity of the German nation are we today also responsible for our national history and its consequences. That is precisely the reason why the GDR denies its identification with the totality of German history.

And finally, we come to Habermas's pitting "the conventional forms of national identity" against "binding universalist constitutional principles anchored in conviction." Here I can only warn of the consequences. As laudable as his reference to constitutional patriotism as a raison d'être for the Federal Republic is, it is problematic to polemically and categorically set this concept off from national identity. The actual point at hand is the old and very German theme of freedom and unity and the experience that the price of the one has always been the atrophy of the other. But history can also offer another relevant experience: that the constitutional patriots of the first German republic had nothing effective to set against the powerful emotional appeal of the nationalists. No doubt, the experience of National Socialism has dampened the German leaning toward nationalist extremes. But whether this dampening will last more than one or two generations is doubtful—despite all the political pedagogy, about the effectiveness of which there should be no illusions.

Questions about German unity and national identity continue to be asked, and it is not only a matter of scholarly interest but also of political prevention when historians take up these questions and rationally and soberly take a position on them in order not to abandon the topic to other, perhaps more dangerous forces. For this reason we always have to tell and explain the *whole* story. This includes freedom, the constitution, *and* the nation, but also Auschwitz *and* Weimar.

There is nothing wrong with a heated dispute. But the discussion should not be conducted with a Manichaean reduction of reality and artificially constructed hostile images. [The discussion that Jürgen Habermas initiated is good, as is any dispute that leads us back to fundamentals. And there is nothing better than a good polemic. On the contrary, our scholarly enterprise will be enlivened by it. But the discussion should not be conducted with a Manichaean reduction of reality and artificially constructed hostile images, nor with willfully distorted quotations if the clarification of problems and facts is what is intended and not only an exchange of political pamphlets. It is important to give one's opponent the chance to objectively refute what has been said. And this is only possible if all participants learn to do without moral sledgehammers and are prepared to grant their opponents the legitimacy of scholarly pluralism.]* Otherwise the dispute will be unfair—which is a devastating verdict in the realm of Western (but only Western) political culture. The "greatest intellectual achievement of the postwar period" that Habermas praises, the "unconditional opening of the Federal Republic to the political culture of the West," has not, at least judging by the debating style of German intellectuals, been fully achieved.

Source: *Die Zeit*, September 26, 1986

Author's Note: The original manuscript contained the bracketed passage here.

HANNO HELBLING

A Searching Image of the Past: What Is Expected from German History Books

Is a specter haunting us? Or are spiritualists having their heyday? The one does not preclude the other. Three months ago in *Die Zeit*, Jürgen Habermas spoke about "apologetic tendencies in German historiography." He put together quotations from books by Andreas Hillgruber, Michael Stürmer, Ernst Nolte, and Klaus Hildebrand in such a way that one was led to believe that a phalanx of German historians had assembled to revise—which means to illuminate—our understanding of the National-Socialist past.

Some of the sentences quoted there no doubt sound horrifying. For example that the history of the Third Reich has been largely written by the victors and made into a "negative myth." Or that the "so-called" annihilation of the Jews realized understandable intentions in an extreme way. Or that the "victims" of the system were not just its opponents but also its lackeys. Or that those twelve years should be understood within the overall context of totalitarianism—for in this way the events could be stripped of their "ostensibly singular character."

It is strange enough that historians should strive to contest the uniqueness of past events. Are their efforts not usually dedicated to the contrary, and are they not otherwise in danger of emphasizing the extraordinary aspect of the events they describe? Doesn't a kind of historiography that desires to assure us that what it describes is not all that particular appear a little forced? And now it is German history between 1933 and 1945 that is to be "categorized," to be leveled.

No reasonable person, "victor" or not, has ever claimed that National Socialism simply fell from the sky in 1933. A series of events led to the Hitler movement, no doubt about it. But the assumption that what then became a historical unity has been constructed over a period of decades is itself misleading—even if this idea is repeatedly and skillfully expressed. It is correct that a trend toward totalitarianism had been afoot for a long while and had even asserted itself here and there—although by no means everywhere. But the continuities that led to National Socialism only came together here, creating an absolutely singular form of totalitarianism;

"1933 did not only mean intensification and radicalization; it brought about a new combination of continuities—it meant something new" (Thomas Nipperdey).

Revisionists who gloss over the evils of National Socialism and deny its atrocities have raised a ruckus lately. What they claim is without scholarly substance and cannot influence our understanding of history in the long term. However, they may, using the mass media, succeed in sewing seeds of doubt about solidly supported facts—within people who cannot come to grips with these facts. After all, who could come to grips with such facts—on a moral level? And it makes sense that it is easier to simply reject on a factual level what is morally unacceptable. The unholy concept of *Vergangenheitsbewältigung* [coming to grips with the past] is in part cause for the conflation of the factual and the moral. Why, oh why, couldn't people speak of working on [*Verarbeitung*] the past?

Today, this working on the past is not only prevented by the fools who want to convince us that Jews did not have it half bad in the Third Reich; it is also prevented by the people who are, at least in the academic world, in possession of their senses. They are undertaking to overthrow the "negative myth" of the Third Reich, not only by revising our inevitable understanding of this reign of terror but also by restoring the national past. The German people have been "robbed of their history"—this or something similar is frequently argued. And only through historical stock-taking can these people renew themselves spiritually.

What Günther Rohrmoser and others have been striving for is a history of which one can by and large be proud (again)—a German history that does not have to be read as a prehistory of National Socialism. It is hard to determine how consciously this tendency is aimed by those who emphasize continuity at leveling the years 1933 to 1945. But, if German history is to have nothing or as little as possible to do with Hitler, then the singularity of the Nazi regime that other patriots cast doubt upon should be made to stand out all the more sharply. In any case, many people are still looking for German history where they sought—and found it—a century ago: in Germany. The restoration, in other words, reaches back behind the broad comparative view that has liberated our understanding of history from its nationalist, statist, and political confines. These people want their "own" past—as if there were such a thing.

One is justified in seeing the formation of new myths at work where one suspects that history is being written so that certain theses or simple wishful projections can be implemented. This suspicion is often justified—as it was in connection with the reasoning behind the discussion of guilt for the outbreak of the First World War or with the assertions about the German defeat in 1918. But rarely has such suspicion been less justified than in connection with our prevailing understanding of the Hitler regime. "Negative myth"—as if myths were necessary to make our understanding of

National Socialism negative. The restorers of the past are wary of attempts to demythologize the past. Such attempts, they suggest, would lead nowhere. But then these people want to construct a countermyth, a "positive myth" about an honorable national history that can be balanced with the dishonorable history of the Third Reich. Who is holding the scale—down here on earth?

Or one can take refuge in countermyths of the negative kind and thus come close to a leveling strategy, just as announcements of horrors from the distant past are not suited to proving that back then, too, murderous deeds were committed. And what about the recent past: "Didn't Stalin . . ."; "in Cambodia, didn't they . . . ." These are sad calculations—which in a strange way have propagated themselves into the political view of the present. For if all things are equal, what does this all mean for differences between the great powers? Peter Graf Kielmansegg and Ralf Dahrendorf discussed this in *Die Zeit*. The former emphasized the difference that it makes when a government is freely elected, when the forum of public discussion is free, and when the courts are independent. The other sounded a different note, which in essence suggests that these differences are losing meaning, that a convergence between East and West will come about and that for this reason the necessity of a political decision in favor of the one side or the other might be sidestepped altogether.

Is there an agreement, or an affinity, between this convergence theory and the continuity thesis discussed above? Both cases amount to leveling. One has taught that the path to Hitler's Reich was the German path into totalitarianism, parallel to Italy's road into fascism, Spain's road to the Falange, and Russia's so thoroughly trodden road to Bolshevism. In other words, unavoidable and inevitable—if we could overlook the fact that other European nations maintained their freedom or lost it only through external intervention. But what is freedom, say the convergence theoreticians? How free are we really, and how unfree are the others? What is of duration are the continuities in the oppositions of power and individual self-assertion. Thus nationalism and neutralism appear to be the desired outcome.

Do a majority of readers in Germany expect history books to be nationalistic? Certainly not. But books that treat the greater German past are not unpopular with readers. Do they also expect the naturally negative view of the Third Reich to recede? Not necessarily. But a certain degree of saturation is quickly reached. Is, however, a positive revision expected? No. But the mass media are making sure that something can be gained from the theme of National Socialism and the debate with the revisionists. Are more books about the resistance to Hitler expected? Without doubt. Is there today a predominance of "apologetic tendencies in German historiography," as Jürgen Habermas has warned? Who knows?

Source: *Neue Züricher Zeitung*, September 26, 1986

HANS MOMMSEN

Search for the "Lost History"?
Observations on the Historical
Self-Evidence of the
Federal Republic

Recently, in the weekly *Das Parlament* (No. 20/21, May 17, 24, 1986) Michael Stürmer gave eloquent expression to the trauma of the conservative Right, which is now consolidating. This is a trauma that derives from the insight that the Right can no longer shore itself up on an adequately consensual national image of history. Stürmer fears that this "lost memory" will lead to a lack of continuity and reliability in the Federal Republic's foreign policy. We can set aside for the present whether a closed image of history is really desirable in a world subject to rapid changes. Likewise, we can set aside for the moment the hypothesis that a stronger connection to historical tradition makes foreign policy more reliable. Is the complaint about the loss of historical identity, which has almost become a stereotype in this country, justified? And is this complaint a reflection of the fact, argued on the conservative side, that in the Federal Republic a new political self-understanding has developed, accompanied by a fundamental change of the historical paradigm?

In comparison to the fields of economics and politics, the regrouping of historical-political thought comes about in a slower rhythm. This can explain how the debate about the historical self-understanding of the Federal Republic is beginning in a period characterized more by political stagnation than by rapid change. The debate is, in the meantime, the expression of a creeping crisis of legitimation of the Federal Republic's political system. This country has just emerged from a phase of uninterrupted and unquestioned economic growth and can derive no further bonus of trust from the undeniable accomplishments of reconstruction of the early postwar period. The political polarization, which is becoming more and more acute, touches not insignificantly on central sociopolitical questions. It touches in increasing measure our understanding of politics itself. It is no wonder that therefore the transmission of history also is becoming the object of fundamental controversies.

It may be surprising that distinguished historians like Michael Stürmer present the Federal Republic as a land without history, despite the fact that in contrast to the 1950s, the interest in history has gained breadth and intensity. Even the politics of the day makes reference more and more frequently to historical events. For the early postwar years one could speak of an extinguishing of historical memory; the traces of the catastrophe of the Second World War were evident to everyone. Despite the deep wound of a shared sense of the loss of national unity, there was no fundamental break in historical continuity. Hour X, longed for by Helmut James von Moltke and which would have created a tabula rasa for an epochal new beginning, did not happen. The hopes to be able to exploit the downfall of the Third Reich for a fundamental societal upheaval revealed themselves to be misplaced.

The period of reconstruction oriented itself throughout to political norms that went back to the Weimar period. Only in exceptional cases did the Allied policy of reeducation prevail against the habitual structures of public administration in the party system and in economic life. At the outset there was no lack of pronounced conservative-national parties, which increasingly gave up their votes to the CDU/CSU. This larger party proved to be a catch basin for groupings that had belonged to the older conservative Right. This contributed to the fact that if one does not count neo-Fascist splinter parties and parts of the *Vertriebenenverbände* [associations of people resettled from the German East after 1945], the political Right was not able to form a clearly delineated grouping. Within the spectrum of the political parties, the CDU took over this role without being defined as a conservative party.

In contrast to the founding phase of the Weimar Republic, the political Right after the war possessed no reservoir of conservative values to which it could connect without interruption. The weak attempts of the chancellor democracy to revivify the legacy of Bismarck on the one hundredth anniversary of his death came to nothing. Likewise the incantation of the Christian-Western tradition lost credibility to the extent that the various strategies of the cold war were incapable of changing the status quo in Central Europe as had been agreed to in Allied conferences during and after the war. Konrad Adenauer's anti-Bolshevism could be effectively and successfully industrialized for the fancy of right-wing groups of voters. In foreign policy matters this anti-Bolshevism stumbled in 1961 with the erection of the Berlin Wall. Significantly, Washington pressed then for détente. For the long term, a conservative position with reminiscences of the cold war could not be founded.

The expression coined by Rüdiger Altmann in the later years of Ludwig Erhard of the "molded society" represented a first attempt to carry over certain conceptualizations of Weimar neoconservatism to the parliamentary system of the Federal Republic and to lend the conventional liberal motto, the "social market economy," a sociopolitical support. Important preconditions were lacking for a revivification of neoconservative ideological currents. The obvious success of and expansion of the industrial society refuted the ideas of the neoconservative ideologues of the 1920s, which essentially had arisen from the preindustrial structures. Even if corporativist ideas were taken up one by one under the motto of corporativism, the emphatically antiparliamentarian alignment of the conservatism of the Weimar period precluded direct connection to it.

Furthermore, the political Right, by making itself into the unreserved advocate for the Altantic Alliance, ended up in a skewed political alignment. Foreign policy considerations ruled out the possibility of the Right's making itself the advocate of national sovereignty and of its encouraging more independence in foreign, economic, and military policy for the Federal Republic within the framework of NATO. The ghost of the neutralization of Central Europe deprived the Right of the possibility of being the advocate for specific national interests against Western European partners; under duress it had to leave this to the SPD and to the neo- and post-Fascist splinter groups. So long as the Federal Republic found itself so completely on the lee side of the Western Allies' foreign policy, the theoretical dilemma of conservatives remained a low priority. In the face of the open appearance of a specific U.S. policy under President Reagan, the German position is transformed into a strange rigidity. Clinging to the Western Alliance, something not earnestly contested by the opposition, is stylized as a domestic political dogma.

The escape route of conservative thought in the Federal Republic was at the same time obstructed by the fact that it had all too incautiously let itself be taken in by the theory of "total dictatorship." The equating of National-Socialist dictatorship and Communist dominion, which was the consummate principle of totalitarianism theory, met the need in the cold war to gain a stalwart ideological platform that could not only decorate itself with the epithet "anti-Fascist" but could also rule out and criminalize leftist efforts. The separation of totalitarian dictatorships has served since then as the basic pattern for the justification of a bellicose democracy and for propping up the idea of democracy, reinterpreted in the constitutional sense as a "liberal-democratic order."

The reliance on the theory of "totalitarian dictatorship" served at the same time as the theoretical underpinning for bracketing out the period of the Third Reich from the continuity of German history. Friedrich Meinecke had already postulated this in his *Deutsche Katastrophe* [German Catastrophe] in 1946, and it asserted itself in the chancellor democracy on a broader front. The interpretation of the Third Reich as a capricious regime that subjugated the German people, one that is traced back to the demonic power of Hitler's seduction of and successful manipulation of the "atomized masses," contains an indirect exculpation of the predominantly conservatively predisposed functionary elite. Their decisive coresponsibility for the origin and stabilization of the National-Socialist dictatorship thus steps into the background. Their coresponsibility corresponds to the psychological repression of the criminal politics of the Third Reich, a repression justified by Hermann Lübbe as the means to a psychological self-assurance.[1] This manifested itself in the neglect of the criminal prosecution of the war crimes by the justice system of the Federal Republic. Serious prosecutions only began when the Ulm *Einsatzgruppen* and the Eichmann trial caused a stronger pressure on the Federal Republic from the public abroad.

The interpretation of National Socialism as the result of "ballot democracy" held on until deep into the 1950s. Even today the classical repertoire of conservative thought includes the thesis that the rise of the NSDAP is primarily attributable to the mass unemployment of the early 1930s and that the "power grab" would have been unthinkable without the consequences of the Great Depression. It is significant that the Weimar Republic was viewed in the years immediately following 1945 as an experiment failed from the outset; not until the success of the chancellor democracy did this image brighten. Then the Weimar experience could be trotted out for the additional legitimation of the Federal Republic and the fundamental superiority the Federal Republic asserted. However, cause for doubt is given by the fact that the political Right condescendingly refers to the Federal Republic as the "most democratic" and the "most liberal" constitutional order, against which critique from the Left is inadmissible.

For the profiling of domestic conservative positions, the wholesale rejection of the GDR won a place of central importance. It culminated in the West German claim to be the sole representative of all Germans. The demand for reunification was made serviceable for purposes of domestic politics until it turned out that this was unpopular with the majority of the populace, who saw Brandt's *Ostpolitik* with relief. The lack of recognition of the GDR, and its function as the anticliché to "liberal-democratic order," resulted in West Gemans' national solidarity with the population of the GDR being undermined. To the same extent, the nation-state tradition of the Kaiserreich lost its psychological binding power. For large parts of the West German population, in particular for the younger generation, referring back to the founding of the Reich by Bismarck proved itself to be historically blind. Such references were soon exhausted as a source of legitimation of the pan-German claim.

The dilemma of conservative politics consists not least of all in the fact that the specifically national interests of the Federal Republic are hindered by the fixation on the claim for reunification. Reserving the term "nation" for the people of both German states lends ambivalence to the attempt to appeal to a national sentiment; it throws up the question of the difference between these views and the rightist-nationalist and neo-Fascist tendencies. Neoconservative journalism, which has grown steadily in the past two decades, frequently mixes its claim for the return to the "German nation" with hardly redeemable demands for revision. The line between these views and unambiguously neo-Fascist positions has proved to be fluid. A comparison of the publications of the study center Weikersheim e.V., led by the former minister president Hans Filbinger (and conceived of equally as a retirement residence), with the contributions to the *Deutsche National-zeitung* makes this all too clear.

The politics of revision propagated by the new Right was very difficult to bring to terms with subscribing to the status quo in German-German policy, to which the Federal Republic as a satellite in the Atlantic Alliance was bound, in the absence of any alternative. Similarly, the neoconservative authors pushed the criticism of Allied reeducation in the years after 1945 more than seemed supportable for the continuation of good relations with the United States. Except for the incantations of pan-German visions, which occurred with fine regularity and achieved their most painful apogees with Chancellor Helmut Kohl's visit to the Silesia conventions, the refuge in decidedly nationalistic positions was blocked for conservative politics. The debate about the German question, which has largely gone politically sterile, moved itself not coincidentally to the level of conflicting images of history.

Until the end of the 1960s the self-understanding of the Federal Republic had been predominantly directed to economic growth. During this time the question of historical legitimacy characteristically was assigned a subordinate weight. The debate with the critical Left changed this and led to the call for an intensification of historical education. The CDU/CSU hoped to prop up its endangered domestic consensus. The legitimacy debate took on greater importance after the proclamation of the politics of the *Wende* [the change in 1982 to a conservative coalition government in Bonn]. It proved quickly to be the case that there was not sufficient resonance in public opinion for recycling the formulas of the 1950s. After the honeymoon had passed that had allowed the Kohl-Genscher government to profile itself in comparison to Chancellor Helmut Schmidt's divided social-liberal cabinet in his last years in office, the lack of an integrative political concept became evident. In the politics of the *Wende* this lack took on the blemish of unadorned restoration. As opposed to the social-liberal politics of reform and the program "dare to have more democracy," the new government was only able to refer to its higher level of economic reliability. There was no real shortage of efforts of rightists, nor of intellectuals who had gone over to the Right to fill this vacuum. And they did not shy away from borrowing from U.S. neoconservatives. But in the last analysis these efforts, accompanied by distinctly conservative cultural politics, could come up with no long-term perspective that was suitable to providing an ideological cloak for advancing the politics of naked self-interest.

Precisely in this constellation the long-smoldering debate about the contours of the West German image of history grew much sharper. Whereas previously the debate had always developed in the context of a supposedly widespread antipathy toward history, now it could take shape with regard to the actual content of history. In the central position stood the evaluation of the history of the Third Reich. The commemorative ceremonies, forced on the Federal Republic from the outside and only accepted against its will, in honor of the fortieth anniversary of the German capitulation gave the external impetus for this evaluation. The ineptness of the government of the Federal Republic on the occasion of President Reagan's visit to Bitburg made surprisingly clear that the burdens of the Second World War now as before possess traumatic meaning. These burdens disturbed the dramaturgy of the Bitburg spectacle, which, under the fiction of final reconciliation among friends, was supposed to replace the idea of a crusade by the Allies against a Hitler dictatorship with the idea of a crusade against Communist world dictatorship. Consequently, in the official speeches, the Second World War was pushed back into the sequence of normal wars and the Third Reich appeared as a tragic but, in the face of the threat of Bolshevist aggression, understandable entanglement.

The domestic policy arguments that followed immediately on the Bitburg episode likewise made plain that the view of the National-Socialist period, which had set the tone in political education and in the history books, no longer had any adequate binding force. This view was stamped with the problematic acceptance of the internal programmatic consequence of Hitler's ideology of domination. This acceptance had been combined with the totalitarianism theorem, which had originally purposefully not been framed in terms of personalities. On the one hand, the emphasis on Hitler as the decisive initiator of the criminal policies of the Nazi regime grew out of the reaction to the assumption that Hitler's good intentions had been turned into the opposite by his subordinates. This assumption was already predominant in the ruling elites before the defeat and was bitterly disappointed in 1945. This point of view became a necessary lie to precisely the extent to which the dictator usurped the monopoly of national identity. As a matter of policy, every attempt to turn away from the "Hitler cult" had been stigmatized as antinational. On the other hand, Hitlerism in historical interpretation had the aim of unburdening the conservative leadership groups by presenting the complexity of the domestic and foreign policy decision-making apparatus as the simple derivative of the omnipotent will of the führer. This made possible the wholesale rejection of the Third Reich in the first years after the war; it was seen as a kind of historical foreign body. The analysis of causes was therefore preoccupied by the topic of the erroneous estimations of the National Socialists by the other parties and interest groups before 1933. However, these historians avoided detailing the various and frequently nonhomogeneous motivations that induced in particular the representatives of the upper middle class to loyalty to Hitler. These were people who were inwardly opposed to and rejected the NSDAP and the SS, and especially, as they were characteristically called, the "methods" of Himmler, Heydrich, and Goebbels. Describing the Third Reich as a monolith caused the fact that it was also characterized by an open political process to recede from public understanding. Still, one sought the "guilt" for the catastrophe of the Weimar democracy in the extreme opposition of Left and Right that supposedly strangled the political center of Weimar. The foreign-policy complement to the comfortable and altogether too easily grasped model explanation consisted in the grotesque conclusion that the British policy of appeasement, especially the British pacifists of the 1930s, had to bear the burden of responsibility for the ominous escalation of the National-Socialist politics of violence.

The evaluation of the Third Reich as an event, complete in itself, and only conditionally connected with the Weimar Republic, was also reflected in the complete equation by conservative historians of the Russian October Revolution and the Nazi power grab of 1933, as it was called. This terminology itself is an incorporation of National-Socialist vocabulary and in this way describes the Nazi rise to power as a "revolutionary" upheaval. Thus the history of the Third Reich was stylized as a fated doom from which there was no escape and from which no concrete political impulses could reach the present. Similarly the conservative historians reacted to the persecution of the Jews and to the Holocaust primarily with moral shock, leaving the events, only inadequately reconstructed by the West-German research community, on the level of a purely traumatic experience. Chancellor Kohl captured this political consequencelessness, which becomes visible here, of the National-Socialist experience with the phrase "Gnade der späten Geburt" [blessing of a late birth].

Precisely against this ubiquitous tendency to "shake off the mortgages of a past now happily made morally neutral" (Jürgen Habermas), Martin Broszat directs his plea for "historicizing" National Socialism.[2] In the international as well as in the West German writing of history, a far more open view of the Third Reich has predominated for some time, a view that has freed itself from the originally predominant dualistic interpretation, which compared the traditions of the "other Germany" to the center of terror of the SS state and prescribed an ideological-historical determinism. Significantly, it was the foreign-policy research, in particular the ground-laying works of Andreas Hillgruber, that suggested the view for continuities of German policy from the late Wilhelminian period up to the capitulation. At the same time it became ever more plain that the availability of extensive segments of the predominantly conservative leadership elites for the Nazi regime rested less on ideological indoctrination than on this regime's promises, only inadequately fulfilled, to reverse the loss of status brought about by progressive social leveling.

It is significant that this line, which had long been under way in concrete research in the Federal Republic, was fought less by means of scholarly than legalistic arguments. The highly emotionalized debate about the question of whether a formal order by Hitler for the policy of genocide was necessary illuminates this tendency, reaching up to the threshold of agnosticism to reject unpleasant facts that cannot be ideologically compensated for. This can be demonstrated analogously to the research on the resistance to Hitler, which, due to the slackening of interest, is accused of demythologizing, an accusation for which there is no justification. Similarly, an increased softening of the fossilized image of the Nazis makes itself evident not least of all in the light of the attitude of the younger generation, which has difficulty coming to terms with the interpretation of the National-Socialist period that attributes this period primarily to a fateful entanglement.

Where conservative scholars once bracketed the Third Reich out of the historical continuity, they now want to relativize it. With the demand that National Socialism be placed in larger historical contexts, Ernst Nolte agrees with more pronouncedly progressive historians, as he does with the warning against taboos motivated by "folk pedagogy." When, however, he understands the genocide as a naked psychological reaction to Lenin's White Terror, characterized as an "Asiatic" deed, and describes the genocide in the tradition of "the tyranny of collectivist thinking," then he is moving in an arena in which all actions directed against Bolshevism appear justified as such and every political responsibility disappears behind dispositions determined by the specific epoch. In his view, the tyranny of collectivist thinking has been answered by the "decisive turn to *all* the rules of a free society."[3]

One can perhaps understand this argumentation as an inadmissible construction in the history of ideas without any political intention. But Nolte's justification years ago of the deportation of the Jews and his view of Auschwitz as a mere outgrowth of an anomalous apolitical constellation had led to his being criticized as an "ordinary German nationalist" (Felix Gilbert). The alleged apoliticality is therefore insufficient to account for the defense carried out on his behalf by conservative colleagues. Klaus Hildebrand explicitly took sides with Nolte's view when he gave up his previously stubbornly claimed singularity of National Socialism (failing to appreciate this was, as is well known, the standard criticism of the comparative fascism theory).[4] Similarly, Michael Stürmer called on Franz Oppenheimer as an unsuspecting witness. Oppenheimer had appealed in the *Frankfurter Allgemeine Zeitung* to the Germans to free themselves from the traumatic ballast of this part of their past and argued against holding on to the "collective German pre-occupation with guilt."[5]

It is no wonder that this new view of things found well-meaning applause coming out of Washington. In a lecture entitled "Beyond the Zero Hour: The Creation of a Civic Culture in Postwar Germany," given at a Nuremburg symposium, the U.S. ambassador to Bonn fervently entreated the

Germans on May 23, 1986, to develop a greater self-consciousness and a higher sense of national pride in view of the accomplishments since 1945 that had their roots in national history. As far as he was concerned, Burt emphasized, there was no "zero hour." May 1945 meant "the reanimation and consolidation of German democracy," which in Weimar had stumbled above all because of hostile economic conditions and not from any internal necessity. The Germans must free themselves from the "tragedy of 1933–1945" and be mindful of the positive elements of German history, which for a long period had borne democratic features.

The exhortations from Washington to clear up at last the relation of Germans to their history give cause to prick up our ears. These exhortations touch on the concern of Michael Stürmer, expressly brought up by Burt, that without a consolidation of the German image of history the foreign-policy alliance of the Federal Republic with the West would be put into question. The exhortations are at the same time connected to his complaint about the putative "ahistoricality" of the Federal Republic and the challenge to reclaim lost terrain. Only through the collective endowment of higher meaning by means of historiography could the endangered domestic political consensus be secure for the long term. The alternative would be, Stürmer emphasizes, that the conflict between opposing interests and values, "if it found no common ground," would necessarily lead to a civil war.[6] With this the instrumental character of the restitution claimed by the ruling parties of the "thousand years of healthy history beyond National Socialism," (from a 1978 CDU statement on the reform of instruction in history) is clearly revealed.

One could hardly impute to West German historical scholarship that it is committed to this politically motivated tendency. It is too apolitical in attitude for that, despite its strongly conservative stamp. This tendency does however meet halfway the broad current of the discipline that takes a skeptical stance on the trend toward social and regional history and research about everyday life. This current is directed back toward the classical history of politics and ideas. It is difficult to estimate to what extent the neorevisionist tendency championed above all by Stürmer and Hildebrand will meet with agreement. At any rate, their technocratic instrumentalization might just run into rejection from conservative scholars; even with them, as in the case of Hillgruber, there is a certain affinity for a stronger emphasis on national factors. His historiographic association of resettlement and the Holocaust indirectly supports the plan, so aggressively posited by Stürmer, of relativizing the crimes of the Third Reich. It allows for revisionist misunderstandings by its demand for "a reconstruction of the destroyed European Middle."[7]

By viewing the experiences of the Third Reich exclusively as a national burden and assigning the shock about the crimes of the National-Socialist domination predominantly to the category of "guilt," the representatives of neorevisionism actually block the way to a measured treatment of this epoch. The phrase "collective obsession with guilt," apart from its apologetic tendency, diverts from the actual consequences, which are not primarily of a moral but of a political nature. A 1986 memorandum of the Federal Republic's minister for construction on the erection of the House of History in Bonn states that the "mortgage of the Third Reich" must be balanced against German history's "capital of venerable parliamentary, democratic, and especially federal traditions." He acts as though the recent past could be neutralized by simple accounting measures. This only proves that the constitutive meaning of the experiences of the National-Socialist epoch for the historical and political self-understanding of the West German society is being denied.

In fact, from this experience we should derive the commitment to hold firm to the parliamentary-democratic principle and defend liberal principles even at the cost of reduced state efficiency. For only before the backdrop of the dissolution of the state systems of norms and institutions was the collapse into Nazism conceivable. It was a political structure characterized by cynical contempt for human beings and by the application of violent force without bounds. It was a structure that furthermore was promoted by the German elite's practice, reaching back into the late imperialistic phase, of an increasing moral indifference. What made the way clear for Hitler was the turn against Western constitutional traditions. The turning away was in fact not completed in National Socialism and succeeded under the affirmation of the idea of the state based on power and anticommunist resentment. Thus, it was not the continuation of democratic traditions that founded the democratic consensus of the Federal Republic.

The prevailing mistrust in the Federal Republic, independent of every party affiliation, of any cult of community organized by the state, of appeals for national willingness to make sacrifices, and of sentiment against national pathos and national emblems has its roots in the political sobering up that arose from the experiences in the Third Reich. Whoever wants to see in this a lack of patriotic sentiment should be clear once and for all that there is no lack of willingness for democratic participation, although this frequently takes place outside of the corrupt apparatus of the large parties. If Theodor Mommsen bitterly accused the Germans in his political testament of not getting beyond the "*Dienst im Gliede*" [feudal service to the bond of vassalage], this has changed decisively in recent decades despite a growing tendency for external accommodation. This is reflected in the mistrust of the broadening of apparatuses of state control, of data exchange, and of police surveillance, even if signs of political resignation are impossible to overlook.

It is therefore absurd to want to rehabilitate older authoritarian attitudes through historical relativizing. It is a mistake to characterize as a wrong path the consequences of action inferred from the flawed developments of the period between the wars. These developments by no means touched only the German nation. The pacifist current recently making itself felt in the general critique of the U.S. commando attack against Libya may be somewhat uncomfortable to the government, but is the necessary consequence arising from the experiences of two wars that from today's perspective lack justification. The arms race of the world powers meets in both parts of Germany with undisguised mistrust. This does not have to do in the least with the assumption that because of their "memory of past wrongs" Germans are hindered from advocating their true interests. On the contrary, they have been put in a position to recognize these interests. They now counter doctrinaire claims with skepticism, from whichever side the claims may come. The extensive repression of nationalistic resentment, which has led to a normalization of the relationship with the neighboring peoples and even has reduced xenophobia, is being described from the conservative side as a potential danger to political stability and as a putative "loss of identity." However, it is not primarily national feelings, but rather examples of a politics of self-interest, that give neoconservatives like Michael Stürmer reason to ponder that with the loss of religious bonds, only "nation and patriotism" ("Kein Eigentum der Deutschen: Die deutsche Frage" [No Property of the Germans: The German Question]) are able to provide a consensus that transcends social classes. The helplessness of neorevisionism becomes clear at this juncture. For both of these dimensions can be manipulated only at the cost, as the history of the Weimar Republic impressively shows, of losing control over them. Furthermore, the fulfillment of the nationalist claim raised from the neoconservative side is necessarily diffuse and politically fanciful.

It is significant for this dilemma that the sought-after consolidation of nationalist feeling is supposed to be undertaken via a detour: strengthening national consciousness. This is the deeper meaning of the plans of the federal government to erect historical museums in Bonn and Berlin. If it were a matter of strengthening the democratic consensus through a critical treatment of national history, the government would hardly have hesitated to accept the offer of cooperation from the opposition.[8] Just how authoritarian a path the chancellor is following in this area is demonstrated by the founding of a German Historical Museum[9] without regard for plans, already completed in Berlin, for the establishment in the Gropius Building of a Forum for History and the Present. The German Historical Museum was supposed to be established and built for Berlin as a "birthday present" on its 750th anniversary. The new museum building planned for the vicinity of the Reichstag has the task, in keeping with the suggestions made by experts who consulted for the Federal Republic's minister for construction, to present the whole of German history, from the ninth century to the present. How strongly desire for external representation is commingled with neoconservative interest in revitalizing German national history is revealed from the models for this project. They range from the National Museum in Mexico City, the Diaspora Museum in Tel-Aviv, and the Air Space Museum in Washington to the Pompidou Center in Paris.

The plan for a mammoth historical museum in West Berlin, which in contrast to the East Berlin Museum for German History will have no authentic items to exhibit, presents, despite all the expertise of the historians willingly working on the project, an artificial fossil of the nation-state mentality of the nineteenth century. It is supposed to realize what the German unity movements since the wars of liberation have not achieved: a representative national image of history. The special expert committee did agree in the publication of their first concept that they did not want to create a "national shrine" and that they wanted to make allowances for pluralistic views of history. They also said that they wanted to illuminate not the history of the German national state but the history of the Germans in a Europe of changing borders. Whatever one may think in the face of the objective constraints of the chosen medium about assurances of that sort, the intent at any rate will be pursued by those responsible in the government. As in the Bonn House of History, they intend to deliver belatedly to the Germans, as it were, their "national identity." While the idea of the Forum in Berlin was open to various views and interpretations, the German Historical Museum will without hesitation become an event aimed at the middle class. At the same time it will be a self-presentation of the discipline of history.

The recourse to a museum, to a rounded presentation of the national tradition, is significant in double measure for the intentions of the government and its close academic advisers. What is being asked for is not a critical view of history founded on research but balancing accounts. At the same time, the history of the period between the wars is to be thinned out. In Bonn this period functions as a brief introduction; in Berlin it takes up less than a tenth of the exhibition's area. Both plans have the goal of refuge in past normality. In both cases a historically grounded awareness of values is supposed to be transmitted, one that puts the Federal Republic in a position to accommodate the ways of national power politics, not, as in Bismarck's days, as the strongest power in Europe but as a "centerpiece in the European arc of defense of the Atlantic system" (Michael Stürmer). Such a project would indeed require a new image of history, one that takes lightly the warning sign of the National-Socialist epoch and that wants to make us forget the Holocaust and Project Barbarossa under the slogan of "normalizing." This intention has nothing to do with the understanding of history that has grown stepwise in postwar Germany, an understanding that has come about apart from the classical monumental history and frequently independently of the scholarly discipline.

Source: *Merkur*, September/October 1986, pp. 864–874

NOTES

1. Compare with Hermann Lübbe, "Der Nationalsozialismus im deutschen Nach-kriegsbewußtsein" [National Socialism in the German Postwar Consciousness], *Historische Zeitschrift* No. 236, 1983.
2. Martin Broszat, "Plädoyer für eine Historisierung des National-sozialismus," *Merkur* No. 435, May 1985.
3. Ernst Nolte, "Die Vergangenheit, die nicht vergehen will," *Frankfurter Allgemeine Zeitung*, June 6, 1986; also "Between Myth and Revisionism: The Third Reich in the Perspective of the 1980s," in Hans W. Koch, ed., *Aspects of the Third Reich*. London, Macmillan 1985.
4. See the discussion of Nolte's contribution in the *Historische Zeitschrift* No. 242, 1986.
5. See Stürmer's letter to the editor in the *Süddeutsche Zeitung* of June 25, 1986.
6. Michael Stürmer, "Kein Eigentum der Deutschen: Die deutsche Frage" [No Property of the Germans: The German Question], in Werner Weidenfeld, ed., *Die Identität der Deutschen*, Munich, Hanser 1983.
7. See Andreas Hillgruber, *Zweierlei Untergang: Die Zerschlagung des deutschen Reiches und das Ende des europäischen Judentums* [Twofold Fall: The Destruction of the German Reich and the End of European Jewry], Berlin: Siedler 1986. It is today an open question "whether more than regional initiatives in Western Europe will be possible for a reconstruction of the destroyed European Middle—as a prerequisite for a reconstruction of the whole of Europe or as a consequence of the reconstruction of all of Europe getting under way." Habermas's critique "Eine Art Schadensabwicklung" [A Kind of Settlement of Damages] in *Die Zeit*, July 11, 1986, goes too far with regard to Hillgruber.
8. Compare Hans Mommsen, "Verordnete Geschichtsbilder? Historische Museums pläne der Budesregierung" [Ordained Images of History? Museum Plans of the Federal Government], *Gewerkschaftliche Monatshefte* No. 1, January 1986.
9. Compare Dieter Hoffmann-Axthelm, "Geschichte ohne Ort und Schatten: Deutsches historisches Museum in Berlin" [History without Place and Shadow: The German Historical Museum in Berlin], *Die neue Gesellschaft* No. 7, July 1986.

HANS MOMMSEN

The New Historical Consciousness and the Relativizing of National Socialism

The battle order of conservative thought in the Federal Republic has changed. For decades conservatives insisted on interpreting National Socialism as a singular rupture in the continuity of German history. Germany was seen as the first country occupied by National Socialism. This in turn reflected the tendency to attribute the catastrophe of the Third Reich and its criminal politics to Adolf Hitler and in the last analysis to speak of Hitlerism. This tendency was already setting in after 1945 and it solidified afterward. Supporters of the comparative theory of fascism were rudely met with the reply that to subsume National Socialism under fascism was inconsistent with National Socialism's reputed singularity; indeed, it was argued, this came close to "trivializing" the revolutionary character of the National-Socialist system of domination. This, however, did not keep conservative writers from equating National Socialism with Bolshevism as a central explanatory model, an equation that had been pounded into the Western thought since the Stalinist purges; nor did it prevent them from garnishing it with the theory of "total dictatorship."

For some time, however, things have been different. Suddenly, not only the "singularity" of National Socialism, but also its crimes, are being denied. The debate was ignited by the evaluation of the Holocaust. Ernst Nolte was among the first in this in that he emphasized that the liquidation of millions of European Jews did not represent something unique in world history; instead it needed to be "relativized" in the universal historical perspective. At that time, prominent historians like Peter Gay and Felix Gilbert disagreed strongly with Nolte. The German public was silent; the debate was nothing more than a marginal problem for them. Recently, Ernst Nolte has presented this thesis anew, first in an English-language anthology, then in a contribution to the *Frankfurter Allgemeine Zeitung*, originally intended as a lecture at the Römerberg Talks. Unlike before, criticism of Nolte now elicited a defense by prominent historians, among them Joachim C. Fest and Klaus Hildebrand. Characteristically, the defensive polemic was directed against Jürgen Habermas, who in *Die Zeit* came out against the efforts to present an image of German history completely "equilibrated" as Helmut Kohl would want it, and also against the efforts to help the German people to a new "national pride." (They find in this effort explicit support from the U.S. ambassador in Bonn, Richard Burt.) Hildebrand's partisan shots can be easily deflected; that Habermas is accused of a "loss of reality and Manichaeanism" and that his honesty is denied is witness to the self-consciousness of a self-nominated historian elite, which has set itself the task of tracing the outlines of the seemingly badly needed image of history.

More serious is Joachim Fest's anticriticism in the *Frankfurter Allgemeine Zeitung*. Fest goes to great lengths in the defense of Ernst Nolte and does not hesitate to insinuate that Habermas attempted a "personal character assassination" and made a careless reading of the texts he criticized. One must be impressed by the sensitivity with which Fest reacted to the criticism that this was not at all about isolated articles by serious scholars but rather about the Pandora's box opened up by the politics of the *Wende* [the conservative shift in the government in 1982], which was accompanied by an attempt to drop historical taboos. These accusations in fact fall far short of the point to which West German political culture has progressed. This causes concern. The *Frankfurter Allgemeine Zeitung* has increasingly made itself the platform for advocates of revising the "image of history." This fact is overlooked by Fest's claim that Habermas is obstinately wrong-headed about this "most absurd kind of conspiracy theory," which, according to Fest, "is nothing other than an expression of uncomprehended contexts." Fest's claim also ignores the fact that efforts of this kind are in no way isolated. This is all the more surprising, since Michael Stürmer, the editorial writer of the *Frankfurter Allgemeine Zeitung*, has repeatedly announced such a program, and announced it under the slogan that he who is master of history would also have the future for himself. It may be that Joachim C. Fest does not mean what is intended here: that the fixing of the image of history also has the function of consolidating political power. The chancellor has lent his full political support to this reconsolidation of the national image of history in the form of a German Historical Museum. He expounded on the project as a "national task of European rank." Along with him, leading representatives of the CDU/CSU have picked up on Stürmer's ideas exactly in this sense.

At any rate, Fest is correct (and Habermas never did assert this) that there is no conspiracy. The goodwill in German academic circles, on which efforts of this sort can count, is much too great. What is happening is much more like freeing lines of thought that until then had been repressed because they seemed politically questionable. These lines of thought include equating the Holocaust with resettlement; calling into question the purposefulness of the assassination attempt of July 20, 1944, in the face of the threat by the Red Army; shifting German responsibility for the Second World War and Auschwitz to the British politics of appeasement and its pacifistic practitioners; the notion that Weimar had failed primarily because of the bonds of the peace treaty, the "edict" of Versailles; the notion that the nonexistent national consciousness of the Germans was also a consequence of postwar reeducation; and the notion that in the last analysis it was the Communists who (along with the National Socialists) had buried the republican system. Certainly this last, in its crude form, is not advocated by the scholarly community; implicitly, however, it is being accepted and paid no further attention.

This revisionism of the neoconservative stripe is not new as such. It has flourished in neoconservative niches of West German society for some time and is reflected in a widespread literature, whether it is financed by the Siemens Foundation, by Minister President Filbinger's Study Center Weikersheim, or by other tax-sheltered sources. It is not even mentioned in the *Frankfurter Allgemeine Zeitung* that the renowned Ullstein Press has recently begun a series like this, although it seems spooky that this previously representative Jewish press today supports publications that cannot and will not deny their affinity to post-Fascist positions. It is all a matter of financial transactions in the publication business. There is the greatest excitement about the "leftist" literature found in the Goethe Institute in Kyoto; however, it bothers no one that this dubious genre of neoconservative and neonationalist provenance is completely indexed in the Goethe Institutes. What is taking place at present is no conspiracy. A better description would be that national sentiments, long dammed up and visible only in marginal literature, are coming together in an unholy alliance and seeking new shores.

It is evident that Joachim Fest, one of the outstanding historians of the Nazi period, is not in agreement with tendencies like this; likewise, the language of U.S. neoconservatives, which is ultimately resentful and characterized by internalized anti-Bolshevism, hardly fits in his vocabulary. But Fest should employ a somewhat more thoughtful approach than to accuse Habermas, the outsider, of intellectual dishonesty and of being a "mandarin of myths," especially since Fest has taken on the role of several "dominant" historians of pressing their opponents into the corner of obscurity. In Hildebrand's reply in *Frankfurter Allgemeine Zeitung* this happens indirectly: Hildebrand alleges that Habermas divides the German world into "government historians" and Habermas. Implicitly, the Bonn historian claims with this accusation to represent the whole of the German discipline of history. It is consistent with this position, then, to accuse the nonhistorian Habermas of inadequate expertise. There is a reason for employing this technique: fundamental polemics, if they take place outside of the disciplinary journals (where else then?), are labelled "uncollegial," and one's opponent is described as a hopeless outsider, as a "Manichaean." Whoever believes that this is an isolated case should read the critique by "Dagens Nyher" of Karl Dieter Bracher's work published by the Bundeszentrale [Federal Center], *Nationalsozialistische Diktatur. Eine Bilanz: 1933–45* [National Socialist Dictatorship. A Balance: 1933–45].

In the context of the current debate one must warn against such "Stop! Thief!" phrases. Precisely for this reason, it is regrettable that Joachim C. Fest does not separate his accusation of inadequate expertise from the methodically difficult question of the singularity of the Nazi crimes. That historians like Hildebrand and Stürmer have taken Nolte's position has from the outset deflected the question from the path of straight-and-narrow historical research, because for Hildebrand and Stürmer the question is about direct political conclusions, that is, to quote the *Frankfurter Allgemeine Zeitung* writer Franz Oppenheimer, it is about dismantling the notorious "German obsession with guilt." The concept of "singularity," raised by Karl Dietrich Bracher in connection with National Socialism, is for the historian first of all a triviality, since historical events hardly demonstrate identical structures and frameworks of causation. "Incomparability" in this sense does not exist methodologically; each comparison has to legitimate itself by its epistemological fruitfulness, while there is no criterion *a limine* for holding it to be illegitimate. It is therefore equally justified to interpret National Socialism as a specific form of fascism as it is to compare it with Communist regimes. The question is rather whether correct or misleading conclusions are drawn from the comparison.

In connection with the politics of "genocide" such a procedure, for understandable reasons, is especially controversial. From the Zionist position that sees anti-Semitism as the sole deciding factor for the implementation of the Holocaust, the murder of Soviet prisoners of war and Gypsies does not seem to be parallel. With justification it can be pointed out that the murder of the Jews corresponded to the unreal projection of a "world enemy" that, however much it played a role in the original anti-Semitism and the persecution of the Jews before 1938, is to be assessed as of completely subordinate importance in contrast to the motives of the politics of interest. In accord with the perspective that mass murder for racial or ethnic reasons was by no means, either then or now, limited to the Holocaust, the policy of genocide must be seen as the most extreme form in history of the cynical and systematic destruction of undesirable peoples and minorities. For this reason, Hannah Arendt, after the experience of the Eichmann trial, pled for the creation of a form of punishment for genocide that would be valid in international law.

From this consideration it becomes important to uncover the mechanisms that, motivated by a thorough but not complete ideological indoctrination, made it possible to set into political reality the murderous dreams of the racist anti-Semites. Here, too, the notion of comparability plays an important role, although in a different sense than was applied to the indictment of the Eichmann trial. That indictment saw in the National-Socialist genocide the end-stage of the anti-Jewish genocide striven for by Christians. Hannah Arendt protests passionately against this concept, because in principle this makes eternal the role of anti-Semitism as a historical factor.

Yet there is a relative singularity of the Holocaust. Fest addresses this indirectly when he recognizes the "arrogance" of the "old master race attitude" in the argument that an old "cultured people" are to be held more strictly accountable for crimes of this order of magnitude than would be the case for "more primitive people." Certainly there is horror over the fact that the nation of "German idealism" had sunk down to a level of contempt for and destruction of humanity that has not been exceeded. The journal of Jochen Klepper, who chose suicide in the face of the unavoidable deportation of his married Jewish daughter, demonstrates this clearly. Previously achieved stages of political and moral culture are not relevant in evaluating of the murder of the Jews, which was made possible by terrorist dictatorship and propagandistic indoctrination. This argument should surely not be foreign to those who speak of the regeneration of German identity arising out of the awareness of a "thousand years of healthy history before National Socialism." To accept with resignation the acts of screaming injustice and to psychologically repress their social prerequisites by calling attention to similar events elsewhere and putting the blame on the Bolshevist world threat recalls the thought patterns that made it possible to implement genocide.

The terrifying thing about the debate continued by Fest, a historian who tortures himself precisely with the question of the reaction of the populace (and not just the German populace) to the Holocaust, is that Hitler's "will to annihilate" suffices as an adequate end cause. The real question is why the many who actively took part in the exclusion of Jews from German everyday life, which stands at the beginning of the Holocaust, did not try to refuse to participate in the technical details of the deportation, the exploitation of Jewish property, and the melting of the gold of Jews' teeth. Why did they not refuse membership in the *Einsatzgruppen*? This is certainly not a problem of the German mentality alone, although a certain form of obedience to authority and a misdirected love of order presented additional factors without which the dimension of moral indifference and human apathy cannot be explained.

If, however, the connection between Bolshevism and National Socialism is going to be the topic of discussion, a connection that, as mentioned, was essentially a social-psychological one, then it has to first be established that the characteristic response was the overreaction in Germany of the political elites, not the October Revolution or the Nazi seizure of the apparatus of power, and that the political culture of Weimar was characterized by unquestioned acceptance of violent force in political debates; and this violence came, to recall Josef Wirth, predominantly from the Right. The hybrid anti-Bolshevism on whose wave Hitler came to power contributed in great measure to shutting off even the quasi-moral inhibitions of those who assisted the SS hangmen. And this pertains equally to the role of the *Wehrmacht*.

In light of these questions, which thinking people encountered repeatedly, it seems superficial and insincere to narrow the discussion to the question brought up by Ernst Nolte about the extent of the similarities between the National-Socialist mass murder and the Gulag Archipelago. Translated into contemporary consciousness, this would amount to equating Katyn and Auschwitz, but with a similarly reversed point of view from those in the opposition who bravely wrote this equation on the wall. If one puts any stock in the opposition in the Third Reich, then one should not forget its reaction to Goebbel's Katyn propaganda: The opposition refused to accept, considering the murder of the Jews, the regime's justification for playing up the Bolshevist murders as having transparent purposes. Despite all psychological repression and all the will not to perceive, there was in the broad mass of the populace, though certainly not in the relatively small number of fanatical Nazis, a consciousness of guilt about having allowed deportations and violence and about having condoned them for the most part.

The psychological and institutional mechanisms that explain the lack of reaction in the populace must be the object of careful research. The research must be carried out under the criterion of doing all one can to hinder the recurrence of something comparable, even though the scale of the systematic extermination of the European Jews stands as singular, in particular that it was almost completely and perfectly accomplished. Research is in agreement that the actual explanation consists of the tension between the unsuccessful attempts to keep the genocide secret, though the existence of the death camps was perhaps known, and the lack of protest not so much by the general public as by the people occupying the relevant positions. All comparisons with Stalinism do not help in this connection any further, since the conditions were different. In the Russian struggle for power, after all, explainable inimical feelings also played a part, while the abstract "anti-Semitism without Jews" in the Third Reich represents an anomaly.

There is no talk about all this in Fest's defense of Ernst Nolte's arguments. To some extent he does take up arguments propagated by Martin Broszat and me when he concedes that Hitler himself became a prisoner to a complex context of actions that he himself had launched. But he builds into his argumentation a proposal that a "causal nexus" was probable between the Bolshevist crimes and the Holocaust. The latter is well known to be Nolte's position; he interprets Hitler's radical anti-Semitism as a misguided counterreaction to the "Asiatic deed" of Bolshevism. Causality in this sense, however, still cannot be claimed; at most it would allow indicating the historically necessary psychological constraints on action. The stipulation of a causal connection between the Gulag Archipelago and Auschwitz is, however, not simply methodologically untenable but also absurd in its premises and conclusions. Now Hitler's anti-Bolshevism preceded, as is well known, the Stalinist measures against the kulaks; it is difficult to see how this anti-Bolshevism could have derived from the violence of the Russian civil war. Nevertheless, if one accepts Nolte's hypothesis, one arrives at the following determination: the hybrid anti-Bolshevism, whose "victim" Hitler appears to be in such a view, forced Hitler subjectively to use the same methods (that is, the methods of which he accused the Jews); he succumbed thus to the self-deception of taking Bolshevism as a Jewish invention. Subjectively, it could thus be reasoned that Hitler's anti-Semitism was comprehensible, even if for other reasons his methods were not justified. It is best not to continue working with such constructs.

The anti-Bolshevism of the German Right, but also of the German bourgeoisie, in 1918 was already making use of the equation of Bolshevism and Jewry. The Pan-German Union [alldeutscher Verband] in the First World War had already decided to use anti-Semitism for the purpose of anti-socialist mobilization of the masses. These facts suffice to explain why Hitler, in the immediate postwar years in a Munich shaken by civil war, took up anti-Semitism with its typical anti-Bolshevist trappings. In this respect he was anything other than a special case. In contrast to these irrefutable conditioning factors, Nolte's derivation based on personalities and the history of ideas seems artificial, even for the explanation of Hitler's anti-Semitism. It is beyond dispute that fascism and thus both National Socialism and the folkish movement were able to reach broader acceptance only as a reaction to the October Revolution, as the beneficiaries of the hybrid anti-communist resentments unleashed by the Fascist movement. Acceptance of this anti-Semitism also extended well into the SPD. Other factors, however, were ultimately necessary to make the NSDAP into a mass movement.

If one emphasizes the indisputably important connection in isolation, one should not then force a connection with Hitler's weltanschauung, which was in no ways original itself, in order to derive from it the existence of Auschwitz. The battle line between the political Right in Germany and the Bolsheviks had achieved its aggressive contour before Stalinism employed political methods that led to death of millions of people. Thoughts about the extermination of the Jews had long been current, and not only for Hitler and his satraps. Many of these found their way to the NSDAP from the Deutschvölkisch Schutz- und Trutzbund [German Racial Union for Protection and Defiance], which itself had been called into life by the Pan-German Union. Hitler's step from verbal anti-Semitism to practical implementation would then have happened with knowledge of and in reaction to the atrocities of the Stalinists. And thus one would have to overturn Nolte's construct, for which he cannot bring biographical evidence to bear. As a Hitler biographer, Fest distances himself from this kind of one-sidedness by making reference to "the Austrian-German Hitler's earlier fears and phantasies of being overwhelmed." It is not completely consistent that he admits that the reports of the terrorist methods of the Bolsheviks had given Hitler's "extermination complexes" a "real background."

Basically, Nolte's proposal in its one-sidedness is not very helpful for explaining or evaluating what happened. The anti-Bolshevism garnished with anti-Semitism had the effect, in particular for the dominant elites, and certainly not just for the National Socialists, that Hitler's program of racial annihilation met with no serious resistance. The leadership of the *Wehrmacht* rather willingly made themselves into accomplices in the policy of extermination. It did this by generating the "criminal orders" and implementing them. By no means did they merely passively support the implementation of their concept, although there was a certain reluctance for reasons of military discipline and a few isolated protests. To construct a "causal nexus" over all this amounts in fact to steering away from the decisive responsibility of the military leadership and the bureaucratic elites.

Hitler's fanatical battle against the alleged "conspiracy of the world Jewry" was furthermore an ideological construct that in no way needed support from concrete historical events such as the Stalinist crimes. The process, described by no one better than J. Fest, that caused Hitler to drop all inhibitions in pursuing his real and imagined enemies cannot be explained by his perception of Lenin's "Asiatic methods," despite the fact that Hitler's ideology was rooted more in the folkish anti-Semitic thinking of the prewar period than most biographers assume. The complex process that led from the deprivation of social rights, through forced migration and ghettoization to, finally in 1941, systematic liquidation can simply not be explained ideologically, as Fest admits. It is connected with the self-unleashed dynamic that was necessarily initiated by the total exclusion of the Jews from the everyday life of their fellow citizens, together with Himmler's resettlement policy.

It is not appropriate here to elaborate in detail the fundamental difference between Communist systems and the Nazi regime, nor between Bolshevist and Fascist parties. The specific form of politics that characterizes fascism, that is, the reduction of politics to the mobilization of power and the application of violent force, is very difficult to tar with the same brush as the political concept of communism, despite all the external affinities. For example, the similarity of the Stalin cult with the Hitler cult is misleading. The inner boundlessness that allowed no compromises was especially characteristic of National Socialism (and therefore a necessary condition for the annihilation of the Jews). This form of inner boundlessness is not typical for Communist systems of domination, as tyrannical as they were at times. This explains also why the Third Reich reverted with internal logic to self-destruction while the Communist regimes as a rule observed the relation between available resources and political ambitions. The analogy between Bolshevism and National Socialism is much better suited for tempting one to mistake its merely external similarities for constitutive ones.

Fest's retort, which occasionally becomes polemical, arouses the impression that to let the crimes of National Socialism stand as an eternal moral warning would amount to justifying the crimes of Stalinism. Now the latter have never been disputed; it begs the question, nevertheless, whether it is appropriate to judge the communism of today on the moral standard of the events of the 1920s and 1930s. However, it is dangerous to connect this reflection with Nolte's construct that Hitler borrowed the idea of the Holocaust from Bolshevist writings and at the same time acted out of a psychopathological compulsion, without at least posing these questions: Which social-psychological, institutional, and political-interest factors made it possible for Hitler to make himself the enforcer of the resentments, not merely of the "masses" but also of the ruling elites? What made it possible for the elites to practically adore him in this role?

The *Frankfurter Allgemeine Zeitung* published Nolte's planned contribution to the Römerberg Talks with polemical intent. In so doing it has made itself the tool of those with an interest in linking the derivation of the Holocaust from the instinctive fear of the "Asiatic hordes" to a debate that took on its political character primarily because of Michael Stürmer's resonances. On first glance the derivation seems esoteric; the reference to Asia, however, reflects a syndrome still laden with sentiment in Germany, clearly a product of racism. It is significant that Fest refers to the concept of *"conditio humana,"* so happily overused by Stürmer, in order to classify as unrealistic "optimists" those who draw out of the National-Socialist experience the obligation to alter the societal foundations that contributed to making the Holocaust possible. Realistic thinkers are satisfied with the insight "that the genocide which he (Hitler) set in motion was not the first and will not be the last" as if, after the experience of incomprehensible horror, a transition could be made to the international world-historical agenda.

In this it is not, as Fest suggests, so much a matter of the "perfectibility" of human beings and their educability. It is a matter of preserving institutions that can stop a process like that of the Third Reich in its beginnings. It is a matter of sharpening the sensibility for individual responsibility in a political and moral sense so that constellations in which terroristic force extinguishes possible resistance do not even arise. In Germany, particularly, it involves fighting the tendency of accommodation to authority as a norm of social behavior. "Holocaust" is a constant warning flag for that because it signifies the renunciation of the civic virtues in all decisive moments. Precisely this experience teaches one to tread cautiously with the syndrome of anti-Bolshevism. This experience explains the sensitivity encountered by Nolte's derivation of Auschwitz from the Gulag Archipelago, not only in the survivors of the victims but also in those who see their life's mission in destroying the seeds of similar developments.

Emotionally, one finds oneself on the side of those whom Fest wants to exclude. Hildebrand's polemic clearly suggests that he barely considered the consequences of making Nolte's constructs the centerpiece of a modern German conservatism that is very anxious to relativize the National-Socialist experience and to find the way back to a putative historically "normal situation." For everyone who assesses the epoch of the Third Reich in its political and moral consequences, this "normal situation." cannot be achieved without violating the facts. The spreading spirit of intolerance is reflected in the accusations that, by arguing sharply in this matter, Habermas had committed personal slander. Now suddenly, the accusation of "revisionism" is derogatory; when the accusation was coined against the structuralist interpreters of National Socialism, with conscious political intent and in analogy to David Hoggan's position, there were no such sensibilities evident in the *Frankfurter Allgemeine Zeitung*. In fact, for the self-nominated ideologues of the *Wende* like Michael Stürmer and Klaus Hildebrand, this is all about shutting out competitors. They sense that they have the support of the majority of their colleagues, who tend to conservative positions, who in other daily political matters are indifferent, and who find arguments of this kind disruptive.

With regard to the historical treatment of National Socialism, Joachim C. Fest speaks, not without grounds, of rituals of a "fake obsequiousness." The idea about the knowledge that is undesirable for reasons of "national pedagogy" clearly does not stem from the camp of those who sympathize with Habermas. Habermas had offered a fundamental warning against a historical neorevisionism that presses for national good conduct. The Hitlerist fixation of the Nazi image, to which Fest contributed less as an author than as an editor, belongs likewise to the conformism that he denounced and that still today earns me the popular criticism of "trivializing" National Socialism. To these rituals belongs, however, the extensive psychological repression of the fatal coresponsibility of German society: it was possible in the span of a year and a half to let the Holocaust become a reality.

To write about this dimension of the Holocaust and to let the impression arise that the course of events was decided by Hitler's image of Bolshevism and that the rest was terroristically realized compulsion reflects a particular conceptualization in which one period of psychological repression is followed by another, broader one. The first repression of the National-Socialist experience, described by Hermann Lübbe, employed the slogans of the singularity of what Hitler brought about. Beginning in the late 1960s, the second, broader period of repression has been letting the reality of the persecution of Jews disappear in universalist consideration about "totalitarianism, genocide, and mass displacements as the signature of the twentieth century" (Hildebrand). This second displacement follows on the attempts at genuinely clarifying this most difficult chapter of German, certainly also of European, history. It covers the "shame" about what happened by suggesting that every people had its Hitler and then returned to normalcy. Although the anti-Bolshevism and anti-Semitism always appeared as Dioscuri, this form of "coming to grips with the past" [*Vergangenheitsbewältigung*] sees its justification in having sought out the Soviet Union as the root of all evil. If there is a lesson to be drawn from the National-Socialist catastrophe, then it is this, to free oneself from all "collective" hostile images.

Source: *Blätter für deutsche und internationale Politik* [Journal for German and International Politics], October 1986, pp. 1200–1213.

MARTIN BROSZAT

Where the Roads Part: History Is Not a Suitable Substitute for a Religion of Nationalism

In view of the considerate and collegial style that historians maintain not only for reasons of opportunism, it was obvious that the reckless aggression of Habermas's July 11 polemic should not only be welcomed as a breath of fresh air that might purify the atmosphere but should also be rejected as an unwelcome denunciation by an outsider. If one of the weakest points of the attack by the Frankfurt philosopher was that he lumped together politically agile professors such as Michael Stürmer and Klaus Hildebrand with the phlegmatic Andreas Hillgruber and that grand eccentric of contemporary history, Ernst Nolte, then this "most absurd kind of conspiracy theory" (Joachim Fest) seems to have been at least partially validated. Recently an ideologically conformist group of historians, inconspicuously sponsored by the Schleyer Foundation, has been meeting in a symposium ("To Whom Does German History Belong?") under the leadership of Klaus Hildebrand, with Stürmer and Hillgruber as additional speakers.

The selection of active participants and the timing of the symposium, one week before the beginning of the Historical Convention in Trier, suggests the programmatic intention with which the voices of only one partisan group are holding court about the troublemaker Habermas.

It is no less important to keep in mind that the controversy set in motion by Habermas must be seen in the context of an older discussion about several key questions: In what way is the fashionable lament about the loss of history and the desire for a new sense of identity that might be posited by historians related to the critical and Enlightenment-oriented trend, which after 1945 took shape in the discipline of history in the Federal Republic? After all, this discipline had been the product of sad experiences of history being used as political theater. When we consider the Nazi period, what new relationship between historicization and political sensitization is produced for the historian forty years after Hitler? And aren't we running the danger that the ever-overworked national question and the desire not to abdicate to the GDR responsibility for the cultivation of our national history might gradually make us blind to the postulate of West

German constitutional patriotism, the priority of which has been generally accepted until now?

In the case of the recent dispute, hypersensitivity drove Jürgen Habermas to overreaction. Cologne historian Andreas Hillgruber hardly deserves to be accused of trivializing National Socialism, even though the compilation of Hillgruber's lectures, which was quickly patched together by the Berlin publisher Wolf Jobst Siedler for a new volume in his bibliophile series and which treats two quite heterogeneous topics (the collapse of the German eastern front and the National-Socialist mass murder of the Jews), is no masterpiece. The explanation for the interdependence of the two processes that was announced in the title (Twofold Fall) was not forthcoming. This misleading linkage to a grand theme caused Hillgruber's original intention to come perilously close to being apologetic. He had set out to express his understanding for the "ethic of responsibility" of German soldiers, civilians, and party officials who, toward the end of the war in the East, attempted to slow down the inundation by the Red Army. But the material was just not sufficient to justify the scandal that Habermas made of it.

SPLITTING HAIRS IN AN APOLOGETIC WAY

What Ernst Nolte recently formulated—and not for the first time—on categorizing and relativizing the Nazi act of genocide is all the more astonishing. If we generously concede that even in this area scholars are to be granted the freedom to engage in experimental inquiry, a freedom that should not be limited by sensitivities, the final criterion for judging scholarly quality is conscientious argumentation. The fact that Nolte has once again, in arrogant disdain for empirical and historical procedures, exceeded such limits, causes many of this renowned scholar's arguments to appear to be querulous hair-splitting. This is sufficient to shock all those— myself included—who owe many an impulse to Nolte's thought.

The most offensive thing Nolte had written to date appeared in a 1985 anthology in London (W. Koch, *Aspects of the Third Reich*). Long before any notice of Auschwitz reached the attention of the world, Nolte wrote here, Hitler had good reasons to be convinced that his opponents wanted to annihilate him. Nolte then places Jewish Agency leader Chaim Weizmann's statement that in the event of war the Jews of all the world would fight against Hitler on the side of England in this context. He concludes that this could support the thesis that Hitler was justified in treating Jews as prisoners of war and interning them.

In this way, Ernst Nolte associates himself with the thesis that Jewry "declared war on Germany"—a notion that for years has been a hallmark of right-wing pamphlet literature in the Federal Republic. The fact that the World Congress of Zionists in whose name and mission Weizmann spoke in 1939 was not an entity in the definition of international law and the fact that the message Weizmann communicated in the name of the congress never had the legal meaning and status of a "declaration of war"—these facts may be overlooked by a right-wing publicist with a dubious educational background, but not by the college professor Ernst Nolte.

This is the point where, objectively, his argument turns into apologetics. Aside from his motivations and despite the fact that Nolte is, as everyone knows, not intentionally an apologist, this kind of trivialization cannot be allowed, nor can attempts such as Joachim Fest's to restylize these thoughts. These kinds of argument should not be made respectable— particularly since they stem from such a respected scholar.

For this reason Klaus Hildebrand should also admit that he at least secretly disapproves of or simply overlooked Nolte's thesis when, in this spring's issue of the *Historische Zeitschrift* (no. 242, p. 466), he praised Nolte's article. He did this, as he wrote, because the essay "undertakes in an extraordinarily provocative and fruitful way" to "reinterpret for the history of National Socialism central elements of the destructive capacity of Nazi ideology and of the regime." It is not to be assumed that he lacks the ability to read, or that this is a case of political opportunism. The fact that Hildebrand failed to invite Nolte (who lives in Berlin) to the Berlin symposium of the Schleyer Foundation could lead us to conclude that this is a slight, diplomatic attempt to distance himself.

Through all the dispute, most people failed to see the keystone of Habermas's polemic—his commitment to the integration of the Federal Republic into the West. The main passages deserve to be repeated: "The unconditional opening of the Federal Republic to the political culture of the West," this "greatest intellectual achievement of the postwar period," as Habermas puts it, "has been achieved precisely by overcoming the ideology of Central Europe," which is again being warmed up by Michael Stürmer and others with their "geopolitical drumbeat about the old geographically central position of the Germans in Europe. The only patriotism that will not estrange us from the West" is the kind of "constitutional patriotism" that unfortunately was only able to take shape after Auschwitz. For this reason, he adds, it is hard to accept the recent use of phrases such as "obsession with guilt" to drive the shame about these facts out of the Germans in an attempt to call them back to the "conventional forms of their national identity." This process, Habermas says, destroys "the only reliable foundation for our ties to the West."

A LACK OF COMMON SENSE

Here, too, one is faced with the question of whether Stürmer deserves this vehement attack. Of course Habermas knows that the Erlangen historian is neither a German nationalist nor a political romantic. Quotations from his recently published collection of essays (*Dissonanzen des Fortschritts*, Munich, 1986) can be put together to demonstrate him to be a skeptical rationalist and a decisive supporter of the Atlantic Alliance. And in this way and by using his own quotations, Stürmer defends himself against Habermas (*Frankfurter Allgemeine Zeitung*, August 16, 1986)—without, however, being able to deemphasize the quite different sounding quotations that Habermas took aim at. It is not hard to add other quotations to those (all from the essay collection *Dissonanzen des Fortschritts*):

History promises signposts toward identity and other anchors in the cataracts of progress.

A community that separates itself from its history will not survive long in the consciousness of its citizens.

It is hard to mistake the fact that the loss of history and the destruction of the constitutional consensus are among the dangers that threaten the present.

If we do not succeed in agreeing on an elementary culture curriculum so that we might continue to work for continuity and consensus in this country and for moderation and a measure of patriotism, then it could be that the Federal Republic of Germany has the best part of its history behind it.

If this is not an example of neoconservative "ideology planning," as Jürgen Habermas interpreted it, then this kind of pessimistic Cassandra rhetoric represents, at the minimum, a grave lack of mental precision and common sense, embedded as it is in pretentious language that suggests more profundity and significance than it contains. The reader of the more recent Stürmer articles is confronted with a kind of thinking and speech that attempts—in vain—to reconcile two things: on the one side a rational affirmation of democratic pluralism and the universalist principles of the Western constitutional state, and on the other side an invocation of premodern, community-producing elites, conventions, cultures, and historical traditions—all in a priestly tone.

In this context, history is far more than the simple story of man's experience and suffering. It also has the function of an ersatz religion and thus must, for reasons of state, be propagated to achieve a democratic consensus—especially if we are to stand up to the challenge of the tyrannical systems of totalitarianism and their historical myths.

HISTORY OVERTAXED

Stürmer accords history a leading role in social and national integration. And this overtaxes the discipline. In the Bundestag budget debate of September 10, Alfred Dregger said, "Historylessness and ruthlessness toward our own nation worry us. Without the kind of elementary patriotism that is a matter of course in other countries our people will not be able to survive. Those who misuse so-called *Vergangenheitsbewältigung* [coming to grips with the past], as necessary as that was, in order to rob our people of a future, will meet with our resistance." When Stürmer speaks of the "erect posture" that is supposed to be made available to the Germans again, he means the same. Habermas formulated it succinctly: These are attempts to drive the shame out of the Germans.

Here the roads part. Those who want to talk the Germans out of self-critically dealing with their older and their more recent history rob them of one of the best elements of the political culture that has been developing since the late 1950s. The most revealing aspect is the fundamental misunderstanding inherent in these thoughts—as if the moral sensitivity to one's own history, achieved through necessity, puts us at a cultural and political disadvantage compared to other nations, as if it were a matter of copying their more often robust or naive and usually politically harmful historical sense of self.

Such perversions of the desire for history threaten to deprive us of the only thing we gained from the experience of the Hitler period. And it was precisely these experiences that placed the West Germans in a position to gradually make themselves at home in the legal and social structures of the Federal Republic—without needing emotional nationalism. For the first time in German history, Germans have affirmed the political reality— not in a grand nationalistic consciousness of their special status, but rather in a simple sense of well-being in their civilization.

The complaint that this is not sufficient and must be complemented by national history has, it seems to me, little to do with reality as it is perceived by the younger generation in the Federal Republic. Rather, it reflects the political ambitions of the elites in our country who desire to be bearers of culture. Having arrogated political leadership roles to themselves, they now believe they cannot manage without some kind of national-pedagogical watchdog office.

Source: *Die Zeit*, October 3, 1986

RUDOLF AUGSTEIN

The New Auschwitz Lie

Five years ago one could hardly have believed possible what is taking place today among historians, philosophers, and sociologists. Only a few historians, philosophers, and sociologists are involved, and the majority of the public has no part in it. But the discussion is taking place. Those following it can only rub their eyes in astonishment.

It is about Auschwitz. Previously, one only had to argue (with those incapable of learning about the question) over whether it really was six million Jews and whether one had not merely furnished the gas chambers; and these questions had been cleared up by the Cologne historian Andreas Hillgruber. By his account, which he details for us with careful precision, it was "over five" million people. Since there were also other death camps, Hillgruber sets the number of Jewish victims at Auschwitz "according to reliable estimates" at approximately one million.

Up to this point, no problem. In the wake of the fortieth anniversary in 1985 of the German capitulation, however, new concerns have developed. We must deal in all seriousness with the following questions: Was it reasonable, no, was it necessary for Hitler to feel threatened by the Jews of the whole world after the president of the Jewish World Congress, Chaim Weizmann, in September 1939 "declared war" on the side of England? Was the Jewish World Congress a state to which all Jews of the world, whether they knew about it or not, belonged?

Could, no, should Hitler feel justified in treating Jews as prisoners of war and interning them? Ernst Nolte, the scholar of fascism, answers yes. Hillgruber asks, "Was the systematic annihilation of the Jews in the whole territory controlled by Germany 'really pre-determined'?"

Is it the expression of a new "master race mentality" when it is argued that a highly civilized people should not have been capable of such an atrocity? Joachim Fest asserts so. Does one have to place anew the accents of historical writing on the Hitler epoch because until now the victors have dictated the content of historical writing? Nolte asks whether one is allowed to ask how the history of Israel indeed would be "accented" if the Arabs had been successful in throwing the Israelis into the sea. Had Stalin already demonstrated for Hitler how one was to deal with one's enemies? Are Hitler's racial war and Stalin's class war comparable things? Fest thinks so. Is it productive to note that Hamburg was bombed in 1943 without the Allies knowing anything about Auschwitz (Nolte)? Was that, in Nolte's view, also an "Asiatic deed"? Was Auschwitz?

Had the Allies planned, also without knowledge of the "so-called" (Nolte) annihilation of the Jews, to amputate Germany and cut it in several pieces (Hillgruber)? Yes, after two wars of expansion, that was their intent—after 1942. Are the Jews in Israel blackmailing us by always referring to Auschwitz? (Nolte expresses it more elegantly.) Well yes, they probably are. But it was left to the German government spokesman in 1984 to warn, on Israeli territory, that one should "not instrumentalize Auschwitz." Must we really discuss today whether Hitler alone desired the annihilation of the Jews against the will of all his paladins (Hillgruber); or whether the circumstances of the war drove him to the annihilation of the Jews so that he himself was to some extent the last one to find out about it (David Irving's overstated thesis)?

Without Hitler, according to Hillgruber's frank assertion, the Jews would have been discriminated against, but not a man, woman, or child would have been gassed.

In this regard one must consider State Secretary Hans Globke, the second most important man in Adenauer's Reich. In 1938 he had been responsible for the legal and formal deprivation of Jews' rights. Although he could not read the Hebrew lexica, he invented mandatory names, which he assumed would be recognizable as Jewish names: Faleg, Feibisch, Feisel, or Feitel for the men; for the women Schewa, Schlämche, Slowe, or Sprinzi.

One is not supposed to quote the dust jackets, but here we must. Thus the text from *Zweierlei Untergang*: "Hillgruber's sensational work directs itself against the current opinion in Germany, according to which the destruction of the German Reich was an answer to the atrocities of the Nazi regime." He who thinks and talks in this way is a constitutional Nazi, one of the kind that would exist even without Hitler. For such a historian the extinction of the European Jews is "tied up with the Germans' fall." Every teacher who teaches his pupils something like that ought to be fired.

Why? Hillgruber knows and demonstrates that no one was threatening Hitler's Reich in 1939. Chamberlain, Great Britain's prime minister, went to extremes—in my view properly—in order to spare his country a new war and the loss of the whole empire. He had in mind a kind of four-way balance between Great Britain, the German Reich, the Italy of Mussolini, and France. He could not know how crazy Hitler was or what he was willing to try. Even continental statesmen without umbrellas made this mistake.

The discussion among the so-called experts cuts a ghostly figure, even on the side of those who contradict the revisionists, who are the new accent setters. A nonhistorian, Erich Kuby, has convincingly described the matter in *Als Polen deutsch war* [When Poland Was German], in my opinion the best of his recent books:

One can only understand Hitler if one starts with the notion that he lived for what one can call his life's work. Until his relatively early death he understood his life's work, although it dwelt solely in the negative region, not as a piece of the real world but of a world of historically graspable substance. He was like a magician who pulls a rabbit out of a seemingly empty top hat but who distinguishes himself fundamentally from this magician in that his hat really was empty, the rabbit was originally not present. He then nevertheless pulled it out, to the amazement of the world, even more to his own amazement. And he never got over it.

But we know how he then really did get over this: he murdered in completely real and certain ways. Kuby's book treats Poles and it touches on more than Jews, though on Polish territory there were certainly more Polish Jews killed than Polish non-Jews. Here one has to read the bills of the *Reichsbahn* [National Railroad] for the transport—a 50-percent discount was given to the government for transport of the Jews and annihilation trains were declared military trains so that they obtained the highest priority. One is acquainted generally, if at all, with the gas chambers in the six death camps. However, mass murder was committed before that, with gas wagons or with engine exhaust in sealed rooms. All the philosophers, historians, and sociologists should take serious notice of the following invoice:

> The firm Motoren-Heyne, Leipzig C1, Anton-Brücknerstraße 8, delivers for the latter purpose at a price of 140 Reichsmark (net) a used, reliable, diesel motor on November 2, to the SS Special Command X, SS Hauptsturmführer Crim. com. Rothman, Kulmhof/Post Eichstädte (Wartheland)

One knows in the meantime that approximately a million German-speaking people were directly involved with the annihilation of the Jews, and this does not count their relations. One cannot believe of the leaders of the *Wehrmacht* that they knew nothing of the state of events described by Kuby: "The German policy of occupation in Poland was, from the first day of the war on, a policy of extermination and annihilation. They divided the assignments up cleanly." Just when the officers wanted to carry out a putsch—and precious few wanted to—news of a victory would intervene. In September 1941, the same General Halder who supposedly wanted to carry out a putsch in 1938 during the "Sudeten crisis" (pretty phrase, but false), wrote, almost crazily, in his journal that Russia had been defeated in two weeks. He was at that time the chief of the General Staff of the army.

These Teutonic warriors did not really hate their führer. They were afraid of failures. As long as there were none, the compact between the *Wehrmacht* and Hitler was ironclad. As the enforcers who failed to recognize the insanity of their master, they actually believed they were building a great Reich in the East in which their grandchildren and great-grandchildren would live as members of the master race. For validation of the fantasy, they could look to Hindenburg and Ludendorff, who indeed had subjugated the Ukraine and had almost subjugated the Crimea.

Unfortunately, one must mention here Ribbentrop's state secretary between 1938 and 1943, Baron Ernst von Weizsäcker, who thought the war against Russia was harmful but who, in his private sketches and letters, made no bones about heartily despising the whole Soviet pack. He must have known of the annihilation of the Jews. Nevertheless, he served his führer as ambassador to the Vatican up to the last day.

Hitler's "ideological atrocity" necessarily followed from the basic elements of his politics, writes Nolte. This does not mean, however, "that these foundational elements in themselves are at the same time historically groundless and morally reprehensible." Was it time for this discussion? It does seem so: The German crimes under Hitler had to be incorporated in the crimes of all millennia so that we could once more be a normal state among others. This is what one calls "normalizing history." We cannot be an upstanding member of NATO if after forty years the criticisms and accusations do not stop.

This time we have to be on the right side. For this it is essential that Hitler's crimes are over and done with but those of Stalin and his successor Gorbachev continue. The past cannot be dealt with ("the labor of grief"); it has to be actively put to use in the future, that is, once and for all it must be mindlessly used against Bolshevism.

Not for nothing did Nolte let us know that the annihilation of the kulacks, the peasant middle class, had taken place from 1927 to 1930, *before* Hitler seized power, and that the destruction of the old Bolsheviks and countless incidental victims of Stalin's insanity had happened between 1934 and 1938, *before* the beginning of the Hitler war. But Stalin's insanity was, in contrast to Hitler's, a realist's insanity.

After all this drivel comes one thing worth discussing: whether Stalin pumped up Hitler and whether Hitler pumped up Stalin. This can be discussed, but the discussion does not address the issue. It is indeed possible that Stalin was pleased by how Hitler treated his bosom buddy Ernst Röhm and the entire SA leadership in 1934. It is, however, not possible that Hitler began the war against Poland because he felt threatened by Stalin's regime.

Hitler was one of the most reliable of politicians. He announced and then carried out his program. In 1927, the thirty-eight-year-old Hitler wrote in *Mein Kampf*: "In Russian Bolshevism we can see the attempt of the Jews, undertaken in the twentieth century, to complete world domination." He argues respectfully with Bismarck, but then writes: "The giant empire in the East is ripe for collapse. And the end of the Jewish domination in Russia will also be the end of Russia as a state. We are chosen by destiny to be witnesses of a catastrophe that will be the violent confirmation of the correctness of the national theory of race."

The poor führer: he was not able to witness Stalin's pogroms against his Jewish physicians. One does not have to agree in everything with Konrad Adenauer. But in light of the crass tendency to deny the coresponsibility of the Prussian-German *Wehrmacht* ("The oath! The oath!"), one gains an understanding for the point of view of the nonpatriot Adenauer that Hitler's Reich was the continuation of the Prussian-German regime.

Certainly, even with regard to Hitler, this last great individual criminal of the world, there remain difficult problems and problems that one cannot solve at all. Should the planet one day be devoid of people, it certainly will not be his fault. What should we make of the Pol Pot regime, which exterminated almost a third of the population of Cambodia? Recognized by the UN, this must be a useful regime for Nolte's and Hillgruber's view: it proves that the Hitlers go but communism remains.

Maybe the fortieth anniversary of the capitulation came forty years too early. The speech by the president of the Federal Republic on that occasion was praised throughout the world. He wanted to draw a line under a long period of "European history." He said: "Israel was supposed to stay in the desert for forty years before the new chapter of history could begin with the entry into the promised land. Forty years were necessary for a complete change of the generation of fathers who were responsible then."

Responsible for what? The comparison was bold in two respects. In the first place, the Israelites were condemned to forty years of punishment in the desert by their tribal god Yahweh because they had refused to conquer land that belonged to them. They refused "to swallow up" (this expression is used in the Bible of both German denominations) the Amalekites, the Canaanites, the Hittites, the Jebusites, and the Amorites. They were, quite simply, afraid of this war of conquest. It is quite clear at this point that their power-hungry Yahweh became powerfully angry.

Forty years ago the trials began in Nuremburg, in which the present president of the Federal Republic defended his own father, Ernst von Weizsäcker, one of the "generation of fathers who were responsible then," not only with the love of a child, but also, as he publicly said to Günter Gaus, "out of deep conviction." He did not believe, so said the son, that his father had "placed himself at the disposal of the regime." If not that, then what? One should have delayed the absolution forty years.

Source: *Spiegel*, October 6, 1986

CHRISTIAN MEIER

Keynote Address on the Occasion of the Opening of the Thirty-Sixth Conference of German Historians in Trier, October 8, 1986

[. . .] We cannot yet determine the meaning of the dispute about our relationship to the past, especially to the years 1933 to 1945. Is it only a debate between philosophers, publicists, and historians that was caused by various publications, particularly the essay by Jürgen Habermas that was published in *Die Zeit* of July 11 and that caused controversy far beyond the borders of this country? Or is this perhaps a debate that was long due among us historians? Or is it a dispute between the Right and the Left in a situation in which a consciousness of history seems to be stirring in the Federal Republic? For that would have political consequences. In the final analysis, we are once again seeing an example of the politics of history.

Or is this dispute effecting a much deeper, more elemental process, perhaps the end of the postwar period or the dissolution of the anathema under which we have lived in the past decades? Or is it the explosive breakup of an ice floe on which we are living? Last year, when we were considering whether and how to commemorate May 8, the forty years since 1945 were not long enough for many people. But maybe these years represent the time period after which an enduring change in our historical memory had to force itself upon us. This could be for biological reasons, since those who could have been involved in the Nazi regime have reached an age where they could be grandparents. It could be because certain preconditions that were present in the postwar period are today used up— perhaps because we failed to reproduce them properly and introduced them into public imagination and into the roots of general knowledge.

Perhaps the new turn to history can be seen in a greater context, for this kind of renewed interest in history is also taking place—in a different way—in the GDR and in Turkey. There are important movements beginning in Europe. Hopes for progress have met with broad disappointment so that nationalist elements seem to have become more important. Political forms of fundamentalism are flourishing. In the past two years, the successor states of the old *Großdeutsches Reich* are showing signs of deep change.

I know no example of a people that have experienced the remembrance of its history in such as painful way as we have in recent decades. An exception might be a people that accepted and understood their history as divine punishment, but we can hardly do that. And, after all, we are doing quite well despite all that we lost in the war. Thus we are burdened by our history while at the same time faring well. As far as I know, that is something quite new in history.

The German crimes between 1933 and 1945 were, as I see it, singular in that they qualitatively surpassed by far those of other peoples (for example, the Stalinist Soviet Union). But even if that were not true, the way in which these deeds were and are known in this country and abroad is singular, which is hard to take, especially for younger people who were not participants of the time. One can know about these atrocities, but one will always compartmentalize and repress this knowledge. And the farther we get from these events, the more a gap opens up: With every passing day the number of people who want to have nothing to do with the crimes of that time grows—as does the number of people who do not understand why they are supposed to be members of a marked people. At the same time the horror, the gruesomeness, of these crimes themselves is growing since they are increasingly viewed in the light of potential, of what might have been—instead of in the light of the experiences of the hard reality of the first half of the twentieth century. Even if we are primarily occupied with thousands of other things and appear to have a grasp on the present, the past is, as I see it, a point of great vulnerability, a festering would that occupies us and absorbs much of our attention—even though it does not prevent us from "walking upright."

In this respect it is no wonder that many people want to leave the crimes of that time be, or at least to relativize them. And it is no less surprising that this endeavor cannot succeed. When the past that has troubled us so long is brought into the open, many things are set in motion—although not necessarily just old Nazis, even though they too reappear together with the anti-Semitism that is particular to them. If this is the case, then the current debate is by no means "as superfluous as a tumor."

But no matter how we interpret the present situation and its deeper background, we have been drawn into a dispute. We have to face up to it, for we have always claimed, when our discipline was threatened; that history contains such important conditions for the present that it is urgently important to study it.

A dispute such as this, however, does not only have to be scholarly; it must also be political. This is unavoidable because of the object itself and because of its importance for the political situation in the country. This is evident from the fact that the media seek to claim our attention and naturally simplify, exaggerate, and provoke.

In principle, that is not a problem. Quite the contrary: Disputes re-invigorate, clarify, and bring progress, even if they are not, as Heraclitus says, the father of all things. Thus disputes are welcome. Direct debate is usually better than manifestations of intellectual alliances-in-arms, which now appear to be becoming fashionable—and competing with the History Conference. But it is also troubling that *Die Zeit* is printing articles one after the other that all seem to be written at the same time. In this situation, there is no dialogue taking place. Instead, people are taking positions on much earlier positions of other people, who in turn are taking a position on other positions.

I do not want to dramatize the situation. We should not take ourselves too seriously. Probably what we lack most at the moment is a good dose of humor. It seems appropriate to use this place and time to decisively and openly make a few points that I address—although not exclusively—to the public.

As substantive and fair as most of the publications on this topic have been, there are some that cause concern. It is not acceptable for historians to refuse to set foot in rooms where other historians are present—just to be able to resist the temptation to shake hands with them. It is also not acceptable that participation in this conference has been refused to some with the justification that allowing them to participate would only pretend a liberality that in reality does not exist. It is not liberal to claim liberality only for oneself and one's intellectual allies—even if others do just that. He who glibly declares liberality to be dead is himself contributing to its death. But we should do everything to maintain it. For it is up to us to determine what content this concept has. And it is a valuable asset. Incidentally, those who pull no punches should not be exaggeratedly sensitive. With all due respect to our discipline, not every harsh word, not every misunderstanding, can be seen as an insult.

One of the foundations of liberality in disputes is that the opponent should be taken seriously. That begins by precisely studying what he wrote or said. Unfortunately, in disputes people tend toward errors and mis-understandings. And they like to stick to quotable material that, if need be, can be taken out of context. That is part of polemicizing, especially when it becomes political. And it is anything but just. We do not have to just accept as an accomplished fact things that we perceive as being unjust, but it is not permissible to declare that your opponent is a bogeyman just because he is doing the same thing that you yourself are doing. Each side of the dispute reads with partisan eyes. If one accuses the other of endowing meaning through scholarship and the second calls the first a self-anointed prophet and a self-appointed judge, then neither side is likely to give in.

Despite all the passion of the dispute, should we take mistakes, mis-understandings, and exaggerations as examples of malevolence? We should oppose our opponent's opinions, but not the person himself. Otherwise the foundation on which we can carry out a fruitful debate will be eroded. It appears that old wounds incurred around 1970 heal damned slowly.

As far as historical publications have been drawn into the critical debate, it must be said—particularly regarding the downright scandalous treatment by the press—that historians are not guided by simple wishful thinking. That can happen, but historians do not usually simply give in to the political interests that guide their search for knowledge. It should be a part of the historian's everyday experience that he challenges his own questions. This is often a matter of recognizing and understanding unpleasant things. Some of the great historians, from Thucidides through Polybios and Tacitus to Tocqueville and Jacob Burkhard, knew why the things they did not like happened, and their greatness came from their willingness to recognize and even respect the facts to which their nation, their class, or their world was subject. They showed their respect by continuing to question until they understood. Recent German history presents just this kind of challenge.

By the same token, not every finding and not every attempt to understand is guided by a political intention. Historians cannot be sorted politically by whether they think Hitler gave the order to exterminate the Jews. It is not evident why those who believe that would do so because of a conservative political conviction. Why are the "power elites" of the Third Reich who accepted and executed such an order exculpated by its existence? Why does this kind of thesis serve today's conservatives? One can take things too politically.

There are, however, certain political interests that guide knowledge, and there are intentions, despite all attempts at objectivity. Historians do not write *sine ira et studio*, or if they do, what they write is all too boring. They take part in the words and concepts of their time, consciously and unconsciously. Their questions are as much posed—and maybe even promoted—as they are prevented or repressed by the world in which they live. That is common knowledge for everyone who has worked in the field long enough and has observed himself doing it. Thus it may be justified to perceive political tendencies in historical studies, but this can also lead us astray. In this point we must exercise extreme caution.

Our colleague Andreas Hillgruber has seen how quickly intolerable accusations can come about without this caution: in *Vorwärts*, in *Der Spiegel*, and in *Die Tageszeitung*! Unfortunately, Jürgen Habermas has aided and abetted this. It is really nonsensical to try to insinuate that Hillgruber was attempting to trivialize the Nazis, in spite of the methodological dubiousness that he—or his publisher—should have stricken from his book.

It is also not permissible to simply ignore all the concerns—and tendencies—that Habermas noted in recent historiography by simply pointing out that his quotations are too short or that he used an incorrect distribution of direct quotation and paraphrase. It seems to me that, insofar as he made mistakes in the reproduction of other people's opinions, it was due to a misunderstanding that perhaps arose from a kind of reading that is guided by suspicion—which incidentally was in part inspired by the quoted authors themselves. However that may be, he deserves a different response from historians, a response to his main point. "One must make his opponents stronger if one wants to be smarter than they are"—this is the way Gadamer formulated Heidegger's principle in interpreting Plato. One should also respect the other's caliber, for only then can the dispute be fruitful—and only then will it be most likely to do justice to this truly difficult and oppressive topic.

It must also be said that we cannot allow questions to be prohibited. The comparison between the crimes of Germany under Hitler and those of the Soviet Union under Stalin is not at all illegitimate. Quite the contrary, it casts light on the topic and is useful. There is also good reason to recall the totalitarian characteristics of both regimes, especially in their presuppositions and in how they executed their crimes. This can also be said about other mass murders. The result will be many parallels, but also important differences. People who accuse others of using the harmless formulation "the end of Jewry" should for their own part not speak of the "expulsion of the kulaks."

It is just that we should take care not to pose the question about the singularity of German crimes in a way that encourages new attempts to relativize or to divert attention away from these deeds. This—and this alone—earns justified criticism. To be more precise; no one will forbid Ernst Nolte to ask questions; no taboos will be established. But the way Nolte poses these questions must be rejected simply because one should not reduce the impact of so elementary a truth; because German historical scholarship cannot be allowed to fall back into producing mindless nationalist apologies; and because it is important for a country to not deceive itself in such sensitive—ethically sensitive—areas of its history. The truth, no matter how bitter it is, stands. If Mommsen's formula about the "duty of political pedagogy" has a meaning, then it has rarely had it as much as here.

This dispute about singularity should not divert us in an undignified way from important themes. Even if our crimes were not singular, how would that be advantageous for us and our position in the world? What good does it do us when the annihilation of the Jews is set next to the persecution or liquidation of the kulaks or the exterminations carried out by Pol Pot? Earlier, we engaged in a pointless dispute about whether we killed one, two, or three million Jews. We must prevent our dispute from taking that kind of unfortunate turn. These are arguments that remind us of the helpless laughter that children caught in the act produce, when they do not want to show their surprise.

We should act as though it would make no difference whether we or the Turks or the Soviet Russians committed millionfold murders. If we suggest that our long history created different civilizing and ethical preconditions than in Russia, Turkey, or Indochina, are we supporters of a master race theory? No privileges arise from such historical developments. But responsibilities do. If millionfold murders are a reality of the twentieth century, then the fact that these things did not happen in western, southern, or northern Europe or the United States is no less a reality. Should we be measuring by those nations' yardsticks?

Then there remains the question of why there is always talk about the German crimes and not about the comparable crimes of other peoples. In my judgment, that is not the result of an obsession with guilt—even though there is such a thing, just as there are people who try to rouse and exploit it. But the reason is more likely to be found in the fact that our democracy was founded on the experience and the rejection of Nazism. And that with freedom we were given responsibility—including responsibility toward our own history. It is for this reason that these events lie so deeply embedded in our remembrance of history, and this is not subject to our caprice! It represents a monstrous truth that repeatedly forces itself upon us—a truth that is still able to have its effect despite our attempts at repressing it.

One cannot escape this fact. Every attempt to escape will just increase our helplessness. We all have to suffer through this, and we should respect ourselves because of it. Nobody should think that he has cornered the market on inner reparation. Even if one draws ethical postulates from the past that others do not like, one is by no means just styling oneself as a high priest. One should strive to show that these postulates are false, unjust, or impractical and that one has better ones. The memory of Nazi Germany does not permit us to draw some conclusions and not others.

No matter how one comprehends the present situation, no matter how one views the place and significance of our dispute, its theme, as Habermas has suggested, is the question about which consequences we can today derive from this history and how we are to deal with them. It is not only we historians—though in an essential sense it is we in particular—who are competent to do this.

On the one hand, it is a matter of whether there are particular symptoms of a new neglect in dealing with National Socialism—the symptoms that can be observed in many places—in the language, the method, the identifications, and the argumentations of historians.

On the other hand, there is also the question of whether patriotic loyalty to the constitution can be the only form of national identity remaining for us. Michael Stürmer thinks otherwise, and reasons can be found to support him. Then the next question would be whether, as Habermas suggests, a national identity that is linked to all of German history would only be a conventional form of identity—or whether history would not and could not offer a new form of identity. This identity may be linked to older forms, perhaps in many ways similar to the mode in which other peoples connect with their predemocratic past—in a thoroughly democratic identity that enables them to critically process the many inherent tensions. German history should not be viewed *sub specie* of National Socialism. Perhaps a national identity is necessary if we want to completely subject ourselves to German history as our own history in order to establish a productive relationship to it. Perhaps it is only in this way that we can learn to live with our history and also learn to have a historical consciousness.

It is also unavoidable that historians consider these questions. We can derive a regulative principle from them to guide "the duty of political pedagogy," to cite Theodor Mommsen again. As the history of the past eighteen years has shown, this principle can be used by the various sides of the political spectrum to instrumentalize history. But the principle itself, aside from any kind of instrumentalization, contains a good part of truth. Historical research is not entirely harmless.

Behind this stands the problem of how we can resolve the hypnotic paralysis that large segments of our population feel in the face of the Nazi past. This paralysis stems from the need to somehow reconcile, on the one hand, condemning all that was German in the Nazi period, with, on the other, repressing knowledge about parts of the period and engaging in spiteful fascination with the period. I personally believe that a solution will only be possible if we remain clear in describing and condemning all the crimes that Germany committed while attempting to understand what can be understood about the actions of our parents and grandparents. This includes understanding the principles according to which they acted and the traditions in which they were rooted. Certainly not everything was wrong. It is just that we must discover categories of reason and imagination and perhaps also of the heart in order to bring together into a comprehensible relationship the grand scale of the gruesome crimes and the small scale of the ordinary lives led by so many people who were devoted to duty and decency. In this way, so it seems to me, we are most likely to succeed in finding a way to live with this piece of history in the long term without constantly being haunted by it—although my personal answer is not decisive here.

It just seems important to me that the questions Habermas posed—and they are significant enough—should be seriously discussed. Only then will the debate have the usefulness that it could have. I do not know what meaning there is in speaking of attempts to sanitize the past. I feel myself being reminded of the figure of speech that so happily confuses the grave digger with the murderer. I find grave diggers and cleanups useful once dangerous events have passed. But there is also no doubt that there are impatient attempts to normalize our historical consciousness; and that will not be so easy to do.

I am not trying to bring the discussion to the point where it loses itself in complexity, but I would like to make the debate more difficult. I am chiefly interested in two things: that our relationship to that difficult period of our history be clear, truthful, and responsible; and that we respect the borders within which the dispute can be carried out fruitfully and without damage.

In contrast to many other disciplines, history survived the shake-up of the years after 1968 and benefited from this experience. The discipline's standards have remained intact. It has discussed its problems in a fair and hard dispute. Its unity and its standards of quality have really not suffered. This was presumably in part because our subject was challenged from the outside so that we had to defend it together. Occasionally I ask myself whether it is not regrettable that no West German historians became Marxists at that time. For then others could have studied under them and learned what that means and would not constantly have to call non-Marxists Marxists.

Ladies and gentlemen, it is said that humor is when one laughs in spite of it all, and it can also be said that ideology is when one can believe in spite of it all. I would like to suggest the following formulation: Pluralism is when unity prevails in spite of it all—in the fundamental and mutual sense, that is. And I would not like to have that undermined.

Source: Keynote address on the occasion of the thirty-sixth Conference of German Historians in Trier, October 8, 1986, pp. 7–16 of the recorded and later supplemented transcript. An abbreviated version appeared in the daily *Rheinischer Merkur/Christ und Welt* of October 10, 1986.

THOMAS NIPPERDEY

Under the Domination of Suspicion: Scholarly Statements Should Not Be Judged by Their Political Function

[It would be nice, dear Eberhard Jäckel, if this "great debate" could be focused on a scholarly problem—to what degree Gulag and Auschwitz are comparable, i.e., simultaneously similar and/or different, or even causally related. Although this is controversial, it can be decided. And with Jürgen Kocka one can also soberly ask whether what one learned from this or from comparison with Pol Pot was worth the effort. Or whether Nolte's interpretation of Weizmann was not a wild misconstruction. But Habermas's attack cannot be played down in this way. One cannot ignore his attack on Hillgruber by saying that it overstated its case—even ignoring its bogus quotations; nor can one agree with Hans Mommsen, Habermas's comrade-in-arms in the political mispositioning of historians.]*

From quite diverse historians, Jürgen Habermas constructs a group of "revisionists" and facilely designates them as part of an ideological-political program that Michael Stürmer is supposed to have formulated. Habermas inquires about the motives, the social and moral consequences, and the political functions of historical statements. And since he does not want to be just an observer of politics, these statements are given moral valuations. Morally unassailable colleagues are associated with Nazi apologists. The goal of these men, it is argued, is not to compare and differentiate but to exonerate the past and to turn to a kind of historical thinking that is ideologically in league with NATO and the *Wende*, or conservative shift.

He equates his own political tendency with truth, and, almost incidentally, the "annihilation" of the kulaks becomes their "expulsion." It is the old tune: The interpretation of National Socialism is used as a weapon in the political fray. But this time it is more: It is the dominance of "suspicion" (Hegel), of self-confident virtue, and of a monopoly over the truth—the differentiation of good from evil. For this reason, it is correct to speak of insinuation, of prohibiting questions. The mere publication of Nolte's

---

Author's Note: The original manuscript contained the bracketed passage.

article in the *Frankfurter Allgemeine Zeitung* was for Habermas almost a sin in itself. The notions that Tacitus did not write *sine ira et studio* and that the criticism of ideology is legitimate do not carry as much weight for Habermas as this one ideological error. The moral imperative of scholarly investigation demands that the arguments of participants in a discussion be examined independently of origin, motives, and consequences. The level of the argument must be separated from that of the context. Everyone knows enough examples of scholarly and political positions not being identical. The "moralizing" interpretation of contexts cuts off the process of scholarly discussion, which can only be sustained by new discoveries and new perspectives and sometimes even lives on the inventive force of ideological interests. The Habermas kind of interpretation also cuts off freedom and the duty to permanently engage in revisionism. [I do not believe that that is an overreaction. Of course, we are humans, and our political and moral convictions carry over into our discipline. But here there is a method to the madness. Habermas, the "crafty sleuth on the trail of conservatives" (Henrich) has also branded a whole group of his fellow philosophers as intellectual constitutional police (as if we did not all want to protect the constitution) and Henrich as being a conservative philosopher prior to the establishment of a conservative shift. His philosophy of historical scholarship is "like [that of] a missionary in search of consensus" (Udo Marquard)—in search of forced unity. And what can be universalized is to be determined, in domination-free discourse, by the administrators of progressive morality. There are still "readings," but only of one text, i.e., the one from the project of modernity. But it is also a part of the discipline and of the morality of scholarly work to limit such excesses. The domination of suspicion is undermining the thin ground of pluralism.]*

I am thus opposed to judging scholarly statements and the knowledge they bring with them by their asserted political function. Now, one can proceed from individual statements to general perspectives. Then, to take an example, we arrive at the contrast between "apologetic" and "critical" historical scholarship. That there is such a thing as apologetic history is trivial; what is in question is the discipline itself. The so-called "historicists," who desire to understand the past on its own terms, are viewed by their opponents as apologetic or affirmative. Habermas, too, points out such traditions, and since the beginning of the "great debate" lesser intellects have been blowing this same horn. On the other side there is the branch of the discipline that calls itself critical—not because it, like every scholarly discipline, employs critical methods but because it subjects the past to its critical view. The past is demasked, politicized, moralized, and

---

Author's Note: The original manuscript contained the bracketed passage.

even hypermoralized using the omnipotent principle of emancipation. This is the only way the road can be cleared for the monopoly on the future claimed by the utopias.

Previously, also in this newspaper, I argued against this critical history, written by prosecuting attorneys and judges, which does more to block than to open up access to the past. In the end, the moralized past destroys real history. We must "historicize" National Socialism.

But that remains to be done. Beyond apologetics and criticism, beyond conservative and progressive partisanship, there is objective history, which we, despite the limitations of our—transnational—scholarly endeavor, are closing in on. Everyone knows it: There simply is, beyond our bickering about values, history writing that is more or less valuable, outmoded or merely provisionally valid. Scholars dedicated to critical-emancipatory or apologetic endeavors and those committed to a search for identity can contribute to this.

It is the first commandment of a pluralistic scholarly morality to recognize the coexistence and open competition of such larger trends in scholarship. In the present case, that means that one must oppose the monopolistic claim of critical history writing and its damning judgments. Today the purpose of enlightenment is to defend objectivity and pluralism and, taking recourse to that movement's skeptical heritage, to resist militancy, to resist the cocksureness of compact morality and the all-encompassing desire to force consensus on others. The type of scholarship envisioned would insist on the finiteness of man and, to speak with the enlightener Max Weber, endure the struggle of the gods and the value-neutrality of knowledge.

History has meaning for life. History has to do with our identity—that is nothing new. My identity is always a piece of the common identity. Why we are how we are and why others are different—we can only understand this historically. For identity is also always heritage. And since it is difficult to recognize the way we are and the way we are different, this recognition is also an achievement of history. Granted, history also has other functions, and here, too, a part of the morality of pluralism is to recognize this multiplicity. Emancipation is a universalizing project aimed at unity. Identity, on the other hand, including national identity with its program of pluralization and multiplicity, acts as a counterweight to the difficulties stemming from the leveling tendencies of modernism. History assures us of our identity and stabilizes this identity—politics also lives on this process.

National identity exists prior to and parallel to scholarly activity. Scholarship clears up questions of memory and disempowers traditions. The more plural—and the more scientific—the discipline has become, the richer in tension is its relationship to identity. It is not a Machiavellian idea of Stürmer's that there is a political right to memory—it is a simple fact. Today there is a postscholarly identity. A political question in the realm of scholars' responsibility is how they will treat our shaken national identity, which can have a critical and stabilizing function.

Government-ordered history writing cannot exist in this country. That notion is just as absurd as the claim that only history writing aimed against the ruling government, in this country or in the United States, is true history. But here rests a twofold misunderstanding of the pluralism argument.

Despite the interpretation of many historians, history by no means consists of a plurality of perspectives. There is a foundation of secured knowledge. There are stronger and weaker perspectives, more objective and less objective portrayals. There are more than just questions and discussion forums at which all questions are again and again on the agenda. There are tested results, and one should not discredit them. There are exonerated and exonerating truisms. The knowledge that something is a certain way and the question of whether it is that way make for a balance. And even where it is a question of competing perspectives, there is still always the basic democratic consensus between conservatives and progressives. We battle about the past, but the past itself is beyond such battles—as is the discipline.

This simple truth is hard to practice. But it is necessary. Habermas's useful sentence about reflexive memory in the autonomous association with an ambivalent past can be generally agreed upon—but his countermodel, the nationalist bouying up of conventional identity, simply does not exist. That is phantasy born of animosity. All of German history is indirectly related to Hitler, and indirectly related to the Federal Republic. But it is directly related to something else—namely to itself. Both sides belong to our identity, to our heritage. History disturbs our identity. But it also stabilizes it. And this forgotten truth should be paid its due.

I think that the debate initiated by Habermas is unfortunate. The areas under discussion are highly sensitive, the moral and political commitment of the participants is strong, the difficult distinctions and differentiations will get lost in the fray. The German tendency toward making things into fundamental principles is beginning to triumph. Gulfs are being opened, the guild of historians and the public are being polarized. The ground on which both the discipline and our liberal culture exist is thin enough. For this reason we need the virtues of history writing: soberness and distance. We need pluralism beyond moralizing suspicion and political partisanship. We need pragmatism to oppose moral absolutism.

Source: *Die Zeit*, October 17, 1986

IMANUEL GEISS

Letter to the Editor of
Der Spiegel, October 20, 1986

I read Rudolf Augstein's essay in the *Spiegel* with dismay and sorrow because for me *Der Spiegel* has for decades been an organ of critical enlightenment. But in 1986 Augstein damned dissenters and excluded them from the consensus of our liberal republic. Jürgen Habermas was hardly oversensitive in his use of quotations by various authors in his attempt to paint a portrait of an antidemocratic, reactionary revision of the German understanding of history by several West German historians (in *Die Zeit*). Augstein exacerbated this with a headline ("The New Auschwitz Lie") and the accusation that Andreas Hillgruber is an enemy of the constitution (a "constitutional Nazi").

Of course there has been recent criticism of the majority consensus among West German historians, much of which is strongly based on economic and social history—this in contrast to the earlier imperial-patriotic and German-national orthodoxy. The revision of the new progressive revisionism is, however, normal by all standards of the discipline and in no way justifies people's blowing this process up and making it a kind of subversive political activity.

Political consequences cannot be ruled out, just as the progressive revisionism of the past twenty-five years had political consequences. Not the smallest gain from heated debates such as the "Fischer Controversy" was that younger historians were able to laboriously achieve our present liberal pluralism. They struggled against the unyielding guild of historians and, with Augstein's help, gained a space in which scholarly innovations could be achieved and discussions could be conducted without automatically triggering insinuations and sanctions of an ideological-political kind. It would be unfortunate if now the insinuations and sanctions were to occur again, only this time under a different banner.

With this kind of attack against alleged or real neoconservative historians, Augstein and Habermas threaten our scholarly and political pluralism—from the other side. They denounce those who disagree as being close to Nazism (Augstein) and suggest to their unwitting readers, who are unlikely to take the time to compare Hillgruber's original quotations with those of his censors, that the neoconservatives are attempting to either entirely deny or to trivialize the fact or the historical relevance of Nazi crimes.

That, however, is not the case with any of the historians under attack, not even with Ernst Nolte, as much as one must reject his thesis that Hitler's "Asiatic deed" was committed as a reaction to Stalin's crimes. A scholarly dispute with its theses must be permitted.

On the other side, the new trend could initiate a swing of the pendulum with unpleasant apologetic and political consequences, which Habermas is justified in warning against. But this kind of warning must, if it is to be constructive, always distinguish between intention and effect, without simplifications and hysteria. Those people in particular who desire to defend the liberal values in this country must also practice them in dealing with dissenters.

Otherwise we will be threatened—which Augstein and Habermas surely do not want—by the "intellectual civil war" that Michael Stürmer invoked in a more allegorical sense.

In any case, it is unjust to today impute to Hillgruber negative intentions concerning things that might occur in the future—and might only occur then as an escalating reaction to "lie" and "Nazi" defamations à la Augstein, which tend to evoke the envisioned condition. In the long run, a democratic state can neither be sustained solely with the moral dogma of singularity and incomparability nor with an abstract "constitutional patriotism" (Habermas). The accretion of history since 1945 forces us to dare to take the step of reinterpreting incomprehensible events such as Auschwitz—looking backward from Auschwitz as well as looking forward all the way to the present—but also considering events that were then contemporary.

Every historical reconsideration necessarily ends up in comparisons and relativizations. Augstein should provide an opportunity—particularly to Hillgruber—to respond in kind.

Source: *Der Spiegel*, October 20, 1986

Publisher's Note: This letter appeared under the title "Auschwitz, an Asiatic Deed."

ERNST NOLTE

Standing Things on Their Heads: Against Negative Nationalism in Interpreting History

People who review books must pick out certain main points and neglect others. Those reviewers should be willing and able to formulate the question, to outline the entire thought process, and to correctly reproduce the results before they provide their verdict. In some cases a glance at the author might be appropriate. I feel that the polemical articles of Jürgen Habermas and Eberhard Jäckel have not done justice to these postulates.

I did not select the topic "The Past That Will Not Pass" myself. But when I was asked to express myself on this theme at the Römerberg Talks, it fascinated me as no theme had before. The seemingly slight alteration of a well-known book title suggests a quite unusual situation: a past that blocks itself off from its very nature of being past and not present, a past that will not be content in allowing people to remember it, to research it, to glorify it, or to lament it, but which "hangs like an executioner's sword above the present."

Of course this is not literally possible. It is a kind of metaphor by which the relationship of the Federal Republic's present to the National-Socialist past can be characterized. I then described this past by placing two opposing series of arguments next to each other—one still perceives National-Socialist characteristics everywhere, while the other describes just this pattern of thought as deriving from specific interests or as a diversion from really pressing questions.

The predominance of the first series of arguments has led to a paradoxical situation in which all attempts to make the National-Socialist past knowable like any other past and to strive for "objectivity" is stigmatized with the word "apologist." I assumed it to be understood that what the Germans experienced in 1945, in the midst of an incomparable catastrophe and through the revelation of the National-Socialist annihilation of the Jews, the Slavs, and the mentally ill, was a genuine experience that deeply engraved itself onto all those who were alive at the time. But I also indicated that the paradox of the situation would one day lead to consequences that we cannot presently anticipate.

What struck me strongest was the assumption that it would be possible to better understand the motives for Hitler's most reprehensible deeds by using the formulation "the past that will not pass." Hitler used this sentence in a military briefing of February 1, 1943, to justify his fear that the generals taken prisoner in Stalingrad would soon be speaking on Radio Moscow: "Just imagine the rat cage." When I assert that Hitler did not mean Lubjanka, as the editor commented, I certainly did not mean to say that Hitler had had Butyrka or the NKWD Chelyabinsk prison in mind. He meant a process in Lubyanka, a process of unspeakable horror that became known worldwide by George Orwell's use of it in the last scene of his novel *1984*.

This procedure, however, was not a fiction invented by a writer to describe a terrible future. A series of newspapers and other publications had reported in the early postwar years that it was a reality in the prisons of the Cheka. The decisive question, then, is not whether these reports were true. The main point is that Hitler was apparently convinced of their validity—he was speaking to his closest associates and not to a mass meeting. And I do not have to underscore what everyone already knows, namely that not one of the captured generals or soldiers was subjected to this kind of torture. The present had long since become a different reality, but a past that for almost all those who experienced it was just another past was still very present for Adolf Hitler. For him it really was "like an executioner's sword suspended above the present."

But even if the "rat cage" was just a horror story, the perceptions about the Russian Revolution shared by so many contemporaries around 1920 were so well founded that there was a sense that what was transpiring there was something completely new, something never before experienced. For supporters it was the greatest of all hopes. For opponents it was an unprecedented vision of horror. The one side spoke of the "execution" of the czar and saw in this event a shining act of powerful symbolism. The other side noted with horror that the Bolsheviks had killed the czarina, the children, the family's personal doctor, and the ladies-in-waiting, and that precisely for this reason no comparison with the murder of Charles I or Louis XVI was possible. This feeling of something totally new and alien was once again evoked when the news went around the world that in Moscow and Leningrad alone several hundred "bourgeois" and officers had been shot to death "in retaliation" for a social-revolutionary attempt to assassinate Lenin.

A few days after that, *Vorwärts* stated in an editorial: "To hold a class responsible to this extreme degree for the acts of individual persons is a legal novum and could one day serve another social class as a justification for holding the working class legally responsible for the deeds of a fanatic." The author gave no reason why the working class can never be held legally responsible, but he saw correctly what qualitatively new thing was entering world history: the collectivist appraisal of guilt and the acts of annihilation that resulted from it. He could have added that this principle, applied with energy and drawing force from the resistance of the people affected, would demand more and more victims, first thousands, then hundreds of thousands, and finally millions.

But it would be no less correct to state that a series of events such as this cannot be derived from Marxist presuppositions, according to which the "annihilation of the bourgeoisie" only means displacing a tiny minority and not physical "liquidation." Thus it was an obvious next step for both the Left and the Right to commonly use the word "Asiatic" for the murder of a class.

The horror of the "rat cage" was thus only one striking way of expressing a general and genuine experience of the immediate postwar period. I believe that the deepest root of Hitler's most extreme side can be found here. It was obvious for me that the assessment of guilt that Hitler undertook, that is, the indictment of the Jews, presumes this experience. It also means the transition to a new dimension: the transition from a social to a biological assessment of guilt.

The Gulag Archipelago is primary to Auschwitz precisely because the Gulag was in the mind of the originator of Auschwitz; Auschwitz was not in the minds of the originators of the Gulag. Still, there is a qualitative difference between the two. This difference should not be overlooked— nor should the obvious link between the two. Thus Auschwitz is not a direct response to the Gulag Archipelago, but rather a response mediated through an interpretation. I have not specifically stated that this interpretation was false because I consider that to be superfluous. Only a fool could today take up the blather about "Jewish Bolshevism." The profound animosity between the two phenomena has been more than evident for a long time. And no great current of thought or social movement was ever purely national, as emphatically as many Ukrainians speak of Russian Bolshevism and many French speak of German Marxism.

One may cast doubt upon this distinction between experience and interpretation and point out that the young Hitler was already an anti-Semite. But for the young Hitler one experience, namely the horror of the gigantic mass parades of the Social Democrats, and the "key" by which he processed this experience, that is, the insight that the Jews were the cause of it, must be clearly differentiated. This relationship, as I see it, was repeated after the war on a much more intense experiential basis.

Both halves of the article thus merge in the simplest of ways: The situation in the Federal Republic that I characterized as the nonpassing of the past could lead to a qualitatively new situation that has never been achieved before—a situation in which the National-Socialist past becomes a negative myth about "absolute evil." At the same time, there are important insights to be gained by a view of the past that, in the person of Hitler, refuses to pass.

The transition from potential to actual is quite evident in the person of Hitler. Its most extreme consequence is called Auschwitz. But the experience it was founded on is a genuine one that was shared by many people. It is related to the first manifestations of the Gulag Archipelago. If we keep both in mind, we cannot overlook the difference. But then the context also reappears, and with it the possibility of achieving liberation from the "tyranny of collectivist thinking," which still shapes such a large part of the debate about National Socialism.

Presumably this thought process, which doubtless merely intimates many things and presumes others, would not have generated so many misunderstandings and so much excitement if the English translation of an essay of mine had not appeared in print. This essay had been published in an abbreviated form some six years before in the *Frankfurter Allgemeine Zeitung*. The title, "Between Historical Legend and Revisionism," makes it clear that it deals with the same themes, although from a different perspective. In this essay I mentioned a statement by Chaim Weizmann and reiterated David Irving's thesis and suggested that the assurance of the head of the Jewish Agency to the English government that the Jews of the entire world would fight on the side of England was seen as a kind of declaration of war. The most rudimentary sense of fairness should lead those people who found that offensive to at least point out that I said this in a detached way. It was meant to be understood within the framework of self-critical remarks that, taken together, amount to saying that undeniable facts in the "established" literature should not be ignored, if only because in rightist literature they are interpreted in an exaggerated or distorted way.

Thus it is a weakness, not a strength of the established literature that the shameless commentary of the Fascist press about the assassination of Walter Rathenau is often cited, but not Kurt Tucholsky's far worse comments of 1927 in which, expressing himself vividly, he wished German women and children of the educated classes death by gas. I have only encountered these comments in right-wing radical literature, the selective reading of which, it must be conceded, belongs to the occupational duties of a historian. Granted, such citations should not be quoted in isolation as is the practice in these sources. Such practices reveal the differences between the two kinds of literature.

Moreover, my reference to the Weizmann statement, even though it was merely a remark of secondary importance, must be seen within the framework of my main question—the question about the transition to a new dimension that cannot be derived from existing factors. If one concedes that the explanation amounted to the equivalent of a declaration of war—not in the precise sense of international law but as an anticipation of a future reality—then one can understand internment as a countermeasure. But then the Hague convention on war would also have to go into effect. It is worth discussing whether Weizmann allowed himself to be guided by a similar intention. The consequences as they apply to the attitude of the German population and the *Judenräte* are evident. It is doubtless correct that the actual deportations were from the beginning clearly different from any imaginable "internments." And it would be quite simply outrageous to see any kind of justification for the Final Solution in consideration from 1939 and 1940—which were also discussed in Jewish publications.

So what is there to say about the polemical criticism from Jürgen Habermas and Eberhard Jäckel? I do not want to respond to the ugly neologism "imputer" or to the term "NATO philosophy," which are all too familiar to me from the East Berlin *Zeitung für Geschichtswissenshaft*. If Jäckel provides his own definition for the singularity of the Final Solution, then I think that this concept simply elaborates what can be more briefly expressed with the term "racial murder." If, however, he wants to say that the German state, through the mouth of its führer, unambiguously and publicly announced the decision that even Jewish women, children, and infants were to be killed, then he has illustrated with one short phrase all that does not have to be demonstrated in the current intellectual climate but can be "imputed."

Hitler was certainly the most powerful man that has ever lived in Germany. But he was not powerful enough to ever publicly equate Bolshevism and Christianity, as he often did in his dinner table conversations. He was also not powerful enough to publicly demand or to justify, as Himmler often did in his circle of friends and associates, the murder of women and children. That, of course, is not proof of Hitler's "humanity" but rather of the remnants of the liberal system. The "extermination of the bourgeoisie" and the "liquidation of the kulaks" were, in contrast, proclaimed quite publicly. And I am amazed at the coldheartedness with which Eberhard Jäckel says that not every single bourgeois was killed. Habermas's "expulsion of the kulaks" speaks for itself.

The criticism by both gentlemen of my article can only be understood— and then only psychologically—if they assumed I had declared Auschwitz to be a direct and justifiable response to the Gulag Archipelago—and thus as a response on the same level. That, however, would have presupposed the reintroduction of the concept "Jewish Bolshevism," and I did not think it necessary to expressly reject such a presupposition. Still, even for the uninformed reader, the reference to the Chinese Cheka should have sufficed. With Jürgen Habermas and Eberhard Jäckel we should be able to assume knowledge of *Faschismus in seiner Epoche*. And we would have been justified in expecting an expression of astonishment that I have recently been engaged in refuting myself.

I am indeed of the opinion that not only the Germans have a "trouble-some past" and that the troublesome past is not only that of Germany. A simple inversion of nationalism is not adequate to understand the reality of the twentieth century. New ways of rethinking the past and present are required on all sides—especially on the side of the Germans and the Russians—if coexistence is to represent more than an economic reality. Similarly, in the intellectual realm, we must get away from the particularism that seeks above all to prove the guilt of opposing peoples, classes, and races and is thus unable to grasp the fundamental guilt that lies in attributing guilt to whole groups. There are hopeful beginnings in this direction with Soviet dissidents and here and there even in the official literature. Jürgen Habermas would have an important part in a discussion like this, but he would first have to learn to listen even when he feels his prejudices are being challenged.

Source: *Die Zeit*, October 31, 1986

Author's Note: This text was originally entitled "A Mere Inversion: Against Negative Nationalism in History. A Response to Jürgen Habermas and Eberhard Jäckel."

ANDREAS HILLGRUBER

No Questions Are Forbidden to Research

QUESTION: *Professor Hillgruber, in recent months a debate has begun, first among historians, then among other specialists, and then in the general public, about the way we view our history. Are you as a historian happy that such a debate is under way, or do you feel something like horror about what has been unleashed and now is being debated and about the way it is being debated?*

I am not happy about what has been unleashed by Jürgen Habermas's article in the weekly *Die Zeit* on July 11 of this year, and for the following reasons: Habermas, with the insinuation that they advocate apologetic tendencies, carries out massive attacks against four West German historians of completely different stripes, with completely different scholarly fields of inquiry and themes. His attacks are not founded in scholarship but rather are politically motivated. This finds expression, not insignificantly, in his connecting the whole thing with the plans of the Kohl government to erect a German Historical Museum in Berlin and a House of the History of the Federal Republic of Germany in Bonn. The scholarly works of the historians he attacks have nothing to do with that. In each case Habermas brings up a jumble of historical, political, and journalistic problems, which is made even worse by his working with falsified quotations and by his manipulation of quotations, something he must do in order to be able to present his insinuation effectively. I have demonstrated these manipulations in detail, quotation by quotation, in an essay that will appear in the December 1986 issue of the journal *Geschichte in Wissenschaft und Unterricht* [History in Scholarship and the Classroom]. It is a singular scholarly scandal.

QUESTION: *Then you would not see yourself in a line with Professors Nolte, Hildebrand, and Stürmer or with Joachim Fest?*

For two decades I have been closely associated with Herr Hildebrand, who has found his way into this attacked group because of a review in a scholarly journal. I have a friendly collegial relationship with Herr Nolte, and likewise Herr Stürmer, without having to have anything to do with their completely different scholarly motivations, areas of interest, theses,

155

or hypotheses. Habermas "mixes" everything together in order to prove his insinuation of a "revisionism" of recent history, supposedly advocated by us together. Now "revisionism" of scholarly finding is the most natural thing in every discipline, indeed, it is its norm. "Revisionism," although it was not originally so for Habermas, has become a polemically charged concept, a "bellicose" concept.

Habermas understandably has not stayed abreast of historical research in recent decades. With some excitement he now discovers contradictions to what he until now had held to be a firm "image" of the Third Reich. By his "call to arms," he gives the public the impression that something completely new is being published by the historians he has been attacking. In fact Nolte, for example, had already expressed the essential thoughts that he has now formulated more sharply in his large work *Faschismus in seiner Epoche* [Fascism in Its Epoch]. Likewise, what so excited Habermas in my volume published by Siedler is already contained in substance, though not in detail, in my largest studies.

QUESTION: *What motivations are there then to revise the state of facts or the writing of the history of the Nazi period?*

Revision of the results of scholarship is, as I said, in itself the most natural thing in the world. The discipline of history lives, like every discipline, on the revision through research of previous conceptualizations. The accusation of "revisionism" now being raised in public aims at the fact that the "revision" now being played up by Habermas and his followers is allegedly of a more fundamental kind and would bring about a total change in the image of the Third Reich. Here I would like to say that in principle since the mid-1960s substantial revisions of various kinds have taken place and have rendered absurd the clichéd "image" that Habermas as a nonhistorian obviously possesses. The originally predominant Hitler-centrism was, for example, superseded by structural analyses. The role of everyday life in the history of the Third Reich has been researched: consider the large "Bavarian project" of the Institute for Contemporary History in Munich. Resistance research became much more highly differentiated; the original concentration on July 20, 1944, and on the conservative forces in the resistance was superseded by research into the whole broad spectrum of the resistance. In short, revisions have been a permanent feature, granted without the public's having sufficiently taken notice of them.

QUESTION: *Then, in* Twofold Fall *you wrote nothing that you had not similarly already said or written earlier in another place?*

I wrote an essay about the downfall in the East in 1944–1945 that sketches the fighting German armies from the perspective of the populace, that is, not from Hitler's standpoint or from the victorious Red Army's standpoint. I connected this sketch with the presentation of the war aims of the opposing powers in the East and West to the extent that they touched the fate of eastern Germany—on the basis of new research. The attempt to present what happened from the view of those affected fits in with the efforts of colleagues (for example H. Mommsen and M. Broszat) in other fields of the history of the Third Reich similarly to experience things from the perspective of the main body of the populace.

QUESTION: *Recently the editor of the* Spiegel, *Rudolf Augstein, in a "Spiegel Essay" took precisely these publications as the occasion to call you a "constitutional Nazi" and suggested that a teacher who says things like this should be released from school service. Is that pure polemic, or are you willing to have a serious discussion with Herr Augstein?*

I take this attack from Herr Augstein to be absolutely undiscussable, in every respect. It is a low point never reached before in the steady decline of a publicist whose arguments were once of import. I have taken legal advice. Augstein doubtless had his criticism legally "checked on" in advance so that, as things stand, one could not successfully proceed against him in the courts. This essay in *Der Spiegel* and something similarly nonsensical in the foreword of the so-called anniversary edition of the "Frederick" book by Augstein defy any description in this matter; they are absurd and grotesque. I know that I am in agreement with my colleagues, whatever they may think of my scholarly assertions.

QUESTION: *The question is whether the Third Reich is a historical epoch like any other. At least as far as concerns the moral evaluation and estimation of the regime, is it really important whether one comes to one conclusion or the other about whether the Third Reich is unique or not?*

Morally, the Third Reich is characterized by innumerable crimes, above all the mass murder of the Jews. I do not know of a single serious historian who would challenge that. In the current discussion about the "singularity," the following should be established: Everything in history is "singular"— every figure, every epoch, every occurrence. But every occurrence, every event, every personality, has to be compared; that is an essential element of the discipline of history. Singularity and comparison do not exclude one another. If one takes as the yardstick of comparison the Western world, the mass murder of the Jews is singular. Nothing similar existed, for example, in Fascist Italy.

If one incorporates Bolshevist Russia in the comparison, then one can say that the mass murder of the kulaks in the early 1930s, the mass murder of the leadership cadre of the Red Army in 1937–1938, and the mass murder of the Polish officers who in September 1939 fell into Soviet hands are not qualitatively different in evaluation from the mass murder in the Third Reich. Here, as there, a simple characteristic of the people (on the basis of the insanity of race or the ideology of class) led to their murder.

In the case of the Third Reich, because of the availability of sources the mass crimes can be quite thoroughly proven and presented. Bolshevist Russia distinguishes itself even now by its practice of secrecy, so numerical comparisons, which anyway are not decisive for the moral evaluation, remain difficult.

QUESTION: *Can you understand when such comparisons—like those Nolte has just drawn—between the Nazi regime and Stalinism are viewed very critically abroad? Does one have to tolerate the accusation that scholarly work of this kind amounts to exculpation?*

My answer is very decisive here: Either we do historical scholarship, and scholarship is the concern of an international community of researchers in which nationality is of no interest, or we renounce the claims of scholarship altogether. Renunciation would mean falling back into bad times. The West German discipline of history is, like every discipline of history that is worth its name, free in the questions it poses. The answers must obviously be accountable in a scholarly way.

QUESTION: *That means you would say there are no forbidden questions for scholarship?*

Absolutely correct.

QUESTION: *Now comes the accusation, from people like Habermas or others, that the results of scholarly work are being used to view our current German reality differently through a changed description of the Nazi past.*

I am actually not the right one to speak with here. With my book, which deals exclusively with the Third Reich and the downfall in the East in 1944–1945, I have been pulled into a discussion that primarily has to do with the government's plans for museums. They are not my topic.

QUESTION: *Are you participating in setting up this Historical Museum in Berlin and the Museum of the History of the Federal Republic of Germany in Bonn?*

I have nothing to do with the museum in Berlin. As far as the House of the History of the Federal Republic of Germany is concerned, I have just received an invitation from the Federal Republic's minister for construction, Herr Schneider, in which he invites me to participate in the steering committee that has yet to be appointed. The results of the work there are to be awaited.

QUESTION: *What function and what meaning could these museums have, in your view?*

Every nation has its historical museums. In East Berlin the GDR has put up its well-known Museum of German History, erected on the foundation of Marxism-Leninism, in which the visitor gets an overview of the epochs of German history. It is in my view high time that the Federal Republic undertake the attempt, not in view of the East Berlin museum but rather completely independently of it, to lay out for visitors the ever-changing ways of German history since the Middle Ages and to do this on the basis of the results of historical research. This will demonstrate the historical place of the Federal Republic of Germany. I see this as a legitimate task.

QUESTION: *You said that in the mid-1960s there was already a revision in the direction of a stronger social and economic view. It is impossible not to acknowledge that in the past five years a revision reappeared. One can assume that it strives for a stronger national historical view. This assumption is supported by a series of publications that have appeared in the Siedler Press and that include publications by Professors Stürmer and Schulze as well as by you. Is there such a thing as a new orientation to a stronger national view of history?*

The series you refer to has in fact the theme "Germans and Their Nation." It is centered around German national history. But the European context is observed in all the books you named; that even holds for the last volume by Thamer about the Third Reich, which has just appeared. Here the newest results of research are incorporated into the study. The history of the Third Reich is not viewed in isolation. Rather the European context is fully incorporated into the presentation of national history.

QUESTION: *Now the phrases "location in the European Center" and "national identity of the Germans" are cropping up in this whole debate again. What ground actually exists in scholarship or journalism for touching on this stable situation in Central Europe? We have actually done well in this middle situation in the last forty years, haven't we?*

Let us leave the political assertion aside as to whether everything really is so "golden." That would be far afield of this discussion. One has to distinguish two things: On the one hand is the old theme of "Central Europe" that is now being attacked from various sides, not only from the political Right but also from the Center and from forces standing to the left of center. This leading concept latched on to particular traditional connections in Central Europe that were severed by the end of the Second World War and seeks to bring them to life again. It is concerned with, among other things, shaping the relationship anew between the Federal Republic and the GDR, the relation to Poland, to Czechoslovakia, and to Hungary so that these "Central European" connections become viable. I see this as a thoroughly sensible undertaking. Think of the recent visit by the president of the Federal Republic to Hungary.

Something altogether different is connected to the theme "Central Europe," if one wants to latch on to the old concept of Central Europe that played a part in Germany before the First World War. It is the thought of consolidating under German leadership a broader Central Europe, cut out according to German interests. Such an effort is historically hopeless because of the way the Second World War ended. To want to develop such a projection now would mean to bring the powers in the East and the West together against the Germans. I cannot imagine that anyone is earnestly striving for that.

Reminiscences of good cooperation between the German and Slavic peoples in the middle of Europe before the First World War, and in part also still between the wars, are awakened whenever journalists or historians travel to Poland, Czechoslovakia, or Hungary. In that atmosphere it seems imperative to express how closely one feels connected to representatives of these nations. This is understandable, but it cannot all merge into a notion of "Central Europe" that could be misunderstood as taking up the old concept again, which is, as I said, no longer realizable. In a word, I think the effort to latch on to the connections torn apart in 1945, because of the outcome of the war and then in turn because of the cold war, is a sensible political task, especially for the West Germans.

QUESTION: *You said at a conference of historians in the Hanns-Martin-Schleyer Foundation in Berlin a few weeks ago in this regard that in this country one must pay attention to the way the GDR discipline of history goes about the business of German history. I will just name two key examples: the GDR's characterization of itself as maintaining the heritage, and the attempt to present itself as the better German state. Could that not lead one to start thinking again here in the Federal Republic about one's own national history? Is the fear of the GDR behind it all when West Germans concentrate on their own national history?*

It is without a doubt correct that changes in the way the GDR is looking at German history have influenced the political leadership as well as historians. I doubt whether the efforts on the part of the Federal Republic of Germany are to be understood primarily or even exclusively as competing with the developing "modern" image of German history of the GDR. It is a fact that the GDR gave up its originally provincial Marxist-Leninist view of German history in favor of greater self-certainty in dealing with epochs and historical figures that do not fit so cleanly into the traditional rhetoric of a socialist Germany. We can think of Frederick the Great or Bismarck. Certainly one day Stresemann will be discovered in GDR history as a politician between East and West. In this way the GDR raises the claim of being the German state toward which all of German history has coursed and from which one day, by exploding out of the "narrowness" of the GDR, historical development will lead to a unified Germany, a socialist unified Germany.

Before this backdrop it is, in my opinion, sensible to sketch the counterpart image—founded in scholarship—that presents German history (in the frame of European history) as a development culminating in the liberal-democratic order of the Federal Republic, in a unified Germany on the basis of the right of self-determination. This seems to me not only a necessary historical, but also political, perspective.

QUESTION: *Those historians of the Federal Republic who today exhibit a national-historical view are very close to the government, for example, Michael Stürmer. Socially and economically oriented researchers, however, are on the side of the social-liberal coalition. Do you have any sympathy for the critics' assertion that historians are justifying, with what they are undertaking, contemporary political motifs, for example, the "blessing of late birth?"*

An example: My colleague Jäckel, who in his scholarship very pronouncedly emphasizes Hitler's role in the Third Reich and in this matter agrees with me, is a Social Democrat. He is in a scholarly controversy with his Social-Democratic colleagues who emphasize the internal structures of the Third Reich and hold these structures responsible for the realization of the Final Solution in the form of the mass murder of the Jews in the territory controlled by Germany. Jäckel, however, sees Hitler's role as decisive in this. I only want to indicate by this that scholarly position and political preference are not identical.

In the public, nevertheless, a clichéd conception in the sense of oversimplified scholarly and political categorization is connected with individual historians. Political historians cannot work without the research of social and economic history and vice versa. Only when someone sees his research exclusively as a political function is an understanding with colleagues difficult.

QUESTION: *In your view how can one emerge from this very confrontational situation? Could you imagine an international symposium including scholars from East and West at which the various opinions that have been formulated in this debate were presented in order to bring the whole problematic to a head in an objective atmosphere?*

A symposium, a colloquium, by itself would not be enough by a long shot. The profusion of topics that have been addressed necessitates a whole series of colloquia or symposia, which, moreover, would only be sensible in a tolerant atmosphere. To discuss them all together at a single congress is, I believe, out of the question, in light of the incredible breadth and complexity of the topics that are now so excitedly being discussed in the public press.

Source: Rheinischer Merkur/Christ und Welt, October 31, 1986

Publisher's Note: The questions were put by Rainer Krawitz.

JÜRGEN HABERMAS

On the Public Use of History: The Official Self-Understanding of the Federal Republic Is Breaking Up

Anyone who has read Ernst Nolte's sober contribution in the last issue of *Die Zeit* and has not followed the emotional discussion in the *Frankfurter Allgemeine Zeitung* must have gained the impression that this is all an argument about historical details. In reality it is a matter of the newly arrived revisionism in the writing of recent history. This revisionism, impatiently urged by the politicians of the *Wende* government [the conservative-liberal coalition], can be employed politically. For this reason Hans Mommsen sees the controversy as a "regrouping of historical-political thought." With his essay in the September/October issue of *Merkur*, he has delivered the most comprehensive and substantial contribution to date. At the center is the question: *In which way* is the Nazi period going to be understood in the public consciousness? The increasing distance in time makes historicizing necessary, one way or another.

Today those who, at the end of the Second World War, were too young to personally be able to bear any guilt have grandchildren. Certainly there is no personal memory of guilt for the war and its crimes. The discipline of modern history has remained fixated on the period 1933–1945. It does not step out of the horizon of its own life story. It remains preoccupied with sensibilities and reactions that, to be sure, vary by age group and political orientation; but it always has the same starting point: the images of that loading ramp. This traumatic, will-not-pass aspect of a moral imperfection in our national history first stepped into our consciousness in the 1980s, on the fiftieth anniversary of January 30, 1933, on the fortieth anniversary of July 20, 1944, and May 8, 1945. And still barriers are breaking that until yesterday were holding firm.

THE REMEMBRANCE OF THE VICTIMS AND THE PERPETRATORS

Recently there has been a flood of memoirs by those who for decades could not speak about what they suffered. I am thinking of Cordelia Edvardson,

162

the daughter of Langässer, or of Lisa Fitko. We have been able to follow the almost physical labor of memory in which a relentless Claude Lanzmann loosened the tongue of the victims of Auschwitz and Maidanek. In every barber shop, the horror, grown stark and mute, is put into words for the first time. And one does not rightly know whether one should believe in the releasing power of the words. But words are again streaming out of mouths long held shut, words that for good reasons have not been used since 1945, at least not in public. The collective memory evokes different phenomena for the perpetrators than it does for the victims. Saul Friedländer has described how in recent decades a gap has been opening between the desire on the German side to normalize the past and the increasingly more intense occupation with the Holocaust on the Jewish side. A look into the press in recent weeks can only confirm this diagnosis.

In the Frankfurt trial against two physicians who participated directly in the "Aktion Gnadentod," the defense attorney supported his claim that a Göttingen psychiatrist was biased with the argument that the expert witness had a Jewish grandfather and might have been burdened with emotions. In the same week Alfred Dregger announced a similar concern in the Bundestag: "Lack of regard for history and lack of consideration of one's own nation concern us. Without the kind of elementary patriotism that is a matter of course in other countries, our people will not be able to survive. Those who misuse so-called *Vergangenheitsbewältigung* [coming to grips with the past], as necessary as that was, in order to rob our people of a future, will meet with our resistance." The lawyer introduces a racist argument into a trial, the majority leader demands the energetic relativizing of the burden of the Nazi past. Is the coincidence of the two statements really accidental? Or is an intellectual climate gradually spreading in this republic in which those things simply fit together? There is the spectacular demand of the well-known patron that the art of the Nazi period should no longer be "censored." And the chancellor, with his great sensitivity for history, draws parallels between Gorbachev and Goebbels.

Three forces were realized at Bitburg. The aura of the military cemetery was supposed to waken national sentiment and thereby a "historical consciousness"; the juxtaposition of hills of corpses in the concentration camp and the SS graves in the cemetery of honor, the sequence of Bergen-Belsen in the morning and Bitburg in the afternoon, implicitly disputed the singularity of the Nazi crimes; and shaking hands with the veteran generals in the presence of the U.S. president was, finally, a demonstration that we had really always stood on the right side in the fight against Bolshevism. In the meantime we have endured the torturous and festering, but clarifying, discussions: about the planned historical museums, about the staging of a Fassbinder play, about a national memorial that is as superfluous as a tumor. Nevertheless Ernst Nolte complains that Bitburg did not open the floodgates widely enough, that it failed to sufficiently remove inhibitions from the dynamic of settling old scores: "The fear of being accused of settling old scores, and of any comparisons at all, prevented the simple question of what it would have meant if in 1953 the chancellor of the Federal Republic had refused to visit the cemetery in Arlington, arguing that men were buried there who had participated in terror attacks on the German civilian population" (*Frankfurter Allgemeine Zeitung*, June 6, 1986). Anyone who thinks through the presuppositions of this curiously constructed example will be amazed at the ease with which an internationally famous German historian balances the account of Auschwitz with Dresden.

This mixture of the barely mentionable with the unspeakable is probably a reaction to the need that increases with increasing historical distance. At any rate, it is hard to mistake the need that the authors of a series in Bavarian television, "Die Deutschen im Zweiten Weltkrieg" [The Germans in the Second World War] assumed on the part of their older viewers: the desire to remove the subjective experience of wartime from the framework that gave everything a different meaning in retrospect. This longing for unframed memories from the perspective of the veterans can now be satisfied by reading Andreas Hillgruber's presentation of the events on the eastern front in 1944–1945. The "problem of identification," something that is unusual for a historian, poses itself to the author only because he wants to incorporate the perspective of the fighting troops and the affected civilian population. It may be correct that Hillgruber's total work provides a different perspective. But the little book (*Zweierlei Untergang*) put out by the Siedler Press is not intended for the readers who have specialized knowledge, so contrasting views of the "Destruction of the German Reich" and the "End of European Jewry" could already push toward the proper context.

The examples show that history, despite everything, does not stand still. The sequence of dying also carries over into damaged life. Our situation has, as Karl Jaspers wrote in his famous treatise the "Question of Guilt," changed fundamentally. Then it was a matter of making the distinction between the personal guilt of the perpetrators and the collective liability of those who—for completely understandable reasons—did nothing. This distinction no longer touches on the problem of those born later, for whom their parents' and grandparents' act of omission cannot become a burden. Is there still any problem at all of coliability?

JASPERS'S QUESTION TODAY

Then as now the simple fact is that those born later have grown up in a way of life in which *that* was possible. Our own life is connected with this context of life in which Auschwitz was possible, not through contingent circumstances, but internally. Our way of life is connected with our parents' and grandparents' way of life through a web of family, local, political, and intellectual transmissions—through a historical milieu that has made us what we are today. Not one of us can sneak out of this milieu because our identity, both as individuals and as Germans, is permanently interwoven with it, from bodily gesture through the language to the rich interplay of intellectual customs. I could never, for example, when I teach at universities abroad, deny the mentality in which the traces are buried of the very German movement of thought from Kant to Marx and Max Weber. We must therefore stand by our traditions if we do not want to deny ourselves. I also agree with Dregger that there are no reasons for such avoidance maneuvers. But what follows from this existential linking with traditions and ways of life that have been poisoned by unspeakable crimes? A completely civilized populace, proud of its humanistic culture and its constitutional state, made itself liable for these crimes. It is in the Jaspersian sense a collective mutual liability. Does something of this liability carry over to the next generation and the one after that? For two reasons, I think, we should answer yes.

There is first of all the obligation that we in Germany—even if no one else any longer assumes it—must, undisguisedly and not simply intellectually, keep awake the memory of the suffering of those murdered by German hands. These dead justifiably have a claim on a weak amnesiac power of solidarity, which those born afterward can only practice in the medium of the constantly renewed, often confused, always worrying memory. If we brush aside this Benjaminian legacy, our Jewish fellow citizens, the sons, the daughters, the grandchildren of the murdered could no longer breathe in our country. That also has political implications. In any case, I do not see, for example, how the relations of the Federal Republic with Israel could in the foreseeable future be "normalized." Many carry openly the "encumbered remembrance" in name only, while they actually denounce public manifestations of this kind of feeling as rituals of false subservience and as gestures of hypocritical humility. I am amazed that these ladies and gentlemen—if we are going to speak in a Christian way—cannot even distinguish between humility and repentance.

This dispute is not about encumbered remembrance but about the rather more narcissistic question of how we should position ourselves—for our own sakes—toward our own traditions. If we cannot face our own traditions without illusion, then the remembrance of the victims will become a farce. In the officially announced self-understanding of the Federal Republic there was until now a clear and simple answer. It did not sound any different from Weizsäcker than from Heinemann and Heuss. After Auschwitz we can create our national self-understanding solely by appropriating the better traditions of our critically examined history. We can only perpetuate a national context of life that once allowed an incomparable destruction of the substance of human community in the light of healthy traditions. These are the traditions that hold their ground through a perspective trained and made suspicious by moral catastrophe. Otherwise we cannot respect ourselves and cannot expect respect from others.

The official self-understanding of the Federal Republic has until now borne this premise. The consensus is today being abrogated by the Right. One fears one consequence in particular. A critical appropriation of our traditions does not promote naive trust in the moral righteousness of accustomed ways; it does not help in the identification with untested models. Martin Broszat correctly sees the point here where the problems can arise. The Nazi period will be all the less likely to block us from our past the more we view it as a filter through which our cultural tradition must pass, inasmuch as it is adopted deliberately and consciously.

Today, Dregger and those who think like him are against this continuity in the self-understanding of the Federal Republic. As far as I can tell, their discontent feeds on three sources.

THREE SOURCES OF DISCONTENT

First, situational interpretations of a neoconservative origin play a part. According to this interpretation, the moralizing view of the most recent past occludes the view of the thousand-year history before 1933. A repressed memory of this national history, which came about under "thought prohibition," cannot lead to a positive self-image. Without collective identity, the forces of social integration would weaken. The lamented "loss of history" is even supposed to contribute to weakening the legitimation of the political system and to endanger the domestic peace and the accountability of foreign policy. This is supposed to be the reason for the compensatory endowing of higher meaning, with which history is to serve those people who have been uprooted by modernization. The attempt to grasp self-identity through national history demands that the negative image of the Nazi period be relativized; for this purpose it is no longer sufficient to bracket out the period. It has to be leveled out in its onerous meaning.

Second, behind a trivializing revisionism there is a deeper motive, completely independent of a functionalist attempt à la Stürmer. About this, since I am no social psychologist, I can only offer speculations. Edith Jacobson once penetratingly formulated the psychological insight that the developing child must gradually learn to attach the experiences with the loving and nurturing mother to the experiences that come from dealing with the mother who rejects and says no. Obviously it is a long and painful process in which we learn to put together the originally competing images of the good and bad parents to complex images of the *same* person. The weak ego gains its strength only when it copes nonselectively with an ambivalent environment. Among adults the drive to dull the corresponding cognitive dissonances is still alive. The further apart the two extremes are from one another, the more understandable the drive is. As an example, consider the positive impressions, saturated by experiences, of one's own father or brother and the problematical awareness provided to us by abstract reports about the contexts of action and the involvements of these same persons. Thus it is by no means the morally insensitive who felt themselves pressured to remove from the collective destiny in which their next of kin were involved the blemish of extraordinary moral mortgages.

The third motive lies on yet a different plane. It is the battle to reclaim encumbered traditions. Those who were born later, with their knowledge of the course of history, must confront the ambivalences that present themselves. When the view to appropriating these traditions is directed toward these ambivalences, then even the exemplary cannot be free of the retroactive power of a corrupted history. After 1945 we read Carl Schmidt, Heidegger, and Hans Freyer, even Ernst Jünger, differently than before 1933. For many people this is not easy to bear, particularly for my generation, which—after the war—stood under the intellectual influence of towering figures of this kind. That may, by the way, explain the rehabilitation efforts—not only in the *Frankfurter Allgemeine Zeitung*—urgently directed toward the neoconservative heritage.

Forty years later, then, the dispute, which Jaspers was able to settle in his day with great effort, has broken out again. Can one assume the legal successorship of the German Reich? Can one continue the traditions of German culture without taking over the historical liability for the way of life in which Auschwitz was possible? Can one be liable for the context of the origins of such crimes, with which one's own existence is historically woven, in any other way than through common remembrance of that for which one cannot atone other than in a reflective, testing attitude toward one's own, identity-endowing traditions? Can it not be generally said that the less commonality a collective life-context has afforded, and the more it has maintained itself outwardly by usurpation and destruction of alien life, the greater will be the burden of repentance imposed on the mourning and self-critical examination of the following generations? And does not precisely this sentence prohibit downplaying the weight of the burden with which we are saddled by making leveling comparisons? This is the question of the singularity of the Nazi crimes. How must it seem in the mind of a historian who claims that I "invented" this question?

We conduct the dispute for the correct answer from our own perspective. One should not confuse this arena, in which there can be no impartial ones among us, with the discussion of the scholars who in their work must assume the perspective of an outside observer. The political culture of the Federal Republic is certainly influenced by the comparative work of historians and other scholars. But the results of scholarly work must first pass through the locks of the mediators and the media and then return to the perspective of the participant in the public river of the appropriation of tradition. Only here can comparisons become a kind of settling of accounts.

The ruffled feathers about the confounding of politics and scholarship pushes the theme onto the wrong track. Nipperdey and Hildebrand are barking up the wrong tree, or should not be barking at all. They live, it seems, in an ideologically closed milieu no longer reachable by reality. It is not a matter of Popper versus Adorno, nor of scholarly differences of opinion, nor about questions of freedom from value judgments. It is about the public use of history.

FROM COMPARISONS COME SQUARING OF ACCOUNTS

In the discipline, if I see it properly from a distance, three main positions have formed: They describe the Nazi period from the view of totalitarianism theory; or they are centered on the personality and weltanschauung of Hitler; or they focus on the structures of dominance and of the social system. Certainly one or the other position will be more or less well suited for the intentions, brought in from outside the discipline, of relativizing and leveling. But even the view that is fixated on the person of Hitler and his racist insanity can only come into effect as a revisionism that holds harmless and, in particular, exculpates the conservative elite if it is presented in a particular perspective and with a particular tone. The same holds true for the comparison of the Nazi crimes with the Bolshevist acts of annihilation, even for the abstruse thesis that the Gulag Archipelago is primary to Auschwitz. Only when an article is published by a daily paper can the singularity of the Nazi crimes that we appropriate from the perspective of the participants take on the meaning for us that makes it so explosive in the given context. In the public press, for political education, for the museums, and for instruction in history, the question of the apologetic manufacturing of images of history poses itself as a directly political question. Should we, with the help of the historical comparisons, attempt macabre squarings of accounts in order to sneak out of the liability for the encumbered history of the Germans? Joachim Fest complains (in the *Frankfurter Allgemeine Zeitung* of August 29) about the lack of sensitivity with which "people are busy at some professorial desks 'selecting' the victims." This most unsavory sentence from an unsavory article merely falls back on Fest himself. Why does he give credence to the kind of settling of accounts that until now had circulated only in right-wing circles?

That has, God knows, nothing to do with banning questions for scholarship. If the dispute, which has come into full swing through the retorts of Eberhard Jäckel, Jürgen Kocka (in the *Frankfurter Rundschau* of September 23), and Hans Mommsen (in the *Blätter für deutsche und internationale Politik*, October, 1986), had taken place in a scholarly journal, then I could not have taken offense: I would not even have come across it. As Nipperdey sneered, the mere publication of the Nolte article in the *Frankfurter Allgemeine Zeitung* certainly is not a sin, but it marks a juncture in the political culture and in the self-understanding of the Federal Republic. This article is perceived abroad as just such a signal.

This juncture is not defused by the fact that Fest makes the moral meaning of Auschwitz dependent upon preferences for a rather pessimistic or a rather optimistic interpretation of history. Pessimistic interpretations of history suggest other practical consequences, according to whether evil human nature is held accountable for the constants of evil-doing or whether these are seen as socially produced—Gehlen against Adorno. And the so-called optimistic interpretations of history are in no way always fixated on the "new man"; without their meliorism U.S. culture is, as everyone knows, not to be understood. If historical progress consists of reducing, eliminating, or preventing the suffering of a vulnerable creature, and if historical experience teaches that progress, once it is achieved, is followed by a new evil, then we must assume that the balance of the bearable can only be maintained when, for the sake of what progress is possible, we put forth our greatest efforts.

At first, my adversaries avoided a debate on content by attempting to make me out to be scholarly unreliable. I do not need to return here to the adventurous accusations made against me, since the discussion in the meantime has turned to the facts. In order to familiarize the reader of *Die Zeit* with a diversionary tactic that one expects more from politicians than from scholars and journalists, I will give just one example. Joachim Fest claims that I imputed to Nolte in the main matter a completely false thesis: that Nolte "did not really" deny the "singularity of the National-Socialist acts of annihilation." Actually he had written this: that those mass crimes were far more irrational than their Russian models. He summarizes the reasons like this: "All this constitutes its singularity," and then he continues, "but that changes nothing about the fact that the so-called annihilation of the Jews during the Third Reich was a reaction or a distorted copy, but not a first act or an original." His well-meaning colleague Klaus Hildebrand then, in the *Historische Zeitschrift*, praises just this article as pathbreaking because Nolte "attempts to explain . . . what is seemingly unique about the history of the 'Third Reich.'" I was more easily able to understand this interpretation, which sees all opposing assurances as saving stipulations, when Nolte in the meantime wrote the sentence in the *Frankfurter Allgemeine Zeitung* that first got the controversy rolling. Nolte reduced the singularity of the Nazi crimes to the "technical process of gassing." Even at that Fest is not willing to let it rest in the form of a question. With express reference to the gas chambers, he asks: "Can it really be said that the mass liquidations by a bullet to the back of the neck, as was common practice during the years of the Red Terror, are qualitatively different? Isn't, despite all differences, the comparable element stronger?"

I accept the criticism that "annihilation," not "expulsion," of the kulaks is the appropriate description of this barbaric event. Enlightenment is a mutual undertaking. But the public settling of accounts by Nolte and Fest does not serve the end of enlightenment. They affect the political morality of a community that—after being liberated by Allied troops and without doing anything itself—has been established in the spirit of the occidental conception of freedom, responsibility, and self-determination.

Source: *Die Zeit*, November 7, 1986

HEINRICH AUGUST WINKLER

Eternally in the Shadow of Hitler? The Dispute about the Germans' Understanding of History

For some time now there has been no doubt: The end of the century is casting a long shadow. In the middle of the 1980s we have already entered the fin de siecle. A ghost has been haunting the Round Table of the Bonn cabinet, the editorial offices of the *Frankfurter Allgemeine Zeitung*, and the desks of several German historians: "The Past That Will Not Pass." One would like to be rid of it, but it refuses to yield, persistently asking: Why was it you, you Germans, who committed the greatest crime of the twentieth century, the mass murder of the Jews?

Four decades after the end of the Second World War it occurs to several leading representatives of politics and intellectual life that it is time to finally step out of the shadow of Hitler. Does the Federal Republic have a future at all, they ask, if our remembrance is focused on Auschwitz? Doesn't the younger generation have a right to step over the threshold to the next millennium unencumbered by the historical burden of the Third Reich? Won't defeatism and decadence spread farther and farther if we continue to allow ourselves to be determined by thoughts of long-past German guilt?

The appearance of the U.S. president and the chancellor of the Federal Republic at the military cemetery in Bitburg on the occasion of the fortieth anniversary of the end of the war was planned as a signal: The Second World War was to be restyled as a normal European war. Just as the United States of Ronald Reagan did not allow My Lai to disturb its good conscience, the Germany of Helmut Kohl should from now on, despite Auschwitz, once again be able to feel an unbroken sense of national pride. Around the same time, provincial newspapers printed an ad from a Mint Society in their weekend supplements. It was advertising for a collection of commemorative coins on which the outstanding deeds of the German *Wehrmacht* between 1939 and 1945 were celebrated. The last coin pictured carried the half-covered but clearly legible text: "Defeated with Honor."

The ghost of Bitburg leads a tenacious life. The *Frankfurter Allgemeine Zeitung* and others have assured us of that. The "newspaper for Germany" had much more sympathy for the events of Bitburg and thus also much more space for them than for the speech the president of the Federal Republic read in the Bundestag on May 8, 1985. Many articles that have since appeared in the *Frankfurter Allgemeine* read like indirect responses to Richard von Weizsäcker. Thus in an editorial of February 28, 1986, Friedrich Karl Fromme called attention to the debate about anti-Semitism held the previous day in the Bundestag. Fromme considered this debate to be superfluous and unprofitable. His reason: "Anti-Semitism has existed throughout the centuries, and it continues to exist today in the socialist countries, especially in the Soviet Union. Other nations are permitted to ask whether sympathies have been forced upon them. The 'annihilation of the Jews,' the phrase belongs in quotation marks, was carried out discreetly by the Nazi state. There was no weekly announcement by the *Deutschlandsender* [German Radio] back then that so and so many Jews were killed that week."

AN APPEAL TO SENSITIVITY

Despite the fact that the Germans were not in a position to know what had been secretly ordered by the "pathological anti-Semite Hitler" (who in any case was elected by a minority), they are even today (much to Fromme's dismay) not permitted to live their lives without the influence of those deeds. They must "live under this influence in the sense that the otherwise natural process of dividing up people into groups of those whom one likes and those whom one does not like is forbidden toward Jews."

The remonstration to the Germans not to allow their feelings free reign was followed by a warning to Jews not to evoke new anti-Semitism by exaggerated demands. "Young and no-longer-young Germans have a lot of good will toward the Jews. But a generation that no longer feels affected by the past has a limited reservoir of patience. Reason and humanity, two concepts that cannot always be combined into one, must be treated with sensitivity—by all sides." The headline of this contribution to the moral self-assertion of the Germans was "Sensitivity—On All Sides."

Two months later Fromme received support from his colleague Ernst-Otto Maetzke, who, in the context of the worldwide discussion of the political past of the Austrian president Kurt Waldheim, took aim at the Jewish World Congress. He accused it of "hypocritically misusing the dead of a past war and of a violent dictatorship for its own political goals. The fact that this method is the norm in political battles does not make it any better. By comparison, common grave robbers are decent people." Maetzke could have titled his editorial "Let the Dead Bury Their Dead!" But for brevity's sake he chose "Worse Than Grave-Robbing."

Third on the righteous team of the *Frankfurter Allgemeine* rightists was Günther Gillessen. On May 14, 1986, he granted a German who had emigrated to the United States, lawyer Franz Oppenheimer, more than a printed page. Oppenheimer had read a few new books, among them one to which he owed the insight that "even among the devoted core of party members before Hitler's takeover, only a small minority of some 12.5 percent were rabid anti-Semites." This statistic, which stemmed from a U.S. survey in postwar Germany, fit well into Oppenheimer's plan. The great majority of Germans, as Oppenheimer would have it, "bears no greater guilt for Hitler's crimes than do others for Stalin's crimes or Gorbachev's today"—this being the final conclusion of this "collector of historical literature" whom Gillessen presented in his introduction.

Gillessen also made sure that the article had the right presentation. "Beware of False Conclusions from German History" was the recommendation carried in the headline. The subtitle was even clearer: "The Seductions of a Collective Obsession with Guilt."

Thus the stage was already set when Ernst Nolte, professor of modern history at the Free University of Berlin and respected scholar of fascism, stepped upon it on June 6, 1986. Those who read the *Frankfurter Allgemeine* all the way through to the culture section were able to read something under the title "The Past That Will Not Pass" that no German historian to date had noticed: that Auschwitz was only a copy of a Russian original—the Stalinist Gulag Archipelago. For fear of the Bolsheviks' Asiatic will to annihilate, Hitler himself committed an "Asiatic deed." Was the annihilation of the Jews a kind of putative self-defense? Nolte's speculation amounts to just that.

Nolte had expressed the same thoughts before, but in cautious phrases. In an essay that was brought out in 1985 in English by H. W. Koch in the book *Aspects of the Third Reich*, he also asked whether Hitler might not have been justified in interning the German Jews as prisoners of war after the outbreak of the war. (The "right" to do this was given to him by the president of the Jewish Agency, Chaim Weizmann, when he assured the British prime minister in a letter written in the beginning of 1939 that in this war the Jews were on the side of England and the Western democracies.) It is of no account that this sentence or similar passages were present in the parts of the manuscript edited out by the *Frankfurter Allgemeine Zeitung*: No German historian has ever accorded Hitler such a sympathetic treatment.

Nolte is not the only historian who now, with the century approaching its end, has supported a relativization of the Third Reich and its crimes. Andreas Hillgruber and Michael Stürmer, who are also often mentioned in this context (see, for example, Jürgen Habermas's article in *Die Zeit* of July 11, 1986), have not without reason become the subject of controversy: Stürmer because he would like to elevate his rather conservative view of the past to the official German view of history and Hillgruber because of his strong sympathies for the Prussian Junkers and military men, without whom he knows that Hitler would neither have come to power nor remained there long. But neither historian is a "relativizer" à la Nolte, and they do not deserve to be lumped together with him.

The case of the Bonn historian Klaus Hildebrand is different, however. Hildebrand penned an exuberant review of Nolte's essay (*Historische Zeitschrift*, vol. 242, issue 2, April, 1986). In 1983 Hildebrand, on the occasion of the fiftieth anniversary of the Nazi seizure of power, spoke forcefully against the thesis that there had been a German *Sonderweg*—a deviation by Germany from the "normal" development of the West toward liberal democracy—before 1933. He is only willing to concede the existence of a *Sonderweg* between the years of 1933 and 1945, which was the result of the "special case" of Hitler.

At the end of a speech that was published in 1984 but that has received little attention until today (in Wolfgang Michalka, ed., *Die national-sozialistische Machtergreifung*, Padeborn, 1984), Hildebrand appears to revoke even this concession: "It remains to be seen whether future scholarship will initiate a process of historicization of the Hitler period, for example by comparing it with Stalinist Russia and with examples such as the Stone Age communism in Cambodia. This would doubtless be accompanied by terrifying scholarly insights and painful human experiences. Both phenomena could, *horribile dictu*, even relativize the concept of the German *Sonderweg* between 1933 and 1945." (For those of us who know no Latin, *horribile dictu* means "horrible to say.")

Much can be said against Hildebrand's contention that there was no German *Sonderweg* before 1933—little of which has not already been said somewhere else. More instructive in our context is the mention of Stalin and Pol Pot, whose crimes Nolte has already related to Hitler's. What is the sense of this comparison? Culturally, Germany is a country of the West. It participated in the European Enlightenment and in a long tradition of the rule of law. That is not the case for Russia, and certainly not for Cambodia. The crimes of Stalin and the Khmer Rouge are in no way excused by this fact. But Hitler and his helpers must be judged by our Western norms. In this historical context the systematic genocide of the Jews ordered by the German state—but also the murder of Sinti and Roma—is the greatest crime of the twentieth century, in fact of world history.

A SELLOUT OF WESTERN VALUES

In the *Frankfurter Allgemeine Zeitung* of August 29, Joachim Fest suggested that anyone who argued in this way was propagating "the old Nazi distinction according to which there are higher peoples and more primitive peoples who do not even know about the commandment against killing."

It is indeed striking to see to what extremes some people will go when they feel themselves forced to provide rationalizations. Fest exempts Germany from the moral values it participated in creating. And he liberates historians from their most noble task: to provide historically appropriate valuations. Neither Nolte nor Hildebrand nor Fest desire to represent a cynical nihilism, but what they end up bringing about is, *horribile dictu*, a sellout of Western values.

In the article cited, Fest defended Nolte and Hildebrand against Jürgen Habermas's assertion that they were engaged in nationalist excuse-making. Fest even calls this criticism "personal defamation." What was it that Mephistopheles said? "One should not mention in the presence of chaste ears what chaste hearts cannot do without." Those who conjure up Stalin and Pol Pot to "relativize" Hitler are engaged not in historical scholarship but in political scholarship. They instrumentalize history for political goals and thus accomplish from the right side of the political spectrum what the ideologues of the student movement of 1968 did from the left. And does Fest seriously want to suggest that it is not politics but the historical truth and nothing but the truth that motivates his paper in its campaign against "obsessive guilt"?

Continuing to read the *Frankfurter Allgemeine Zeitung* makes it clear where the deeper roots of the nationalist wave of excuse-making are to be sought. Recently, every column in the paper has been shouting the call for German reunification, louder even than in the 1950s. It is important to know whether the newspaper considers this goal attainable. It is important that its incantations help elevate national consciousness. In order to be able to today demand the reestablishment of the German Reich, history indeed does have to be rewritten. The regime that gambled away the national unity of German is no longer supposed to appear to be what it was: the most inhuman of all times. For this reason its crimes are being weighed against those of other nations, no matter what developmental stage these nations might have been in. In the end we will again be at the place where we have been for over thirty years in the beery discussions of pub regulars: that all history is the history of crimes and that there is little in German history that does not fit in this framework.

Perhaps it is of some consolation that not only the century but also the millennium is approaching its end. The Germans can look back and think of what they have given the world in their long history. Of course there will be few political achievements here. The formation of the German national state was, as things stood in the nineteenth century, unavoidable. But the Reich of 1871 failed because of the Germans themselves. In view of the role that Germany played in starting both world wars, Europe cannot and the Germans should not ever want a new German Reich, a sovereign national state. That is the logic of history, and history's logic is, according to a statement by Bismarck, more precise than the Prussian state accounting office.

What is left? We must learn to live with our history without attempting to dispense with parts of it post facto. We must not place exaggerated demands on the future, and we must understand why we should not do that. Remaining from our history is the duty to practice solidarity with all those who were the victims of German arrogance—and this applies in particular to Jews and Poles. A part of our heritage should also be a sense of national solidarity with the Germans in the GDR, who until today have borne a much heavier part of the burden of German history than the citizens of the Federal Republic.

The ghost of Bitburg wants to prevent us from learning from history. It fills us with envy of the real or presumed normality of others. It deceives us into believing that we have a claim that we would only have if in the past we had been different than we were. It tries to lure us onto a path that has already once led to catastrophe. It is time to banish this ghost.

Source: *Frankfurter Rundschau*, November 14, 1986

CHRISTIAN MEIER

Not a Concluding Remark

The "Historikerstreit" that has been fought out in this newspaper and in *Die Zeit* seems to be over. Ernst Nolte, whose article (*Frankfurter Allgemeine Zeitung*, June 6, 1986) was the most important cause, added to his remarks what he had assumed to be obvious, and thus defused his position. Jürgen Habermas, who opened the dispute in July, spoke the last word for *Die Zeit*. However matters thus stand, it is time to sum up the debate.

What has happened? Habermas was of the opinion that he was observing "apologetic tendencies" in various public statements by historians. He feared that the singularity of the crimes that Germany committed under the Nazi regime, especially the annihilation of the Jews, was being denied and that this part of German history was being "relativized" and leveled in order to place the entirety of German history in a more friendly light. He cited Andreas Hillgruber, Ernst Nolte, and Klaus Hildebrand as representatives of this tendency. He associated them with Michael Stürmer's attempts to foster a German historical consensus. He also saw an association with the federal government's politics of history, which is manifesting itself in the foundation of historical museums and in plans for a memorial in Bonn. He also accused them of developing a "nationalistically colored" image of history. In short: He sees these historians as fostering a change in political climate that is manifesting itself in the abrogation of the consensus regarding our assessment of the Nazi past.

After the first responses, which referred to details but also to false or questionable quotations, Joachim Fest (*Frankfurter Allgemeine Zeitung*, August 29, 1986) took up the discussion with Habermas in a lengthy article called "Encumbered Remembrance." Fest aimed at one of the main points: whether the German crimes of that time were singular. With this open and forceful, but also measured, polemic, the dispute entered a new stage. After September it was followed by a series of six articles, concluding with Habermas's piece.

NEGATIVE MYTH

In retrospect, the result appears to be—especially after Nolte's last article—that the problem of singularity is no longer in debate. Eberhard Jäckel formulated this most forcefully: "I claim . . . that the National-

Socialist murder of the Jews was unique because never before had a nation with the authority of its leader decided and announced that it would kill off as completely as possible a particular group of humans, including old people, women, children, and infants, and actually put this decision into practice, using all the means of governmental power at its disposal." Even if the announcement by the führer was not all that explicit, the facts of it cannot be denied. One should add that with this act of industrial extermination what was achieved was not only a new modus, a new point on the scale of the possibility of killing, but a qualitative leap. Nolte wrote that Jäckel's words better expressed what he had described more briefly with the term "racial murder." His original article had tended to place the millions of murders committed by the Germans in a series with mass murders committed by the Stalinist Soviet Union and others. Moreover, he had constructed a causal connection between the Gulag Archipelago and Auschwitz. While he is not willing to withdraw this assertion, he did modify it to the extent of stating that all in all the only disputed questions are the details of Hitler's motivation and of the historical classification of the Holocaust.

It is to be hoped that Ernst Nolte's suggestion that we should remain more keenly aware of the various millionfold mass murders of this century bears fruit. When one seeks orientation about this—and about the role of mass murder in history—one is surprised by how difficult it is to find. This would appear to be an area that historical research should look into. By pursuing these questions, one can recognize more precisely the peculiarity of our century—and certain similarities in its "liquidations." But Nolte's hope to be able to attenuate this distressing aspect of our Nazi past will probably not succeed. If we want, and much speaks for this, to prevent National-Socialist history from becoming an enduring negative myth about absolute evil, then we will have to seek other paths. The consciousness of these crimes is too deeply etched into the foundations of the Federal Republic. It is no doubt desirable to be able to historicize this shocking past and loosen the "hypnotic paralysis" that emanates from it. But we will not achieve this by quibbling about what happened. That would mean fleeing from the facts.

Even if such murders beyond doubt belong to the signature of the twentieth century, they were not committed in the Western countries: And one should not believe—as I would like to assert in opposition to Fest— that it makes no difference whether we or the Turks or even the Soviet Union commit such acts. If we decide that our long history produced different ethical conditions and a different degree of civilization and if we are—justifiably—proud of our history, does that make us advocates of the ideology of the master race? No privileges or prerogatives at all arise from this historical development. But duties do. Fest's objection, if examined closely, can only mean that many cases of self-accusation represent an inverted consciousness of German exceptionality. That has little to do with the present and less to do with the past.

However, one can say that the problem of singularity is not so important under certain conditions. Even if the German crimes were not unique, what advantage would that have for us and our position in the world? Of what use is it to us if the annihilation of the Jews is placed in a series with the persecution and liquidation of the kulaks or the extermination carried out by Pol Pot? In any case, any discussion about this is bound to be touchy. Even if it is true that one must also speak about the other mass murders of our time, the larger ones as well as the smaller ones, and as much as one can agree with Fest when he supposes that moral irritation today follows political intentions, one should leave out the problem of the German past. Otherwise we will end up fighting against each other.

COMPARABILITY

The answer to the question about singularity, however, is also important for other reasons. Because only if one answers this question affirmatively and truthfully can one understand fully why we have to allow ourselves to be repeatedly reproached with this past. Of course there is a complex set of reasons for this. The Nazi crimes are known down to minute details. The crimes of Stalin or Pol Pot are known only in a general way. In this country, the rejection of these crimes has been built into the foundations of the republic. This is not the case with the other successor states of the Third Reich. We are neither a great power that does not have to listen to such things nor are we so poor that there is nobody interested in reminding us of them. There is no doubt that all this is important—as is political reality—in making historical truth take a given direction.

But because that is so, there is no easy escape from this complex. Thus, to examine the matter from its tactical side, it is better for us to understand and to speak the truth than to have others constantly remind us. In this way, we can most easily awaken understanding for the anguish over our history that we and our children increasingly face. In this way, we can counter unreasonable demands differently. Every attempt to sneak out of this past or to mobilize it for political comparisons—especially the wrong political comparisons—only makes matters worse. The events of recent years and weeks unfortunately shows no lack of such examples.

The topic of the *Historikerstreit* was and is less the past than the present and the future. This is the thrust of the question: How we are to live with a past that is so deeply anchored in our consciousness? Are we, seen historically, very different from others? If we are, is that more likely to be an opportunity or a disastrous fate? In this way, the nature of our identity as citizens of the Federal Republic has become a topic of debate.

It is presumably no coincidence that these questions are again imposing themselves upon us forty years after the end of the war. People who could have been active in the Nazi regime are now reaching the grandparent age. In this respect, the *Historikerstreit* has presumably taken up questions whose answers are probably constantly changing. Perhaps a deep-seated, elemental process is taking place here, comparable to a sheet of ice breaking up. Certain tendencies in the writing of some historians offer us little information about these processes—despite the fact that these are in many cases prominent members of the guild. What moved Hillgruber to "identify" with the defenders of the front in East Prussia will probably have to remain a mystery. In my opinion, he wanted to inspire understanding for the situation and respect for the sacrifices the participants made. His publication could have doubtless gained much from multiple perspectives, a more disassociated approach, and more frequent use of the subjunctive. But however that may be and whatever other weaknesses his book contains, it cannot be accused of trivializing National Socialism. In this respect, Habermas's concerns are certainly without foundation.

THERE IS NO WAY AROUND IT

That does not mean that historians are immune to the tendencies of their age. The world they live in certainly influences which questions are posed, which questions present themselves as a challenge—and which questions we see as either less interesting or worthy of being repressed entirely. We should not make this too easy for ourselves. The knowledge that the higher we place the role of Hitler and his regime, the less guilt we can assess to German society should not lead us to make current opinions about Nazi society the guiding star of interpretations of the period, nor should it lead us to suggest that others are doing this. Even if Hitler gave the order for the annihilation of the Jews, that does not exculpate anyone who executed or even tolerated such a criminal order. And that applies to both the individuals and the social structure in which that happened.

Historians should also be able to discern uncomfortable truths—which they do, and the quality of the knowledge they have generated has, since the days of Thucidides, been greatly enhanced by that. There is no reason to believe that historians are softening their condemnation of the Nazi crimes or their abhorrence of the Nazi regime. I know of no historians who want to "cast off the burden of a happily de-moralized past." One should not cast doubt on the fact that we share this conviction. In this sense, our fundamental consensus has not been broken.

HISTORICAL ERRORS

One can, however, observe a new, conservative attitude toward history, especially in Michael Stürmer. This tendency is hard to quote, for Stürmer thinks and argues in an extraordinarily complex and careful way. But if it is permitted to closely examine that which extends beyond widely held opinion and is thus most easily discerned, then it is unmistakable that he instrumentalizes history politically. There is no other way to explain the close parallel in which he invokes dangers facing Germany as a country with a central location while demanding that history be written better and differently so that it can be made more influential than it was in the past. This is not a politically partisan process, and it is certainly not written on instruction from the government (which is fortunately also resisting the temptation to "prescribe" a view of history). On the contrary, Stürmer wants to create a broad historical consensus, which he thinks public policy urgently needs. This consensus, he believes, should be based on recovering all of German history. Stürmer could well be in agreement with widespread tendencies in the Federal Republic. This seems to be the reason for the need for a new historical classification of the Nazi period, just as this also appears to be the reason for a certain negligence in the treatment of this Nazi past—which is not something Stürmer is guilty of.

Thus Habermas, whatever one thinks of his arguments, is right in addressing Stürmer. Of course it would have been nice if he had read him more exactly. For Stürmer is far from supporting a "middle Europe" ideology. In fact what he is getting at is just the opposite. And one absolutely cannot simply dismiss his suggestions that there is a geography of power as "geopolitical drumbeat." In contrast to Hildebrand and Hagen Schulze,* he does not see history as endowing meaning—even though history, as he sees it, should contribute to identity and even though the "tightrope walk between demythologizing and endowing meaning," of which he speaks, occasionally fails. But Stürmer wants to utilize history. He wrote: "In a land without history, the future is controlled by those who determine the content of memory, who coin concepts and interpret the past." If that is intended as a warning, it must also be seen as a challenge. This is the reason he is motivated by the strange and extremely hard-to-substantiate fear (or is it a hope?) that German history could someday belong to someone.

By contrast, Habermas refers to the pluralism of our society, which, he says, must be preserved. We should be allowed at most a kind of patriotism based on the constitution. Broszat points to the great advantages of a "skeptical and soberly modest understanding of historical education"—something Burckhardt had already formulated and that, since the war, has fortunately become part of the consensus. And Habermas finds that the Nazi period is all the less likely to block access to our history the more calmly we see this period "as a filter through which our cultural tradition must pass, inasmuch as it is adopted deliberately and consciously."

Have we thus only been allowed to have a constitutional patriotism since 1945?—or can and should national identity mean something to us? Should

---

Author's Note: The mention of Hagen Schulze in this context was a mistake, and I regret it (see the *Frankfurter Allgemeine Zeitung*, November 29, 1986).

we only establish links to the "better traditions" of German history? Or must we do so with all of our history? That should be discussed.

Stürmer's attempt should probably not be seen as illegitimate. Anyone who in the 1970s referred to the duty of historiography to political pedagogy (Theodor Mommsen) should not accuse Stürmer of wanting the same thing in his own way. But a certain "shared basic understanding" of German history (Richard von Weizsäcker) can only be achieved if we exclude no (or only very extreme) ideas. This presumes a very open debate, very many disputes—and especially liberality. And that can come only from the center. And it can only be undertaken with endless patience and the readiness to listen to others. Otherwise it will remain a deeply self-contradictory undertaking in which one group desires to gain a very broad majority for highly controversial viewpoints. We will also make little progress as long as people claim ownership of history. That does not even exist in the GDR, even though a new access to German history is being sought there. In short, these are things that will perhaps gradually develop and that can be promoted but that cannot be demanded.

THE NATION SURMOUNTED?

However, I cannot see that in this country mere constitutional patriotism is enough in the long run. This despite the fact that a new national identity specific to the Federal Republic is stirring. With all sympathy for postnational identity, can such a thing suffice while we are still living in nations? Habermas's intellectually demanding concept of postconventional identity, too, has little chance of being realized. And finally, "negative nationalism"—even ignoring the fact that it could be inverted and become the real thing—is not sufficient for our most pressing task: to face up to the history of 1933 to 1945 as our own, to open ourselves up to this history.

What speaks against the richness and diversity of our traditions simply unfolding more freely again? Habermas is certainly correct: After 1945, we must read Heidegger, Jünger, Carl Schmitt with different eyes. But does that not make reading them and trying to learn from them and being fascinated by them only more exciting? Can one, should one, read their writings with the viewpoint that they were wrong? And should one warn people about them and about Nietzsche and others?

Why does Habermas not link his thought to the facts that young people, too, must be made liable for our history, that they live in a nation called Germany, and that they are Germans, instead of linking it to "contexts of development in which Auschwitz was possible," contexts he appears to believe are still present today? As if such contexts were proven! In any case, Auschwitz is being drawn into our present and discussed as the product of specific, continuously existing social structures and mentalities. And thus it is also co-opted in a partisan way. I would like to see all this better supported before I could be convinced of it, especially after almost forty years of successful democracy. If we still act like Germans in many ways, is it really this way of acting and not the fact that we are Germans that makes us liable for our past?

INTERIM RESULTS

I have no objections to a properly self-critical treatment of our history. And in many ways it was certainly necessary and good that the Nazi period has acted as a filter. But in the long run, what should be the criteria for this process? After all, the cultural tradition has not been simply filtered away. These criteria have been elevated and placed on a new, democratic foundation. By rationally filtering the past, do we not risk being narrow, intellectually poor, and unfree?

The results that I would like to report on here can thus only be of an interim nature. Now that the *Historikerstreit* is basically over, the problem arises in greater clarity: How are we going to live with this history and what conclusions can we draw from it? In many respects, the discussion should be just beginning now. And it should not be conducted exclusively by historians, despite the fact that society has left this dispute, for which one needed no more background knowledge than what newspaper readers have, to the historians.

We will make no progress if we use the Nazi past as a club in partisan disputes. And as much as focus and clarity are necessary for a dispute, there is no reason to place each other on the defendant's stand. A thought-provoking argument like that of Joachim Fest should not be described as "unsavory"—even if one cannot agree with many things in it. The report for the German Historical Museum, incidentally, is quite balanced. Now the question is what will be done with it. "One must make his enemy stronger if one wants to appear smarter." In this way Gadamer once characterized Heidegger's maxim in dealing with Plato. It could also be applied to this dispute.

Joachim Fest asked what the partisan groupings in this dispute were. That will be clear later. But it is to be wished that the center, especially, will be strong, for in the past, the political middle has always been capable of providing reasonable solutions, results, and maxims. In this case, too, then, there would also be reason for hope in the long run.

Source: *Frankfurter Allgemeine Zeitung*, November 20, 1986

KURT SONTHEIMER

Makeup Artists Are Creating a New Identity

The debate about revisionist tendencies in German history writing that Professor Habermas set off has caused a stir among German historians. Of course the historians quoted by name, all of whom are in the conservative camp, are not willing to accept Habermas's accusation that they, via their new view of the Third Reich and their attempts to shape a national consciousness, are challenging our intellectual and spiritual ties to the West. The historians are striking back more or less vehemently—and acting as if they had been caught red-handed. But one can, happily, still find some voices among the historians (for example Professor Hans Mommsen, Professor Eberhard Jäckel, and Director Martin Broszat from the Munich Institute for Current Affairs) who also see (if not in the same way) the trend identified by Habermas and who also consider it to be questionable.

The long discussion with Professor Andreas Hillgruber from Cologne (*Rheinischer Merkur*, no. 45), who had been attacked by Habermas, in my eyes only confirmed that the accusation of revisionism is correct. There are attempts, as is so often the case, to show up the troublesome critic by dismissing him as being without scholarly qualification. Hillgruber's loudly proclaimed demand for an academic freedom that knows no taboos is an empty phrase, since this freedom had never been challenged—certainly not by Habermas.

Furthermore, there is no such thing as historiography without precondition. Nor can historical knowledge be considered in a disinterested way and without the context in which it stands. The pose of pure and strict scholarly research that is loudly proclaimed by the historians involved in this debate poorly suits those who recently wanted to see history used to shape national consciousness. This is an impermissible attempt to withdraw to the ivory tower of pure scholarship in order to fend off critical questions coming from outside. I am thus of the opinion that the debate—whatever the result may be—is important for our historical and political self-definition and thus should not be broken off. It is not, as Professor Nipperdey recently suggested, unfortunate.

I myself am a political scientist, although I do have a limited past as a modern historian. For me the matter is thus: Some German historians are in the process of supplying arguments for the attempt, favored by the prevailing political climate, to instrumentalize history for political or national interests. They are taking up a tradition of German nationalist historiography from a predemocratic era in order to work on the historical consciousness of the nation.

This program currently has two directions: One is aimed at defusing, relativizing, and normalizing National Socialism (for example, the position of Nolte, Hillgruber, and others). The other is interested in discovering and presenting historical figures, events, and episodes relevant to our national history in the interest of creating a historical consciousness that supports the stability of our political order (for example, the position of Stürmer and others).

This kind of thing certainly is not taking place at the behest of the government. It is, however, taking place within the intellectual horizon of the *Wende*, or conservative shift in government, that is interested in assigning to history the function of providing a sense of national identity. In any case, there is no shortage of eager historians who are glad to represent this program and provide it with content.

The debate comes at a time when historians (please forgive the unavoidable generalization) are in the pleasant situation of being able to look back at their discipline's recent past with some pride. After all, in the preceding decade they succeeded in displacing their main competitors, the sociologists and the political scientists, from the limelight. Conscious of highly official appreciation and encouragement, they felt good about themselves. Here, too, there is a manifestation of an intellectual-cultural shift.

Even though the social scientists had to a great extent reconstituted themselves in the new Federal Republic, they quickly succeeded in winning a great deal of public attention for their research and their work on forming public opinion. History, however—with the exception of current affairs, for which there was always a politically motivated interest—was forced to lead more of a shadowy existence when it came to being a force in education circles. History, which in the second and third reichs played a key—and unfortunate—role in shaping the German national consciousness because it had propagated and legitimized the German *Sonderweg*, found itself, after the catastrophe of the Third Reich, forced to reexamine and reorient itself under altered political conditions. It was no longer able to be a leading discipline for the democratic reconstruction of the Federal Republic. This function fell to the new science of politics—which entered the German public consciousness as a kind of "science of democracy." There is no doubt that political science made a major contribution to forming a political consciousness in the early years of the Federal Republic under figures such as Ernest Fraenkel, Theodor Eschenburg, Carlo Schmidt, and others.

Thus history had to relinquish to the social sciences its once dominant role in shaping political consciousness. Thus it ended up, despite the quality of its scholarship, standing in the shadow of public interest. Historians lamented their contemporaries' lack of historical sense and occasionally found solace in well-attended exhibitions.

Then came the student revolt, and with it the widespread, momentous suspicion that the teachings and theories of sociologists and political scientists were one of the main causes of the student rebellion against the existing order. Now, no one will want to deny that political theories that were popular in these disciplines—in particular the rediscovery of the ideology of Marxism, to which even a thinker like Habermas was able to contribute important elements—became extremely virulent in the student movement and caused the political scene in the Federal Republic to become highly charged. The anger of established politics about this reinstatement of ideologizing and its negative consequences was taken out on political science and sociology, which, despite their pluralistic diversity, went down in the public's esteem.

Aside from a hard-fought debate about fascism, the discipline of German history was largely exempted from the ideological effects of the student revolt. Thus history was able to set out to reconquer the terrain of respect and public effectiveness from the social sciences, which were now considered to be ideologized and politicized. This was successful. At conventions, historians were pleased to note words of encouragement and applause from the highest places, including from the president of the Federal Republic. Historians also succeeded in displacing social studies in secondary schools in favor of an increased consideration of history. Many historians even began to enter the public consciousness via discussions of current issues in German politics. Historians were again a force to be reckoned with.

Moreover, history—as a discipline and as a consciousness—was rediscovered after the conservative shift in Bonn as a means to create a consciousness that would stabilize the existing order. The years-old debate about national identity and views of history that might promote such an identity, coupled with an increased general interest in the Germans and their history, was carried out primarily by historians. Finally, after decades of life in the public shadow, they were handed a political task: the search for a national identity. Many a historian gladly and intensively took up this task.

The result of this effort by a number of our historians is visible today: It was a sense of shock about some of the results that led to today's debate. To lament this debate, as Thomas Nipperdey did, would be to ignore the fact that a part of the discipline is prepared to provide an allegedly historyless nation with—orienting—key words that a government intent upon shaping a positive identity needs. This is clearly a matter of public interest that should be debated thoroughly and publicly.

This undertaking is nowhere near as harmless and purely scholarly an endeavor as its proponents would like to portray it. It is a deviation from the political consensus of the era after 1945 in which German democracy was reconstructed. Back then, it was unanimously held that the principles and foundations of the new democracy were to be sought less in the German past than in the tradition of Western-liberal democracy, and that principles and foundations were to be developed further in this spirit. Searching for vague identities in German history before 1918 and working toward as unified an understanding of history as possible, as some historians have done, is dubious not only because so little is to be found there but also because every attempt to provide political meaning via our predemocratic national history threatens to end the consensus of the postwar era.

In the postwar era we attempted to discover what had led to the fall of Weimar and to the Hitler dictatorship with its consequences and what should be done to finally put behind us the segment of German national history that had ended in 1945. We were attempting to overcome the past, not to invoke it. That by and large succeeded. I simply cannot see what better lesson those who are struggling to provide meaning through history can offer us. The point cannot be to supply the German nation, which in any case tends toward forgetfulness, with a historically good conscience. The point, then as now, is to understand what was and what is—and that under the obligation laid down in our constitution to create a democratic and social state that will place human dignity in the center of its considerations. This meaning of our political existence is clear and unambiguous. It needs no tutoring by professorial bearers of meaning who are busy rummaging through the complex German past to find identity-shaping experiences for the German nation of the present.

The political consciousness of the Federal Republic and thus a central element of the country's political culture would be in bad shape if this culture were to be shaped by identity-hungry historians. Political scientists and sociologists are once again called upon to contribute to forming an enlightened consciousness. A historically informed, liberal social science no longer languishing under the reign of suspicion is a necessary counterweight to the current political afflictions and to the march of the bearers of historical meaning through the political consciousness of the Federal Republic.

Source: *Rheinischer Merkur/Christ und Welt*, November 21, 1986

KLAUS HILDEBRAND

He Who Wants to Escape the Abyss Will Have to Sound It Very Precisely: Is the New German History Writing Revisionist?

The question as to whether the accusation of revisionism is appropriate for the new historiography of the Third Reich is posed so unambiguously that it demands a clear answer. The factual situation, however, demands that we explore the problem in two different respects.

• It is the job of a scholar to relentlessly revise the state of knowledge that he has inherited. To this extent, he cannot be criticized for simply doing his duty. Whether worldviews and interests desire it or not, the search for truth goes on, sometimes supported and accelerated by public discussion, sometimes opposed and hindered by it. For the earth keeps on turning, even when the authorities have forbidden it.

• Thus research on the history of the Third Reich has gone forward steadily and continues to revise, all in all with good results. On the whole the research, which the participants carry out for various motives, is moving toward historicizing the Third Reich.

The answer to our question, Is the accusation of revisionism appropriate for the new historiography of the Third Reich?, is without reservation no, especially if the concept of revisionism is alleged to mean apology and justification for the Third Reich. This is Jürgen Habermas's intent, in what Karl-Heinz Janßen called "a call to arms" against the "apologetic tendencies in the German history writing," and Rudolf Augstein's intent in his *Spiegel* essay about the new "Auschwitz lie."

The moral question about the guilt or innocence of the Third Reich has been answered, and no serious representative of history in the Federal Republic has contradicted that. The scholarly treatment of the Third Reich, however, is naturally very far from being a closed subject. How could it be, when one considers that the progress of historical scholarship over time underlies our changes in perspective and that in the special case of this obstinate object of inquiry, all too many problems are still unexplained? To this extent it is the business of scholarship to use newly available sources to continually examine new questions and new perspectives, as well as to critically examine the state of research and to expand the framework in which it is evaluated.

The overarching question, How could it have come to that?, refers to the origin and development of Hitler's dictatorship. This question is complemented by the question, "What was it 'really' like before 1933, between 1933 and 1945, and after 1945?" In other words, the epochs of German history before 1933 regain their own character without our overlooking the continuities in the historical process. In this way, the individual epochs are removed from the context of the Nazi past, which for them was still an open future.

In the context of free research, in particular within the German discipline of history, first there arose an image of the Third Reich that was a sketch of a total dictatorship. It was characterized by a diabolical mechanism of force that confused people and sucked them in. It also emphasized Hitler's racially determined claim of world domination. Increasingly, the Janus-like character of this system—characterized by force and seduction, terror and cooperation, ecstasy and banality—became evident. The works of Karl Dietrich Bracher and Andreas Hillgruber, on the German side, are representative of works that hold this view.

EVIL, REVERSED FRONTS, BUT OLD CONTENTS

If one disregards the continuing efforts by right-wing radicals to whitewash the Third Reich, efforts that only marginally accompany the history of the Federal Republic, then the first notable approach to revision of the then-valid image of the period of National Socialism came at the beginning of the 1960s from the Anglo-Saxon countries. For example, the American David Hoggan, in his 1961 book *The Forced War: The Causes and Reasons of the Second World War*, tried to remove the blame from Hitler for unleashing the Second World War and to portray the English foreign minister Lord Halifax as the warmonger.

Of a different motivation was A. J. P. Taylor's book of the same year, *The Origins of the Second World War*. It presents Hitler as a politician who stumbled into pursuing a war without really wanting to. In the foreground of the Second World War, the mechanism of power relations is for Taylor both fateful and larger than individuals. This mechanism is supposed to be responsible for the creation of European peoples, something that for him occurs as an automatic consequence of the European national history. In such a perspective, Hitler appears as a "normal" revisionist politician, while Gustav Stresemann is put on a pedestal and can hardly be distinguished from Bethmann Hollweg and Bismarck. Taylor's deep mistrust of a *kleindeutsch* [small-German, that is, excluding Austria] nation-state influenced him in this characterization of circumstances and prevented him from recognizing the differences between Bismarck, Bethmann Hollweg, Stresemann, and Hitler.

A second impetus, begun in the 1960s and continuing to the present, was fundamentally different from its predecessors. It aimed at revising the image of the Third Reich drawn in the 1950s and 1960s and was undertaken by historians who looked less to the political motives of the actors than to the social constraints on their actions: "structures" was the new catchword of scholarship in a time mad for change. In this way Hans Mommsen and Martin Broszat challenged the systematicity of the National-Socialist regime's actions and the goal-directedness of Hitler's foreign policy and racial politics. They see in the total dictatorship of the Third Reich no more and no less than a chaos of rival offices, a process of cumulative radicalization and an explosion of unbridled dynamism. In short, they conclude that the National-Socialist leaders were prisoners of their own politics.

Before such a backdrop Hans Mommsen even calls Hitler a "weak dictator." Moreover, the atrocity of the mass murder of the European Jews appears to this revisionist school in German history writing not as a systematic consequence of a will to destruction originating with Hitler but as a conditioned reaction to crises in National-Socialist rule and in the way Germany conducted the war. Principally its representatives drew on David Irving, who in his 1977 book *Hitler's War* argued the thesis that the dictator of the Third Reich first learned of the murder of the Jews in 1943, and that it was Himmler who had acted as an independent power.

The remonstrance of the revisionists that the traditional position was in danger of overrationalizing Hitler and demonizing the Third Reich was most impressively challenged by Karl Dietrich Bracher. Bracher rejected both the "'new-Left' and Marxist dogma of an overall interpretation of fascism" and the "newer revisionist interpretation." They both

> turn against the "old-liberal" totalitarianism theory and talk about a relativizing interpretation, which emphasizes the "improvisational" politics of power and domination of National Socialism. Leftist interpretations would like to leave behind the questions of guilt and responsibility in favor of a more modern, realistic analysis. But in doing this they slide into the danger of a newer underestimation and trivialization of National Socialism itself. Their analysis also brings with it, in another way, the vague leftist talk about fascism and reaction.

With this, we have reached the current state of the debate, which basically revolves around old issues and is characterized by a reversal in the participants' alignment. Hans Mommsen and Martin Broszat, revisionists par excellence, one with his thesis of Hitler as a "weak dictator" and the other with his findings about the authoritarian chaos of the Third Reich, have lined up with Habermas. For his part Habermas is sniffing out the alleged revisionist and apologetic tendencies in the German writing of modern political history. In this frame he attacks Ernst Nolte, who had reintroduced the term "fascism," long sunk from view, into scholarly studies, and attacks Andreas Hillgruber, who has effectively emphasized the systematicity of Hitler's foreign policy and racial politics.

What has happened? Well, in the course of a scholarly debate, nothing extraordinary—if one disregards the fact that findings, in principle available for decades, have in a particular fashion found their way into public view and been incorporated into a particular concept. For what Nolte wrote in his stigmatized newspaper article "Die Vergangenheit, die nicht vergehen will" [The Past That Will Not Pass] has been available in substance all along in the book he published twenty-three years ago, *Faschismus in seiner Epoche* [Fascism in Its Epoch], namely, the thesis that Italian fascism and German National Socialism arose as countermovements to Russian Bolshevism and are to be understood in this light. Also the idea of comparing National Socialism's annihilation with Bolshevism's annihilations is anything but new; it is contained and developed in earlier works.

The subject of Hillgruber's findings is presented in his stigmatized, elegantly appointed volume *Zweierlei Untergang*. According to his conclusion the Allies' war aims were not planned exclusively in reaction to the German politics of population, resettlement, and race, but were a consequence of the war started by Hitler and were arrived at independently. This idea permeates his works from his magnum opus *Hitler's Strategy*, published in 1965, through the 1982 edition of this work with an extensive afterword, through his book of the same year, *The Second World War*, up to his talk prepared for the Düsseldorfer Akademie, which appeared in printed form as "Der Zusammenbruch im Osten 1944–45 als Problem der deutschen Nationalgeschichte und der europäischen Geschichte" [The Collapse in the East 1944–45 as a Problem of German National History and European History].

What Habermas insinuates about Hillgruber with reference to the second part of the bibliophile volume, which is concerned with the annihilation of the European Jewry, is scandalous. Habermas's criticism is based in no small part on quotations that unambiguously falsify the matter. Example: Hans Mommsen once claimed that between the end of 1938 and the beginning of 1941 "all functionaries" of the Third Reich had advocated "emigration" with regard to the Jewish question but did not go so far as to propose physical murder. Hillgruber had clearly set himself apart from this thesis, in part acknowledging, in part filling in gaps. He concluded, to the contrary, that Hitler had set his sights on a policy that went far beyond the "destruction of the Jewish race in Europe," a policy that the dictator mentioned explicitly on January 30, 1939, in the Reichstag. Habermas makes the following from this: "Hillgruber doubts, however, that *all* decisionmakers between 1938 and 1941 saw a policy of forced immigration as the best solution to the Jewish question. Still, by that time, two-thirds of the German Jews had 'ended up abroad.'"

The latter is actually true, but it has nothing to do with Hillgruber's thesis based on the arguments of Hans Mommsen. In fact these arguments establish the opposite of what Habermas claims in taking on the Cologne historian. A citation garbled like this is in no way a forgivable exception. Rather, Habermas consistently and studiously distorts the texts, which he unfortunately does not study, but more accurately, haunts.

It is incomprehensible to me that the chairman of the Association of German Historians, the historian Christian Meier, attempts to excuse such an outrage. Meier's article opens a new page in the *chronique scandaleuse* of this debate: "It is also not permissible to simply ignore all the concerns . . . that Habermas noted in recent historiography by simply pointing out that his quotations are too short or that he used an incorrect distribution of direct quotation and paraphrase." To sympathize with the "call to arms" of Jürgen Habermas may or may not honor those who do it. To want to justify Habermas's treatment of texts contradicts everything that is customary in historical scholarship and in the area of everyday life. Every student who treated literature in the "Habermas way" would fail his exam!

If one leaves aside all the invective and excitement that unpleasantly accompanies, and to a great extent determines, this debate, then the debate concerns in essence the question whether National Socialism is to be put into a historical perspective and to what extent it stands apart as a singular phenomenon or, contrariwise, appears to be comparable to other phenomena. In this context "comparable" means in principle more or less reprehensible and more or less acceptable. Who is, *horribile dictu*, more acceptable or reprehensible: Hitler or Stalin? A good part of the discussion can be reduced to this alternative. That both dictators are second to none in the "age of tyrants" is an illustration of the essence of the totalitarianism theory that dominated in scholarship and politics from the years immediately following the war into the unruly 1960s.

Therefore it is only half true when Christian Meier, in answer to the question of why the topic is always the German crimes and not the comparable crimes of other peoples, states that it is because "our democracy was founded on the experience and the rejection of Nazism." That the "red Fascists,"* as they were once called by Kurt Schumacher, took on in the same way the value of a negative model for the West-German commonweal belongs to the foundations of the Federal Republic of Germany. But this fact has faded into obscurity since the end of the 1960s, thus contributing to the one-sided focus one but not the other of the totalitarian twins. It is obvious that this one-sidedness is an obstacle to a comprehensive diagnosis of the past.

In order not to be misunderstood, let me explain in four theses what is significant with regard to the singularity and comparability of National Socialism:

Author's Note: The correct quotation is "red-painted Nazis."

• National Socialism is as singular as every historical phenomenon in that it can be seen epistemologically on the basis of a chain of causation that loses itself in complexity.

• The National-Socialist murder of the Jews stands alone as singular in German and likewise in European history, including even the "epoch of fascism." Therefore a common concept of fascism lacks enough viability to encompass Hitler's Germany, Mussolini's Italy, and other regimes and movements, since the quality of National Socialism's annihilation finds no correspondence in Italian fascism, or in other comparable phenomena of the time.

• Precisely with regard to the intensity of annihilation in Hitler's politics of race and with regard to the measure of destruction associated with it, National Socialism appears comparable with the Soviet Union of Stalin. The Soviet Union under the banner of the class struggle was to the same extent engaged in murder. Certainly there are differences and similarities between "Red" and "brown" reign. These are to be carefully determined in their details. An opinion however, that "the German crimes between 1933 and 1945" are "singular in that they qualitatively surpassed by far those of other peoples (for example, the Stalinist Soviet Union)," is just an opinion, and in the case of the historian Christian Meier not even the opinion of a specialist. What I want to say is this: In this field the gaps in our knowledge leap challengingly into view. To be sure we already know enough so that the opposite of the opinion presented above could be true. Contradictory to one another and yet related to one another, the regimes of Hitler and Stalin equaled each other in the intensity of their politics of annihilation. [It has been said that thus comparing National Socialism with Stalinism is not being undertaken in order to relativize or trivialize. Both regimes belong, in their totalitarian practice of human annihilation, to the signature of the time. This points to epochal and transepochal movements of history, in which the "unsuspected commonality of human nature" (Wilhelm Röpke) makes its appearance by degrees. Now both phenomena likewise resemble each other in the common horror of their atrocities while they distinguish themselves in completely different degrees of success in their respective politics. This suggests that their existence, so opposingly connected together, should be studied side by side in order to determine what separates them and what they have in common. Above and beyond Hitler's and Stalin's similarly distinguishing quality of annihilation the question arises, in connection with the worldview utopias of the two systems, whether or to what extent the National-Socialist vision of breeding the "blond beast" finds an equivalent in the communistic idea of the "new man." In other words, does Hitler's biological revolution correspond to Stalin's social revolution?]*

Author's Note: The bracketed material appeared in the original manuscript.

• In the universal perspective, the National-Socialist murder of the Jews remains singular and yet stands in a historical sequence there are both precursors to and successors of this genocide: for example, the murder of the Armenians in the First World War; the "liquidation" of millions of Russian farmers,* the kulaks, during the period between the wars of the twentieth century; the extermination of various peoples inside and outside of the Soviet Union under the banner of the Stalinist war of annihilation between 1939–1941 and 1945; and the regime of terror of Cambodian Stone Age communism.

Whether Germany's level of civilization, as opposed to other, less developed cultures in which comparable crimes were committed, defines the incomparability of the German atrocity has been offered as a matter for consideration in the course of the debate. This is worth considering and leads constantly to new questions that oppugn such a conclusion: What is to be seen in this context as a backward or as an advanced culture? Is such a categorization sufficient for the yardstick of modernization? Does racial murder not in this way seem more likely for a country that is highly armed and, nevertheless, technically backward than for a state characterized by a congruence of the economic, societal, and political dimensions of its culture? Does the Germany of the past belong in this sense so unmistakably to the European West so that only the comparison with England and France are appropriate and the comparison with Russia or the Soviet Union questionable? Certainly not, or there would not be the debate about the German *Sonderweg* [special path] in European history.

Nevertheless, even if we ignore that completely, annihilating millions of completely different large groups in the Soviet Union and genocide in the Third Reich are equally reprehensible, regardless of the regime. What the history of the Third Reich really teaches in this connection lies in the frightening insight that we must acknowledge how ultimately fragile the wall can be that divides civilization from barbarism in our collective and individual existence.

With this insight, a tendency in historical scholarship is being pursued and encouraged that Martin Broszat describes as the "historicizing of National Socialism." He encourages us to understand the history of the "brown" dictatorship as the history of the National-Socialist period, and, in addition, to recognize beside the total uniformity of the phenomenon, the multiplicity of its appearances in politics and everyday life. In this way we can always "see as together and simultaneously hold apart" what was characteristic for this period of German history with its "indissoluble connection between domination, sacrifice, and force, between terror, ecstasy, and normality: And we can see the interdependence of success and criminal energy, of participation and dictatorship."

But, in light of this, what was the cause of all the excitement? It is

---

Author's Note: It should properly be "farmers."

directed against the historicizing, a project that the journalist Hermann Rudolf has determined to be insupportable. Is it one that even Jürgen Habermas, by the way, with express reference to Martin Broszat's position, seems to approve of? Why does he then operate with a heavy-handed assertion of an apologetics for National Socialism? Why did it come to this in part laughable, in part evil insinuation of Martin Broszat and Hans Mommsen that is aimed at anyone who thinks differently?

POLITICAL INFLUENCE PLACED ABOVE THE SEARCH FOR TRUTH

In the end, scholarship, which acknowledges no progressive or reactionary findings, will be at the end of its rope when it tries to answer this question. Then the political battle will begin. Because ultimately, for Jürgen Habermas it seems to be a matter of claiming an intellectual hegemony that places no value on differentiation. Instead the claimed hegemony crudely holds on to an image of history that uses the long shadow of the Third Reich as a uniform foil for grasping past, present, and future.

The threatening loss of public resonance seems to have provoked Jürgen Habermas to attack something that has been established and reported in scholarship for a long time. It seems, thus, that for him what matters is not primarily truth but *influence*. The ritual of persecuted innocence demands that in such a case one loudly invoke the endangered Enlightenment. The question also arises whether his efforts to place public influence above the search for truth, which is obligatory for the scholar, have more to do with philosophy or with its classical opposite, sophistry.

Jürgen Habermas's attacks perhaps reflect shock about how limited and ambivalent is the human ability to do things. This conclusion is unlike the optimistic belief of the "revolutionaries of the 1960s." For one recognizes that totalitarianism, including the genocide and mass expulsions uniquely incorporated in Hitler's dictatorship, in fact belongs to the very character of the twentieth century. To avoid such insights and to punish the messenger of bad tidings opens up the field for myth in two ways.

The task of the historian is to penetrate to a comprehensive diagnosis of the facts. But it is not the task of the historian to precipitously and deceptively convince the patient to adopt a quack therapy. The only way to avoid the abyss, as Cesare Pavese once said, is to take a good look at it, measure it, take soundings, and climb down. Truths that seem destined to precipitate us into the abyss lose their threat when we descend deliberately, examine them closely, and accept them.

There is still much for historiography to do in researching and presenting the history of the Third Reich in a German, European, and universal context. The debate that Habermas started without sufficient reason is not suited to convey the essential priority; instead it rolls an ancient stone of weltanschauung in the way of scholarship.

Source: *Die Welt*, November 22, 1986

MICHAEL STÜRMER

How Much History Weighs

"Do you love democracy? And do you intend to defend yourselves?"
When Andre Glucksman asked this question of the German Left during
the missile crisis of 1983, indignation appeared in place of a response. A
part of the *incertitudes allemandes* of the French is their doubt about which
image the Germans have of themselves, their future, and their history.
After 1945, one was relieved that the defeated Germans looked back with
anger and disgust. It was a precondition of reconciliation that the *Grundgesetz*, or constitution, and the integration into the Western alliance prevented new upheavals and dangers.

A few years ago the influential publicist Pierre Hassner asked: "Is the
German question here again?" He was giving voice to insecurity about the
question: What will become of the German consensus in security policy?
Since that time, the French involvement in Germany has been accompanied by the appeal to have the courage needed for democracy, to face
history, and to affirm the consequences of the *Grundgesetz* and the politics
of the West as a precondition for the future. From Charles de Gaulle's
vision of a Europe of national states that cannot exist without Germany to
the Quai d'Orsay official Jean-Marie Soutou's statement, published in this
newspaper, that Europe needed the responsible and understandable
national consciousness of Germany, French involvement has been motivated by the knowledge that the German partner is needed. Should the
Germans change their minds, however, France could and would carry on.
The majorities in favor of the alliance are reassuring. The dissent about its
foundations causes a sense of unease.

In 1986, industrialist Alain Minc published the successful book *Le Syndrome Finlandais*. It contains a scenario in which a vacillating Federal
Republic draws Western Europe along with it into an irreversible tilt
toward the East. It is a source of concern that the Germans, because of
ecological pacifism, might forget the chasm between democracy and dictatorship and might seek a future in a "Central Europe." As Alfred Grosser
said after the Nuremberg Party Congress of the SPD, it is an important
task to "counteract the minimization of the Soviet Union."

Behind such worries lie cultural dissonances: on the German side much
recent history and little self-assurance, on the French side the blue-white-

196

red consensus about the past and the future, a self-assured patriotism, and the imperturbability of national character.

Would a book such as Ferdinand Braudel's *The Identity of France: Geography and History* (1986) be possible in this country? Braudel, the cofounder of the school of thought associated with the journal *Annales*, while he was a German prisoner of war wrote this outstanding book about the Mediterranean world in the age of Phillip II of Spain. In the foreword of his last book Braudel wrote that he loved France with a passion and without distinguishing between vice and virtue or between "what attracts me and what repels me." Then he described land and people and concluded by asking if geography had invented France.

For Braudel, identity is the central problem: "The determination of France is made through itself, by acknowledging the actuality of all that the human past has deposited, layer on layer. . . . All in all a residue, an amalgam, numerous additions and many crossings. In addition to that, a process, a struggle against oneself that always propagates itself." Why is that so hard to translate into German? That kind of self-confidence has been alien to the Germans since the downfall of the old Reich around 1800. Even Bismarck's state was not for long the unquestioned form of German being. After that, the founding of the Second Reich seemed to many people to be an unnecessary "boyish prank" (Max Weber) insofar as it was the end of something and not the beginning of something far greater. In 1897, Bülow demanded "a place in the sun," and even that was not enough. "There is nothing that is not questionable" (Karl Jaspers, 1931)—this diagnosis of the age stood at the beginning of Hitler and his revolution against all revolution. At its end stood the words with which the historian Ludwig Dehio described German despair: "Wherever we seek a solid place to stand, we find the earth quaking, shaken way back into the centuries by the same catastrophe that is shaking us now." All of our interpretations of Germany have collapsed. How can one live in this rubble?

Is it possible that the popular front and anti-fascism mythology, the opposition to which unified all democrats of 1949, no matter what else separated them, again has a future in the media and the political parties? Can we still count on the antitotalitarian consensus of the constitution, aimed as it is at the National-Socialist past and the Communist present and even at a Communist future?

The German temptations for self-destruction that begin our history and end with the constitution are becoming visible again today. The democrats should thus listen to Helmut Schmidt's warning that no people can exist in the long term without a national identity: "If our German history is only to be evaluated as a single chain of crimes and failures and acts of neglect . . . then our people's present could lose its stability, and that could risk the future." There is good reason to ask how much history weighs in Germany.

Source: *Frankfurter Allgemeine Zeitung*, November 26, 1986

ANDREAS HILLGRUBER

Letter to the Editor of the *Frankfurter Allgemeine Zeitung*, November 29, 1986

Christian Meier ("Kein Schlußwort—Zum Streit um dei NS Vergangenheit" [Not a Concluding Remark—On the Dispute about the Nazi Past] in the *Frankfurter Allgemeine Zeitung* of November 20) writes: "What moved Hillgruber to 'identify' with the defenders of the front in East Prussia will probably have to remain a mystery." Is it really so difficult for a German historian (even if he is, like Meier, a specialist in ancient history) to realize why the author of an essay about the collapse in the East in 1944–1945 identifies with the efforts of the German populace? I identified with the German efforts not only in East Prussia but also in Silesia, East Brandenburg, and Pomerania (Meier's homeland) to protect themselves from what threatened them and to save as many people as possible. For me Meier's remarks on this question (and those of many historian colleagues) support the conclusion of Alfred Heuß—for national history a conclusion full of grave resignation—that the "weak sensitivity about the most serious consequences of the war" (that is, the resettlement of the Germans out of the eastern regions and the loss of their territory) belongs "to the oddest phenomena of contemporary Germany. It is similar to when a Frenchman thinks about the loss of Indochina."

Source: *Frankfurter Allgemeine Zeitung*, November 29, 1986

Publisher's Note: The letter to the editor appeared under the title "So Difficult to Realize?"

RICHARD LÖWENTHAL

Letter to the Editor of the *Frankfurter Allgemeine Zeitung*, November 29, 1986

Johann Georg Reißmüller (*Frankfurter Allgemeine Zeitung*, November 14) has inserted himself with more expertise on the Soviet side than many of his predecessors into the recent German debate on the comparability with or fundamental difference between the mass annihilations of Hitler and the mass annihilations in the Soviet Union—but not without some erroneous judgments. Just as certainly as it is to be welcomed that he rejects the fashionable tendency of "balancing" the crimes of the masters of various nations in various times, is it certain that he is a victim of incorrectly equating the mass killings during the regimes of Lenin and Stalin and therefore of the regimes of Hitler and Lenin.

What Reißmüller has overlooked is the decisive fact that from the beginning of 1918, shortly after the Communists seized power, until spring 1921, after the Kronstadt rebellion, Lenin found himself in a chain of civil wars. This cannot be said of Stalin or Hitler. The same erroneous judgment had already led Ernst Nolte, in his 1974 book *Deutschland und der kalte Krieg* [Germany and the Cold War], to make the observation, which really does sound like a "settling of accounts," that every (large) country has had its "Hitler period." In fact, European, by no means only Russian, history is full of civil wars, including the wars of religion, which as a rule were far bloodier than other wars. But none of the civil wars consisted of the one-sided mass annihilation of defenseless people; nor did Lenin's battle to hold on to power: It was conducted against the military alliance of social revolutionaries with the Czech troops that remained in Russia; against the Cossack uprising; and against the uprisings of General Denikin supported by Allied troops in the South and Northwest, in Koltchak in the East, and in 1920 following the Polish attack and the counterattack that ultimately failed. The Bolshevik troop units consisted of workers and of peasants defending their newly won land and in the Polish war consisted of career officers. In 1920 increasing peasant uprisings and worker dissatisfaction reached their peak in the Kronstadt Sailors' Rebellion. In all these battles there were heavy losses on both sides and horrible torture and murders of prisoners. More than a few anticommunist Germans took part who, once returned to the homeland, reported proudly on the deeds of their side in the literature of the 1920s—and Hitler read these accounts.

These events were certainly not historically singular in their brutality and destruction. Nor was the erection, mentioned by Reißmüller, of concentration camps for opponents whom he, without referring to the civil wars, labels in quotation marks as "enemies." Actually, political opponents, and not opponents captured in battle, were put in these camps; but prisoners were not, as in Stalin's time, held for life. As a student who had just freed himself from his Communist illusions, I became acquainted with some somewhat older Mensheviks, who told me about their fate in these camps.

What Stalin did from 1929 on was something entirely different. Stalin systematically deprived millions of peasants, whom he called kulaks, of their rights. They were by no means generally large farmers but were simply seen as a hindrance to forced collectivization. They were not organized. They had not fought. They were shipped to far-away concentration camps and in general were not killed right away but were forced to suffer conditions that led in the course of time to a miserable death. And—in contrast to Reißmüller's article—this gradual mass murder was for a long time unknown abroad. The foreign journalists, from Germany to the United States, did not travel into the agrarian regions that were undergoing the revolution. When they heard rumors, most of them preferred to be silent. The first systematic portrayal of these camps came, according to my knowledge, in the course of the Second World War from Poles, who had been put in such camps themselves because of the partition of their country. But they had been released, after the Soviet-British alliance forced by Hitler, and reorganized into Polish troop units that came to England on a detour through the Near East. The book on their fate and the fate of the Russians in Stalin's camps appeared in England—with an introduction by Eliot.

What Stalin did from 1929 both against peasants and against various other victims, including leading Communists (among them, incidentally, Bucharin, who in 1929 had already publicly taken a position against the new "system") and returned soldiers, was in fact historically new in its systematic inhumanity and to this extent comparable with the deeds of Hitler. Certainly Hitler, like all his contemporaries, had a preconception of the civil wars of Lenin's time. Just as certainly his own ideas about the total annihilation of the Jews, the Gypsies, the "unworthy of life," and so on, were independent of Stalin's example. At any rate the idea of total annihilation of the Jews had already been developed in the last work of Hitler's mentor, Dietrich Eckart, who died in 1924. For the reference to this source, which leaves no room for "balancing," I am grateful to Ernst

Nolte's first large book, which appeared in 1963, *Faschismus in seiner Epoche* [Fascism in Its Epoch].

Source: *Frankfurter Allgemeine Zeitung*, November 29, 1986

Publisher's Note: This letter appeared under the title "Distorted History."

WOLFGANG J. MOMMSEN

Neither Denial nor Forgetfulness Will Free Us from the Past: Harmonizing Our Understanding of History Endangers Freedom

For several years now we in the Federal Republic have observed a newly awakened interest in history and in particular in our own national history. This has occurred after years of a weariness with history that caused professional historians like Alfred Heuß to lament a "loss of history" as a form of original memory in modern industrial society. The relative weariness with history of recent decades manifested itself in the displacement of history in favor of social studies in the curricula of secondary schools—despite the fact that historical research was running on all cylinders. This development was based primarily on political reasons.

In the period of almost uninterrupted economic growth that the Federal Republic has experienced since the 1950s, the view of the public is understandably mainly focused toward the future. The great social and political problems seemed to be solved, the society seemed to be on the right economic course. The contrasting image of the conditions in the GDR lent these assumptions additional impetus, or so it seemed. The prevalent opinion that social and political problems were fundamentally solvable with the methods of modern science provided the empirical social sciences a key position in the public mind.

Today, we are far removed from these optimistic expectations. It turned out that the trust in the fundamental solvability of all social problems that played such a dominant role in the public mind of those decades was not in sync with the real conditions. The oil shock; the failure of economic strategies, be they Keynesian or purely market-oriented à la Milton Friedman, to secure economic growth and full employment in the long term; the rise in the so-called third world of fundamentalist modes of thought, which for all intents and purposes nullified the optimistic modernization strategies of the 1950s—all these factors have to be mentioned here, as do recent experiences with the peaceful use of atomic energy, which once again demonstrated the limits of our ability to dominate nature and society by rational methods. This again made us more prepared to think about the limitations of our existence. And a part of that was reflection about our historical existence, our place within historical development.

These general factors, which led worldwide not only to an interest in the antiquated but also to an existentially rooted historical consciousness, are joined by special conditions peculiar to Germany. In large parts of the German public sphere of the immediate postwar years there was a tendency to duck a history that included collective guilt and, in many cases, personal involvement. The immediate past was something that one did not talk about and that one was only willing to deal with in a limited way. Because of this, as Friedrich Tenbruck pointed out, a rupture of historical consciousness took place.

DISRUPTED COMMUNICATION

The natural communication between the generations about our own history seemed to be disrupted. The dialogue between fathers and sons and grandsons about a shared historical heritage was only partially successful. Recent history appeared to be tabooed, despite the fact that historical research and the media addressed themselves to these themes with great intensity. The research appears to have reached people who were professionally interested, and, to some extent, the politicians—but it only reached the general public in a limited way. Here the prevailing tendency was to shun the events of recent history and to exclude them from German history wherever possible.

At the same time, professional historians were engaged in critically dealing with the recent German past, partially with the openly declared intention of clearing away the ideological rubble that was preventing democratic traditions from gaining a firm foothold in the Federal Republic. This was also accompanied by the attempt to again establish a link with historical research in the Western countries.

A part of these endeavors was a step-by-step radical revision of the traditional German image of history. This began with an examination of the history of National Socialism and a fundamental stock-taking of the reasons for the fall of the Weimar Republic. It was followed by an examination of the antidemocratic and authoritarian traditions in German political thought and in German politics that led to the national catastrophe of 1933 and to the collapse of the Third Reich. In historical research these "revisionist" endeavors gradually won ground from the late 1950s on, and in the 1960s and 1970s they were even able to conquer a hegemonic position within German history. This, however, does not apply to the same degree to the penetration of this thought into the institutional system of the discipline. Here, a silent majority of more traditionally oriented historians predominated.

For a number of years now, the hegemonic position of the revisionists in the public mind—if not within the discipline itself—has increasingly come under attack. A political shift is apparent. This was in part due to intra-disciplinary reasons: in the eagerness to get rid of the antidemocratic elements in the German tradition, the revisionists had taken their criticism too far. But this political shift also corresponded to a reawakened public need to determine the historical location of contemporary consciousness, which was no longer supposed to exhaust itself on negative criticism. According to an expression that has since become popular, the call arose for a new German national identity or at least a new identity for the citizens of the Federal Republic—an identity that would have to rest on a historical foundation.

Thomas Nipperdey made himself the spokesman of the new tendencies when he, particularly in reaction to Hans-Ulrich Wehler, demanded that the discipline of history in the Federal Republic should stop one-sidedly emphasizing the stream of events in German history that led to 1933. Instead, it should equally—if not preferably—turn to other chains of events, such as those that led to the Federal Republic. Furthermore, Michael Stürmer pointed out that it was of immediate historical impor-tance that once again in the Federal Republic a unified understanding of history was developing that was capable of shaping a consensus. Only nations that possessed a unified, consistent understanding of their history were politically predictable for their alliance partners and thus able to be considered reliable partners. And this rule, he argued, was particularly valid for the Federal Republic.

These processes demonstrate that the shunning of recent German his-tory has given way in the public mind to a lively interest—an interest that is so elemental that its political instrumentalization is an obvious possibil-ity, whether in the sense of instituting a new identity under the sign of existing political and social conditions, or whether for the purpose of mobilizing or consolidating the supporters of political parties and group-ings. It is no coincidence that we are now seeing an increasing tendency to use historical consciousness for political purposes.

The federal government has decided to found two new historical museums. One of these is to be located in West Berlin and devoted to the cultivation of German history from its beginnings. The other, which will be built in Bonn, is to present the history of the Federal Republic. The controversy about the museums, fought with great passion, demonstrates that fundamental questions are at play here. From these projects the government expects to strengthen the identity of the citizens of the Federal Republic. The opposition camp is concerned that this is an attempt to prescribe a one-sidedly nationalist-conservative understanding of history. The Social Democrats have long been involved in utilizing the newly awakened interest in local history and the history of everyday life to politically mobilize their followers. Apart from questions about whether this is a sensible undertaking, it is becoming clear that historical consciousness is again being seen as a factor of great importance for the political orientation of the citizens.

In addition to this, important changes in our historical consciousness are becoming evident. They are doubtless connected to current political interests and political convictions but they also reach into deeper levels. They directly touch on our understanding of the nature of the German nation as well as on the question of the historical location of the Federal Republic in German and European history. Since 1945, three stages of development in the thought of the Federal Republic about the German question can be discerned. However, in light of the lack of clarity about what these questions mean, these stages cannot always be distinguished.

Among the leaders of opinion of West German society in the first decade after 1945, the tendencies to seek orientation in the Weimar Republic for fundamental national questions prevailed without controversy. But this meant nothing other than, in questions of the nation and of the role of the Germans in Europe and the world, linking up with the German—or more precisely, the *kleindeutsch*—national state. Thus the Federal Republic did not find it difficult to publicly celebrate—even in a ceremony in the Bundestag—the 150th birthday of Otto von Bismarck. The reunification clause of the constitution and the determination in its preamble that this constitution would remain provisional until the German nation was unified in freedom support this view. Today, however, we find it far more difficult than did the generation after 1945 to view the German Reich of 1871 as a point of orientation for our national identity. I will get back to this.

From the end of the 1950s on, a slow and cautious partial reorientation of the national consciousness of the Germans in the Federal Republic began. For the minority of Germans who were actively engaged with their own past and its mistaken developments, not only the Weimar period but also the Bismarck era and, in particular, the period of Wilhelm II lost much of the luster that they had possessed for the great majority of the older generation and that, despite the experiences of Weimar, they had never completely lost. For the newer generation the consensus of opinion was that only a thorough revision of the German understanding of history that relentlessly laid bare the authoritarian traits of the Kaiserreich and the antidemocratic mentality of the Weimar period would be capable of opening up space for a new democratic order that was not merely pragmatically accepted but rather internalized as a free consensus of its citizens. For this generation, establishing a link to the liberal and democratic traditions of the West was a fundamental moral obligation. In the area of history writing, this conviction was particularly evident in the critique of the ideology of the so-called German *Sonderweg*, or special path, between Western, allegedly materialistic, democracy and Eastern autocracy. This is a dichotomy that had been articulated in various ways in the past. The ideology of the German *Sonderweg* had always been the backbone of the antiliberal and antidemocratic positions that had prevented a fundamental adaptation of the political order to the rapidly changing economic and social conditions that had taken place in Western Europe.

It was no coincidence that in that period the national idea became discredited. It was becoming increasingly clear that an excess of a hybrid nationalism had caused the series of political catastrophes that began with the First World War and ended with the dictatorship of National Socialism and its gigantic war of destruction, which, in the end, also brought about the end of the German nation.

In the beginning of the 1960s Karl Jaspers had made himself the spokesman of such opinions. He explained that the national idea was outmoded. In the present international historical situation, he argued, a moral mission of leadership falls to the German people. They can fulfill this imperative by making a symbolic act and departing forever from the national idea. In fact, in many circles at that time national orientation, which was no longer present in the younger generation, was displaced by the idea of a united Europe.

Even though the official language relating to reunification continued to be used unchanged in this period—in part under the influence of the cold war—the ground was gradually prepared for the insight that a solution to the German question could only come, if at all, within a European framework—in other words, only as part of a fundamental restructuring of the conditions in East-Central Europe, which for their part would presume the collapse of the Soviet Empire, a premise unthinkable at the time. Many politicians of that period, among them Konrad Adenauer himself, time and time again used the words *nation* and *national*, but usually only in a cautious manner. When important matters were at hand, nationalist rhetoric was always sacrificed for political realities, and at times even for partisan rationale, as was again recently demonstrated in relation to Adenauer's reaction to the Soviet note of 1952 on reunification.

In any case, in the 1950s and 1960s it would have occurred to no one to demand the reawakening of a German national consciousness, much less a German national history museum with the purpose of strengthening the national identity of the Germans. On the contrary, people were still concerned with getting rid of the remnants of old nationalist and German-national traditions. Rather, economic and political integration into the West was on the agenda—without ever doubting that the Germans of the Federal Republic were members of a German nation that was, however, never thought of as a territorial or concretely political unity. The embittered dispute about the German defense contribution to a European army and then the establishment of an independent West German army ended up in a deadlock. These turned out to be rearguard actions of a national German idea that was no longer perceived as real.

From the middle of the 1970s, a fundamental change in these matters became evident. True, the politics of Western integration were no longer controversial, except possibly for the extreme Left and the extreme Right of the political spectrum. The question of reunification, too, and with it the binding force of the national idea, lost much of its previously explosive power in the aftermath of the *Ostverträge* [the German treaties with the Soviet Union and other Eastern European nations]. With the end of the cold war the inner cohesiveness of the political and social system of the Federal Republic lost much of the glue that held it together. The student movement of the years after 1968 signaled that the pragmatic political consensus in the Federal Republic, based upon growing prosperity and the negative example of the Communist dictatorship in the GDR, had become fragile.

THE CALL FOR IDENTITY

The conflict generated by the student movement that pitted the older generation against the younger generation on the question of what moral stance to take toward increasing material prosperity and toward the political order gave impetus to the demand that steps be taken against the severe loss of historical consciousness evident in the younger generation. Step by step, the politics behind the status of the subject history were turned around in the public schools—although not in a short time.

It was of far more fundamental importance that the call for a new national identity, one that could be established on a historical foundation, became increasingly louder. This corresponded to a general trend in the public mind that was more than just the result of political opportunism, although this, too, most likely played a role. The astonishing success of a whole series of large historical exhibits speaks for itself. One of these, the Prussia exhibit, is especially important, for a state that had been declared persona non grata was helped to a new—if largely critical—status. Related to this is the fact that German histories were again in demand, as were books about great personalities in German history—even if they were not written in prose accessible to the general public.

This development can only be termed positive, no matter from which ideological or political standpoint it is viewed. But related to this there was also a partial deviance from historical positions that in many cases had been developed by West German historians of the middle generation in close cooperation with Western researchers. It began when the group of historians that had endeavored to use the methods of social history to develop a new interpretation of recent German history was accused of taking the German past too strongly to task. It was undisputed for this generation that historical research was to orient itself toward the fundamental values of a democratic society and that history was to be written in the light of these—openly declared—values. But just this was challenged by referring to the traditional historical opinion that, as Leopold von Ranke put it, "every epoch has its own direct access to God" and must thus be understood as a result of its own preconditions.

In the same context the thesis of the German *Sonderweg* came under attack as a historically unjustifiable separation of the Germans from the overall European development. This was warranted to the degree that the paradigm of the German *Sonderweg* inappropriately idealized the actual political and social developments in the Western European nations. But the polemic against the so-called *Sonderweg* thesis, which referred to comparable phenomena or processes in other European nations, was aimed at shaking up the normative force of this model and in this way more or less weakening the criticism of the German development that came from the viewpoint of a democratic society. There are many *Sonderwege*, as the formula would have it, and the German *Sonderweg* was only one of these. And the German version was by and large no better and no worse than that of other peoples.

A bitter dispute about the role of Adolf Hitler within the National-Socialist system of rule developed under similar points of view. The central function of the führer in all decisive questions, and in particular in the policy of annihilating the Jews, was frequently emphasized in order to use the concept of fascism to block the political argumentation of the Marxist left. This was coupled with an attempt to limit the responsibility of the German nation for the terrible events during the National Socialist era— which were governed by a strategy aimed at resurrecting a German or a West German consciousness. Recently Ernst Nolte succinctly—and perhaps unintentionally—gave expression to the tendencies of the neohistorical direction within West German history writing, this being a reaction to the revisionist positions of the past decades. He gave a commentary in *Die Zeit* the subtitle "Against Negative Nationalism in Interpreting History."

The reaction to the history writing of the past decades, inasmuch as it was in the main concerned with a critical appraisal of German national history, is the product of political motivation. In fact, in the past few years, Ernst Nolte has spoken with concern about the fact that a radical critical debate about the German past could also generate critical potentials that could turn against the political order of the Federal Republic. Thus in recent years Nolte has distanced himself from the use of a comprehensive concept of fascism—despite the fact that he himself had initially brought this concept into circulation. The reason is that since the end of the 1960s the New Left had used the concept of fascism for a Marxist critique of Western societies. It is doubtless also a good assumption that Nolte's recent endeavors to interpret the National-Socialist policy of annihilating the Jews from a comparative and universalist perspective, and in this way to reduce its singularity, stems from the need to oppose a similarly one-sided political exploitation of the Holocaust.

Of course the protest against Nolte is not aimed at Nolte's attempt to compare the crimes of National Socialism with other cases of genocide, such as the extermination of the Armenian population in Turkey during the First World War or, to an even greater degree, the so-called Gulag Archipelago, that is, the Bolshevik policy of annihilating certain social groups, or the "great purge" of the 1930s. It was his attempt to portray Nazi crimes as a direct reaction to an alleged or real threat by the Bolsheviks' "Asiatic" policy of annihilation that engendered protest from so many sides. This is an explanatory strategy that—intended or not—will be seen as a justification of National-Socialist crimes by all those who are still under the influence of the extreme anti-Soviet propaganda of National Socialism.

In a recently published reply to these protests, Ernst Nolte withdrew this argument to the degree that he now only speaks of Hitler's purely psychological conception of the threat, not of a real causal relationship between the Gulag Archipelago and the policy of destroying the Jews. But this clarification is not sufficient. It is inappropriate to try to justify or otherwise reduce the immorality of the National-Socialist policy of terror by referring to comparable processes in the realm of Bolshevism—precisely because National Socialism was able to untruthfully style itself for German society as a savior delivering the Germans from Bolshevism.

Recently revived attempts to connect the misdevelopment of recent German history—in comparison to Western European peoples or to the United States—to Germany's so-called central location in Europe must also be understood in this context. This is an explanatory model that has neo-Rankean origins and clearly has antiliberal tendencies. It is well known that numerous historians, particularly of the neo-Rankean school, have attempted to justify the relative backwardness of the German constitution in the nineteenth century by suggesting that the Reich was threatened by rival powers. This threat, it is suggested, forced the Reich to organize as an authoritarian state based on power. Max Weber responded to this by pointing out the superiority of Western nations in crisis situations. The experience of the past half-century has confirmed this totally.

It is in the same context that Klaus Hildebrand recently took up the thesis according to which the First World War resulted primarily from the breakdown of the so-called balance of power rather than primarily from the aggressive tendencies as they had developed in the period of high imperialism, particularly in the German Reich, but also in other European great powers and in other, second-rank powers. Thus there is no longer any mention here of the prominent responsibility of German policy for the outbreak of the First World War.

THE FRONT LINE OF CRITICISM
One can be of various opinions about the relative justification of such arguments. They all contain, as do most historical interpretations, a grain

of truth without necessarily being true. But there can hardly be a doubt about the thrust of such arguments in the current intellectual climate. They are aimed at pushing the front line of criticism of Germany's recent past far enough back that the general public can once again establish a less guilt-laden identification with its own national past. This is by no means an attempt to insinuate that this process must always be associated with a conscious political agenda—although this is doubtless the case with Michael Stürmer's argument in favor of founding a new German understanding of history that is at least capable of building a consensus (we have already alluded to this).

It would doubtless not be incorrect to assume that since taboos have been removed from recent German history, the broad public has evinced a certain reluctance to see its own history portrayed primarily in a critical, distanced way. There is a new need for historical assurance and a positive experience of identification with one's own historical tradition.

This recently found expression in the predominantly positive evaluation of the personality of Frederick the Great on the occasion of the two hundredth anniversary of his death. The same can be said for Martin Luther or Otto von Bismarck, and to a lesser degree for Leopold von Ranke—personalities that had already, in the Wilhelmenian period, been elevated to the level of icons for German national consciousness.

The question remains, however, whether it is a good idea to exploit this tendency in a neoconservative sense, as Michael Stürmer recently demanded when he wrote that "in a country without history" the person who "determines the content of memory, coins concepts, and interprets the past" will win the future. It seems to us that history, and particularly our own national history, is not at our disposal in such an arbitrary way as these statements presume. Insurmountable hurdles stand in the way of efforts to find a path back to a harmonious German history—particularly where this entails ignoring events of which we as a nation have to be ashamed. It would only be possible to jump over these hurdles by accepting a loss of the principle of intellectual honesty. I would like to name a few of the hurdles, although I cannot illuminate in detail the problems connected with them.

THE REALITY OF DIVISION

First there is the problem of which actual citizens should assume the recently much-invoked national identity of the Germans. The reality of the division of Germany poses the question whether an—alleged or real—German national consciousness refers primarily to the citizens of the Federal Republic or to the citizens of both German states or even to everyone that could in a general sense be counted as members of the German *Kulturnation* [nation defined by shared cultural values].

This is a problem that cannot be easily solved, one for which fewer and fewer satisfactory answers have been provided from the traditional reference to legal and constitutional traditions—in other words, in reference to the legal succession of the Federal Republic from the German Reich of 1871—assuming that the borders of 1933 are meant. There is little doubt that the historical model of the German Reich shaped by Bismarck has lost much of its attractiveness for political orientation. It cannot be assumed to be a valid norm for a historical or political national consciousness for the younger generation. It is important here that the fateful events that are connected to the history and the prehistory of National Socialism in Germany have become a barrier between the recent history of Germans in the Federal Republic and the rest of German history. It is also important here that the history of the Federal Republic can with some justification be seen as successful and doubtless gives us reason to look back with pride.

It would be simple if we could be satisfied with beginning our own national history with a zero hour set in 1945 or with the reestablishment of a German state in the western zones of Germany, or even with the two states. But this is quite simply not possible. The long-term continuities of our history, the good as well as the bad—cannot be simply eradicated. Their historical force continues to have an influence, no matter how we feel about it. Not only that: We would also be conducting the business of those East German ideologues who wish nothing more than the development of two German national states of distinctly different character—with the additional aspect that the GDR is attempting to claim for itself the positive elements of the German national tradition and of the so-called German cultural heritage.

In both German states these constellations have led, for different reasons, to attempts to establish connections to elements of the traditions of German statehood and German national culture, which after 1945 had been shoved aside. Examples would be the rediscovery of Prussia and the at least partial rehabilitation of Frederick the Great and traditional Prussian virtues. But the dilemma that erected a permanent barrier between the present and the history of the Germans in the Kaiserreich and preceding centuries cannot be disposed of; it can only be ameliorated.

For this reason voices have recently been heard demanding that we should draw a final line under these things and that we should not constantly be called upon to deal with them. In the political arena, the act of conciliation in Bitburg was supposed to be a kind of line drawn under that segment of German history. But it turned out that, at least in terms of intellectual honesty, that cannot be done and that no matter what we do, other peoples will not be willing to accept such an act from us. In his famous speech of May 8 last year, the president said important and valid things about this. It is still a fact that we cannot escape the burden of the past by personal forgetfulness or by a late birth.

BITTER TRUTHS

It is equally true that historical reinterpretations will not reduce this burden. Andreas Hillgruber recently attempted to accord a relative historical justification to the *Wehrmacht* campaign in the East and the desperate resistance of the army in the East after the summer of 1944. He argued that the goal was to prevent the German civilian population from falling into the hands of the Red Army. However, the chief reason, he argued, was that the defense of German cities in the East had become tantamount to defending Western civilization. In light of the Allied war goals, which, independent of Stalin's final plans, envisioned breaking up Prussia and destroying the defensive position of a strong, Prussian-led central European state that could serve as a bulwark against Bolshevism, the continuation of the war in the East was justified from the viewpoint of those involved. It was, as Hillgruber's argument would have it, also justified even from today's standpoint, despite the fact that prolonging the war in the East meant that the gigantic murder machinery of the Holocaust would be allowed to continue to run. All this, the essay argued, was justified as long as the fronts held. Hillgruber's essay is extremely problematic when viewed from the perspective of a democratically constituted community that orients itself toward Western moral and political standards.

There is no getting around the bitter truth that the defeat of National Socialist Germany was not only in the interest of the peoples who were bulldozed by Hitler's war and of the peoples who were selected by his henchmen for annihilation or oppression and exploitation—it was also in the interest of the Germans. Accordingly, parts of the gigantic scenery of the Second World War were, at least as far as we were concerned, totally senseless, even self-destructive. We cannot escape this bitter truth by assigning partial responsibility to other partners who took part in the war.

These unavoidable truths also cast a long shadow on our relationship with the German history of earlier epochs—which we of course cannot, as has been correctly noted, reduce to the prehistory of the "German catastrophe" of 1933–1945. This, however, means that we can only practice German history in a critical way. The first commandment here will have to be to understand the history of the German nation in a European, even in a world context—and not, as has been done so often in the past, in opposition to other peoples.

In the period of the Reformation these other peoples were—particularly in the field of religion—the corrupt Italians. Then, from the late eighteenth century on, France; then "perfidious Albion." This happened because the history of the Germans, as a nation in the middle of a Europe that for centuries formed the cultural, political, and religious bridge between East and West, between North and South, has been tightly interwoven with the history of Europe—or, as Leopold von Ranke put it, with the Roman-Germanic nation. This was already the case for the early phase of the German nation in the late period of Carolingian France and has really never been different. The Germans had to pay for the hegemonic role they played in medieval Europe and their modest position in the Holy Roman Empire with a comparatively late development as a nation. This development also left a third of the ethnic-cultural Germans outside the national borders. The shaping influence of the German Reich—a semiconstitutional state with strong authoritarian traits—on the German national consciousness was extraordinary. However, it showed deep inner fracture lines and accentuated ways of life and values that have largely become estranged from us. Only in the economic-social sector is there still much that connects us with that period; there is little in the area of political culture.

Viewed from that kind of long-term perspective, it seems to us to be an open question whether the German Reich founded by Bismarck could offer us the indispensable standard of political organization for the Germans. Or isn't a plurality of German states in the middle of Europe the European norm—if there is such a thing in history? It appears in many aspects that with the establishment of two German states on the soil of the old German Reich and with the rise of an independent Austria, German history has returned to the era before 1867, that is, to the existence of several German states within one German nation in the center of Europe. This of course does not mean that the German question has been laid to rest. It means that in the improbable and scarcely imaginable case that the deadlocked fronts of the superpowers should again be set in motion, a fedcrative solution would be more probable than a so-called reunification in the sense that the GDR would simply be annexed by the FRG as was envisioned in the 1950s and 1960s.

The history of the German nation is not only more tightly interwoven with the history of other European peoples than that of many other neighbors, it is also to a strong degree a history with a controversial nature. There has always been a lack of national and political unity. Germany has often been fragmented into various groups with often quite independent cultural traditions. This is just as peculiar to German history as is the religious division of the nation since the Reformation or the extraordinary diversity of political forms, with a great number of regional centers of political power existing in the eighteenth and early nineteenth century.

It may be said that many of the national characteristics of the Germans go back to just this situation. However, they are also the reason for many of the great German cultural accomplishments. Max Weber noted with a certain regret that it was not in the center of the Reich that great cultural achievements were produced. Friedrich Nietzsche spoke much more bitterly when he said that the foundation of the German Reich went hand in hand with the extirpation of the German intellect. Nietzsche was doubtless exaggerating. But in retrospect a certain justification cannot be denied them. Critically dealing with one's own national history thus in no way means rejecting specific achievements of German culture.

A DECISIVE ORIENTATION TOWARD THE WEST

Furthermore, we should be conscious of an additional condition. The decisive westward orientation of German policy and the political-social consciousness of the 1950s and 1960s that accompanied the founding of the Federal Republic and its consolidation as a state went hand in hand with the Germans opting for a reorientation of their historical-political consciousness. They consciously turned away from part of the German historical tradition—not by repressing it, but by opting for political models such as were available to us in Western Europe and the United States.

The reason for this was not to shake the burden of history from our shoulders. Rather, the Germans decided to take a more constructive path in the future, a path that would not again lead to insoluble conflicts with our western and eastern neighbors. We have every reason to hold steady on this course. Knowing what historical burden we as a people have to bear is at the same time one of the foundations of freely recognizing and accepting the liberal political order of the Federal Republic as the basis of our social order. If this fact were to be forgotten, it would mean the undermining of the consensus that exists today and binds all important social groups to the notion that this order is worthy of being maintained.

In the years after 1945, the establishment of a liberal order based on freedom was only possible by breaking with important elements of the German tradition and by voluntarily accepting Western European models. It is true that the fathers of the constitution were able to link up with the democratic constitution of Weimar. But this document, too, is the result of appropriating Western constitutional positions whose validity for the German situation had until then been rejected—despite a long liberal and democratic tradition in Germany itself. Viewed this way, the prehistory of the Federal Republic has in an important way not only a German but also a European character. Without the symbiosis of Western and German political traditions as was achieved after 1945, the growth and solid rootedness of these traditions would not have been possible.

In the Weimar period the attempt to achieve the symbiosis of German and Western European thought that Ernst Troeltsch had so passionately supported failed—with destructive consequences. This symbiosis meant a link-up with the intellectual and political traditions of the West—which were supplemented by the addition of many elements from German history. One should not place this synthesis in danger for short-term political goals.

Political decisions since 1947 have meant opting for Western thought— and that cannot be placed in question without risking grave consequences, a fact that should particularly be recognized by those who are part of the political succession of Konrad Adenauer. This by no means suggests a complete break with the German past—especially because German history has always been a European history to a greater degree than has the history of other nations.

Instead of giving in to the prevailing need for harmonizing our understanding of history, we should remain conscious of the plurality of the political, cultural, and religious creations in Germany. This corresponds to the fact that today, too, German history is interpreted from a variety of political viewpoints. One should not try to change that. Losing the principle of free competition of differing views of history would be tantamount to losing freedom. It would endanger the very liberal order of the Federal Republic that is supposed to be "strengthened" by revivifying a so-called German understanding of history.

Source: *Frankfurter Rundschau*, December 1, 1986

HORST MÖLLER

What May Not Be, Cannot Be: A Plea for Rendering Factual the Controversy about Recent History

The criticism, raised in an article by the Frankfurt social philosopher Jürgen Habermas, that there are "apologetic tendencies" in the study of recent history has caused high tempers recently and has reached into the columns of the daily newspapers. Even the recent Nobel Peace Prize winner Elie Wiesel has agreed with this criticism, and in a television interview he characterized the historians attacked by Habermas, without checking the validity of Habermas's accusations, as a "gang of four."

Without a doubt, if "apologetic tendencies" of the sort claimed, that is, a defense of the Nazi dictatorship, appeared in the scholarly writing of history, it would be occasion for the greatest concern. Fortunately these tendencies do not exist. Habermas invented them, and those who follow him uncritically—naturally always with the word "critical" on their lips— do not take the trouble to inform themselves about the state of the scholarly discussion or to read the books of the authors attacked. It is significant that Habermas takes only a few of the authors' lectures to account, rather than any of their larger books. In Klaus Hildebrand's case, he is even satisfied with a review. A review, to be sure, can be more quickly read than this author's countless important books and treatises, which have enriched our understanding of the Nazi period. One can best maintain prejudices without sufficient knowledge. Habermas himself, and not a few others who follow him, are not interested in the historical problem at all; they are plainly led by political motives. They want to unmask a "*Wende*-oriented history" that does not exist.

Those involved are not interested in the fatal consequences that such weighty accusations could have for the political culture of the Federal Republic and the uneasiness the unproved assertion of "apologetic tendencies" must cause abroad. They are taking advantage of the privilege, unfortunately claimed by many intellectuals, of being irresponsible. Controversies are normal in scholarship and must be so. Slander and falsifications, however, should not be a part of the style of scholarly discussion even if a few sensation-hungry journalists are more committed to sensa-

216

tionalism than to scholarly questions. Forged "Hitler journals" keep the presses rolling, while the development of scholarly research on Hitler is pursued by only a few. That would be no problem if altogether too many people did not believe that it was all right to work as a dilettante in writing recent history. Justifiably, however, the assessment of the Nazi dictatorship has a key position for political consciousness in the Federal Republic. Developments in the assessment of this epoch of German history are for this reason often regarded as a seismograph for our political culture.

With regard to any complex of historical topics analyzed by scholarship there is progress, there are changes in the formulation of questions, there are broadenings and differentiations of our state of knowledge. This also applies to the study of the Nazi dictatorship. If this were not so, one could in the future call off research and "reeducate" those who conducted it. The Third Reich is, however, a topic of public discussion and a constituent of the antitotalitarian self-understanding in the Federal Republic. It is fundamentally also a topic of scholarship that over time has produced an abundance of insights on which the experts agree. This part of scholarly findings is not an object for discussion but for the acquisition of established knowledge. No historian engaged in scholarly work discusses indisputable facts. Rather, he discusses solely their arrangement and categorization, their explanation, and so on. Even this is not merely a matter of opinion but the result of objective scholarly argumentation. In order to clarify the background of the controversy, to the extent that it has a scholarly dimension, a few basic positions of the contemporary interpretation of the Nazi dictatorship need to be mentioned. For reasons of space this can be done only sketchily. Even in this it is clear that Habermas's attempt—based on social-political motives—to firmly ascribe a particular image of history after 1933 is a misunderstanding of the pluralistic character of scholarship in the Federal Republic and ignores the fundamental commandment of scholarly freedom.

Habermas ignores, furthermore, a change that has been apparent since the beginning of the 1960s in the posing of questions on this topic. Thus Ernst Nolte's path-breaking work *Faschismus in seiner Epoche* [Fascism in Its Epoch] opened the way in 1963 for a scholarly use of the term *fascism* by delimiting it by epoch and comparatistically defining it in the European context. Even at that time, Nolte interpreted fascism and National Socialism as a response to another totalitarian ideology, that of Bolshevism and its revolution of 1917. With this work Nolte arrested the inflationary political use of the term *fascism*, emptied of its concrete epochal content, within the scholarly community. In the earlier totalitarianism theory, the term had been either dogmatically narrowed in the sense of Marxism-Leninism or degraded as a cheap demagogic slogan against many different opponents.

Habermas discovered this fundamental conception of Nolte's twenty-three years after the fact and felt alarmed. Without a doubt it was a sign of the putative *Wende*. Even Nolte's attempt, using analogies, to grasp the monstrous crime of the murder of the Jews as a product of the self-understanding of the Nazi leadership in no way constitutes an excuse. Rather, it is an attempt at an explanation. An important part of the explanation is the indisputable fact that the Nazi ideology was essentially anti-Bolshevist and that it confounded the declared goal of a Communist-Bolshevist world revolution with the alleged threat of a supposed "Jewish world conspiracy." Such conspiracy theories do not excuse mass murder any more than the proclamation by Chaim Weizmann, the chief of the Jewish Agency—which could not be a declaration of war in the sense of international law—excuses the crime. But the analysis attempts to explain irrational fanaticism by means of rational categories. Herein lies the constant inadequacy of such interpretations. And similarly, the reference to the politically and ideologically motivated mass murders of the Stalinist Soviet Union that preceded them, or to those in other nations up until recent years, is not an attempt to make National Socialism harmless but to make it a simple fact. Such interpretations may have the explanatory value assumed by Nolte or they may not. They are not intended to be an "excuse" for National Socialism, nor can they be. In the strict sense all these crimes are "singular"; that is a banality. Nevertheless, comparisons are possible.

But precisely here we can recognize Habermas's political motive. He measures crime with two different yardsticks. He accuses Nolte of comparing the mass murder of the Jews with—word for word—"Stalin's expulsion of the kulaks." This so-called expulsion is in fact not "only" a deportation but, beyond that, a mass murder of a class of persons that the Fifteenth Congress of the Communist Party had declared to be "exploiters and enemies of the people." The act was organized by the Party and was handed over to liquidation commandos. Every critical reader can see here who is intent on making something seem harmless. The murder motivated by Communist ideology counts for Habermas as an "expulsion," and thus he linguistically preserves a sense of incomparability. With this kind of perversion of history one can, to be sure, prevent any analogy.

Similarly selective is Habermas's critique of Andreas Hillgruber's arguments about the end of the German Reich in 1945. Hillgruber comes to the conclusion, on the basis of British files that have come to light in the meantime, that the destruction of the German Reich was planned before the mass murder of the Jews became known—and that the mass murder does not explain the end of the Reich. This is a fact that the historian cannot ignore, as Habermas thinks. It is a fact that says nothing at all about the responsibility of the Nazi leadership. It is hardly disputable that the attempt to hold the eastern front as long as possible against the Red Army meant protection for the German civilian populace in the eastern provinces against murders, rapes, plundering, and expulsions by Soviet troops. It was not simply the Nazi propaganda against these "Asiatic hordes" that caused this climate of fear. It was the concrete example of Nemmersdorf in October 1944, mentioned by Hillgruber, that had brought the horror of the future occupation into clear view. Even here, the German atrocities in Russia can be brought in as explanation for but not an excuse of the Soviet crimes. The expulsion of the Germans from the eastern regions had confirmed the fears. It was already against international law then, even if one concedes that the war arising from the alliance that Hitler made with Stalin in 1939 was its first prerequisite. And Hillgruber says himself that every way the war was lengthened—regardless through what motives—extended the suffering and crimes in the concentration camps and the death camps. He also correctly characterizes this as an event of inextinguishable tragedy.

Let us turn back to fundamental patterns of explanation. Nolte's historicized and comparatistic interpretation of fascism appeared at the end of the 1960s alongside the similarity typologizing comparatistic analysis of National Socialism that employs a modified conception of totalitarianism. The best examples of this are the extensive studies of the Bonn historian Karl Dietrich Bracher and the works of the Bern historian Walther Hofer. Bracher was also, however, the one who, without sharing its consequences, showed the way for a third direction of scholarship. Since the end of the 1960s, above all since Martin Broszat's foundational work *Der Staat Hitlers* [Hitler's State] (1969), Bracher's direction has led to new perspectives and a new kind of social analysis. Already in his 1956 essay "Stufen totalitärer Gleichschaltung" [Gradual Accommodation and Synchronization to Totalitarian Rule], he had analyzed the polycratic structure of Nazi rule and evaluated as a planned instrument of domination of the führer dictatorship the existence of competing power groups and the overlapping of responsibilities. The question whether the Nazi dictatorship amounted to a planned and goal-directed reign or a chaotic and improvisational reign lies at the heart of a scholarly controversy that extends to more specific problems. For example, about who was responsible for the Reichstag fire. It also discusses forms of and the evaluation of the resistance. Above all, however, it treats the causes of the institutionalized millionfold murder of the Jews.

Besides this voluminous and detailed research, three essential directions of interpretation in Nazi research stand at present beside and against one another, so the most recent ones can be viewed as revisions of the older ones. Revision is thus in this area, as in the discipline in general, something quite obvious and in no way dishonorable, no matter how one judges the revision in a concrete case and whether it actually means scholarly progress.

Such reinterpretations aim at more differentiated explanations of causes or new historical categorizations, but in one regard there is utterly no dissent among serious historians: the equally unambiguous and decisive moral

220 / HORST MÖLLER

and political rejection of the Nazi dictatorship and its frightful crimes.

Naturally historians must analyze the cause of the murder of the Jews and seek to grasp the locus in the Third Reich in German and European history. There cannot be any prohibitions on questions. Not one of these interpretations is or aims at apology. The assertion of "apologetic tendencies" in the German historical research is either ignorant or shameless or both, particularly where the word apology means "defense." And in every book of the defamed historians, from Andreas Hillgruber and Klaus Hildebrand to Ernst Nolte, all of whom have made fundamental contributions to the research and interpretation of National Socialism, the Nazi crimes are called by name and none are defended. The alleged "apologetic" contribution, "Der geschichtliche Ort der Judenvernchtung" [The Historical Locus of the Annihilation of the Jews] in the volume attacked by Habermas, *Zweierlei Untergang* [Twofold Fall], begins with the sentence: "The historical dimension of that millionfold murder of the European Jews, for which the leadership of the Third Reich is responsible, unfolds in three ways." Hillgruber's analysis of the ideological preconditions is oriented toward the modern state of research. It interprets German anti-Semitism after 1933 as an essential part of the state ideology. It also speaks of the massive murder of old people, women, and children. Hillgruber emphasizes explicitly, however, that the historian must go "beyond keeping alive the memory of the millions of victims" and must pose the question of a possible repetition in different ideological conditions or in actual or supposedly extreme situations and constellations.

The search for analogies is no defense and no excuse but instead has belonged forever in the tool chest of the historian, even if every historian is familiar with the difficulties of such analogies. Furthermore, every reader of the books of the attacked authors—Michael Stürmer, whose research specialties lie in other areas than the Nazi period, counts as one of these authors—knows how different the statements of problems, methods, and modes of presentation are. To put them all together as a unified front of "apologetic *Wende* historians" is only possible if one thinks in monochrome images of history and tends to conspiracy theories. Common to all the attacked historian is, however, that not one of them is an "apologist."

Prescribing an image of national Socialism that predominates in public has nothing to do with free scholarship. And the doubtless necessary moral and political condemnation of National Socialism does not replace analysis and explanation. There remains, despite countless important studies, the continual task of the modern historian.

How absurd the present polemic actually is is shown by the scholarly-political goals contained in the oft-cited *Zeit* article. Thus not only are quotations of Hans Mommsen—whom Habermas unwittingly attacks after he praises him in the same breath—attributed to Andreas Hillgruber, but the lines get totally reversed, and some of the most decided revisionists stand closer to the current opposition than to the government. A more decidedly revisionist (and naturally just a little apologetic) school than that of Hans Mommsen has not appeared in the discipline—Mommsen in his articles characterizes Hitler as a "weak dictator" and significantly relativizes his place in the Nazi system of domination. He disputes finally that Hitler and the Nazi leadership carried out their concept in a planned way in their system of terror and that they were responsible, for example, for the Reichstag fire. Mommsen sees the Nazi leaders as prisoners of their own chaotic politics and anarchic structures of domination and authority. These structures led to cumulative radicalization and steady increases of dynamic activities. Mommsen is a Social Democrat and, at least in Habermas's political judgment, not a "*Wende* historian." And others, like Broszat, judge the mass murder of the Jews not—as in the "classical" interpretation—as a stepwise realization according to plan of a murderous anti-Semitism, but as a reaction that grew more or less radical depending on the situation and the crises in the Nazi leadership, under which there was hardly any flexibility in decision-making. Broszat has recently given a vehement plea "for historicizing National Socialism."

In an open and candid discussion these historians would have to admit that they are, with their rejection of the notion of a planned and goal-directed totalitarian dictatorship, much more "revisionist" than, for example, Andreas Hillgruber.

No matter whether one agrees with or rejects the interpretations mentioned above, they all must be possible in the framework of a pluralistic discipline in a democratic nation. They should not have to be defamed by a static—and thus unhistorical—image of history. This is an image of history that furthermore would leave the discipline of history no autonomy but would like instead to put it in the service of social-political pedagogy.

These conclusions are also valid if one, like the present author, holds that the conception of totalitarianism is the interpretation that best explains Nazi dictatorship. In contrast to Habermas, the historians under attack have made essential contributions to broadening our knowledge of the Nazi dictatorship and by doing this have battled "apologies." No one who is interested in scholarly research on the Nazi dictatorship or in the political culture of the Federal Republic should take part in the attempted character assassination.

Source: *Beiträge zur Konfliktforschung*, No. 4, 1986, pp. 146–151

ANDREAS HILLGRUBER

Jürgen Habermas, Karl-Heinz Janßen, and the Enlightenment in the Year 1986

The editors of the weekly newspaper *Die Zeit* chose not to have my book *Zweierlei Untergang: Die Zerschlagung des deutschen Reiches und das Ende des europäischen Judentums* (Twofold Fall: The Destruction of the German Reich and the End of European Jewry)[1] (Berlin: Siedler) reviewed in the column "Political Books" by a specialist reviewer, as is customary. Instead, *Die Zeit* decided to offer the social philosopher and sociologist Jürgen Habermas the "chance" to "take apart" my volume in a partisan way—along with completely different publications by other historians—as supposed evidence of apologetic tendencies. The article in Number 29, July 11, 1986, was subtitled "The Apologetic Tendencies in German History Writing" (title: "Eine Art Schadensabwicklung" [A Kind of Settlement of Damages]).[2] Karl-Heinz Janßen sought to lend special import to Habermas's article by an eye-catching headline—"A Call to Arms"—on the first page of this edition of *Die Zeit*. In so doing, he awarded the label "in the best Enlightenment tradition" (Janßen) to Habermas's "settling of accounts"—which amounts to nothing but the unleashing of a campaign of character assassination against Michael Stürmer, Ernst Nolte, Klaus Hildebrand, and me in the style of the all-too-familiar APO pamphlets of the late 1960s [Außerparlamentarische Opposition, the antiestablishment movement of the late 1960s]. For Karl-Heinz Janßen the whole thing obviously seemed like a good opportunity to continue his attack on historians at West German universities who fail to publish and argue along the one-sided, moralizing, line he has so tyrannically established (as he did to Karl Dietrich Erdmann in connection with the edition of the Riezler Diaries, to Theodor Scheider, after his death, because of a study about Rauschning, and to Walther Hofer in connection with the controversy about the Reichstag fire). Now the four of us have been put on the "blacklist."[3] Just how capriciously these things are being done is illustrated by the fact that, for Hildebrand, that he referred positively to a review in the *Historische Zeitschrift* [Historical Journal] of a Nolte article in an anthology was enough to put him on the blacklist. Who could have given the tip to the layman Habermas, who characterizes himself as "operating without any disciplinary competence," about this fairly obscure passage in a scholarly journal?

As could be expected, the response to Habermas's "call to arms" from his fellow travelers and disciples in the leftist press did not take long to develop. Evidently without having read my book at all, they repeated the philosopher's misleading quotations and varied only the arrangement of the citations, which in part came from other authors. They sought to exceed him in the "level" of the argument and in defaming the "gang of four" (thus an ironic comparison). The rhetoric in the campaign, which has now stretched over many weeks, is not only elaborated but is swollen with personal defamations. High (better, low) points include an article in the Berlin *Taz* about a Heidelberg professor of education, Michael Brumlik;[4] the unspeakably simpleminded and clumsily written piece by a certain Jochen Loreck in the once renowned SPD newspaper *Vorwärts*,[5] which made me an adviser of Chancellor Kohl; and an article by Wolfgang Malanowski in the magazine *Der Spiegel*,[6] which repeats this nonsense in its "scribbling" (one cannot in all generosity call this article anything else), mixing together Habermas and Loreck without bringing any of Malanowski's own thoughts to paper. Habermas fired the opening shot for the campaign himself when, on July 2, 1986, in a public hearing of the Hamburg delegation in Bonn organized by the SPD representative Freimut Duve on the topic of a German historical museum, he took a position on the "neoconservative understanding of history and the role of revisionist writing of history." He demonstratively held up my book and "shaking with rage" delivered the outburst: "This book is a scandal!"[7]

In the following we must discuss a scandal. Habermas's actions cannot be called other than scandalous—scandalous in scholarly aspects, in journalistic perspective, and in view of the "political culture" so often touted these days. Political culture should obligate public discussions to be conducted with a minimum of fair play, or, put less pretentiously, conducted with human decency. A fundamental refutation of the unrestrained criticisms is unavoidable. Then in closing, we will have to discuss, at least briefly, the problem raised or, better, obscured, by Habermas and his followers as the central problem of whether the National-Socialist mass crimes can or cannot be compared with the mass crimes of other twentieth-century regimes. Joachim Fest has already said important things about this issue in his article "Die geschuldete Erinnerung," [The Encumbered Remembrance][8] in the *Frankfurter Allgemeine Zeitung* of August 29, 1986.

Let us begin with the scholarly aspect of the scandal. Günter Zehm is certainly correct when he claims that the opponents of the four historians do not care "about sources and facts" but instead are only interested in political "battle," because the "whole direction" does not suit them.[9] Nevertheless I cannot avoid going through quotation by quotation to compare Habermas's versions and arrangements with the text that actually is printed in my book. Only in this way can we bring to light the partially sophisticated, partially crudely manipulated montage and the implicit and explicit suspicions aimed at me. In this way the seemingly scholarly foundation for the political "battle" of the philosopher can be pulled out from under him.

It seems sensible first of all to go into what Habermas tried to suggest to the readers about my study about the murder of the Jews. Only afterward will I direct the view to his insinuations with regard to my essay "Zusammenbruch im Osten 1944/45 als Problem der deutschen Nationalgeschichte und der europäischen Geschichte" [Collapse in the East 1944–45 as a Problem of German National History and of European History]. Habermas plays the part of the linguistically sensitive person when he tries to read into the title of the volume *Die Zerschlagung des deutschen Reiches und das Ende des europäischen Judentums* [The Destruction of the German Reich and the End of European Jewry] a trivialization of the murder of the Jews. His whole argumentation in this connection would have missed his intended purpose, namely to set the reader against the author, and would have fallen apart if he had honestly given the title of my study "Der geschichtliche Ort der Judenvernhnichtung" [The Historical Locus of the Annihilation of the Jews] or had even quoted from the first paragraph of the foreword, in which I talk of the "murder of the Jews in the territory controlled by National-Socialist Germany."

Habermas talks of the "demonstration" (allegedly by me) that the murder of the Jews was exclusively a consequence of the radical doctrine of race and claims that I "identified Hitler as the sole responsible agent of the idea and decision." He does not tell the readers that my second article, which is the topic here, is the expanded version of my closing address at an international congress in Stuttgart, May 3–5, 1984. Here I summarized the conclusions of the presentations and discussions—to be sure with emphasis on the points that seemed to me to be essential in the controversial exchange of views. I made clear that I agreed with the thesis so convincingly advanced by Eberhard Jäckel[10] that Hitler was the only one in the Nazi leadership clique (including Himmler und Göring) who—over and above all other anti-Semitic activities and plans—had early and deliberately steered toward the mass murder of the Jews. In a situation I have precisely described, he set it into action in 1941. My view was shared by a majority of the participants, including my Israeli colleagues. Jäckel emphatically underscored the results of his research in his newly published book *Hitlers Herrschaft—Vollzug einer Weltanschauung* [Hitler's Reign—Fulfillment of a Worldview][11] with the sentence "It was his (Hitler's) will and his decision . . . no one before him had demanded mass murder." It would be asking too much if one were to demand of the philosopher Habermas that he should be informed about the state of historical research on the complex theme of the Holocaust. Still, he should at least, if he feels called upon to take a position, first get hold of the most essential factual information in order to show his followers his expertise in this field. A citation of K. E. Jeismann is ripped out of its context and included in Habermas's "explanatory" letter to the editor of the *Frankfurter Allgemeine Zeitung* of August 11, 1986:[12] "The greater the role of Hitler in the system of domination, the more forgivable the German society." Including this out-of-context quote does not further scholarship at all. This also applies to Habermas's manipulations of quotations on the theme of "persecution of the Jews in the Third Reich." In the discussion at the convention in 1984, Christoph Dipper presented the thesis (and I mentioned it, citing the author)[13] that if in 1933 the German Nationalists and the *Stahlhelm* [right-wing veterans' group] had come to power instead of the National Socialists, then the life of the Jews in the Reich would have "looked approximately" the same as under the National Socialists until the pogrom of *Kristallnacht* (November 1938). I provided this thesis with a question mark and indicated that all that happened in Germany against the Jews between 1933 and the end of 1938 was not a goal in itself for the regime—as indeed for the German Nationalists—but a manufactured precondition for "completely different, more radical 'solutions.'"[14] A similar falsification of my text by Habermas follows directly. I referred to Hans Mommsen's notion (again by naming the author, something that Habermas omits) that between the end of 1939 and the beginning of 1941 "all responsible parties" in the Third Reich had "agreed on a policy" of forced, systematic "'emigration' (a better term would be expulsion)."[15] This notion, too, I questioned because at this time Hitler was publicly proclaiming a recognizable and far-reaching "annihilation of the Jewish race in Europe." What does Habermas make of this train of thought? He writes: "Hillgruber doubts, however, that *all* decisionmakers between 1938 and 1941 saw a policy of forced emigration as the best solution to the Jewish question. Still, by that time, two-thirds of the German Jews had already 'ended up abroad.'" The latter part is true but has nothing to do with my thoughts connected with the thesis of Hans Mommsen, which expresses precisely the opposite of what Habermas, allegedly quoting me, claims.

Especially insidious are the continued insinuations by Habermas in the following passage. I write: "For Hitler himself the central intention was . . . to decisively advance the 'racial revolution' through the physical extermination of the Jews in Europe. Only such a racial revolution could lend permanence to the world-power status of his Reich. From the winter of 1938–39 this is evident again and again in his speeches."[16] By leaving out the last sentence Habermas plays here again the role of the linguistically sensitive person in that he attempts to use a question ("one does not know") to insinuate to the readers that, since the subjunctive form of the verb is missing, "here again the historian has made the perspective of the participants his own." The clear implication is that I have sympathy with Hitler's argumentation and assent to his views. Habermas must have had reservations about this point later. In his letter to the editor of the *Frankfurter Allgemeine Zeitung* of August 11, 1986[17] he issued me a *Persilschein* [a document issued in the postwar period to certify a party member as merely a fellow traveler and therefore not subject to prosecution] when he writes; "I am convinced that Hillgruber feels the same abhorrence of the Nazi atrocities as most of us do—and he says so, too." I would happily have done without this belated acquittal from this philosopher!

Habermas claims that I "made a sharp distinction between the euthanasia program . . . and the annihilation of the Jews itself." The opposite is true; for I expressly say that the mass murder of the Jews in the so-called *Aktion Reinhard* in Chelmno, Sobibór, Belzec, and Treblinka was carried out with the personnel of the T4 Project (euthanasia project). It is not worth the trouble to go deeper into Habermas's foolish babbling that I "stand firmly in the tradition of the German mandarins," whatever that means. It is, however, significant for its alternation between pretended high-grade linguistic sensibility and crude polemic, and for that reason this sentence should not go unmentioned in characterizing the methods and style of Habermas the agitator.

Finally, I would like to cite the summary of the problem of the murder of the Jews. In my summary I sketch the role of Hitler and of his accomplices, and the attitude of German society in order to confront with quotations Habermas's insinuation that I concentrated my view exclusively on Hitler. "Before the background of broad anti-Semitic tendencies that had gripped Germany since the First World War, the following forces came together: first, the fanatical decisiveness of Hitler, who was driven by an infernal hatred of Jews. In the summer of 1941, after the opening of the war of annihilation against 'Jewish Bolshevism,' he saw the way clear for its 'Final Solution'; second, the readiness to carry out the crimes by a group of people who were not necessarily swept up by the same fanaticism but frequently were to be won over from the most varied apolitical motives; third, the availability of a much larger circle of people within the organizational and technical apparatus who took care of the mass deportation from the German-occupied areas of Europe into the concentration camps; fourth, the expected acceptance by the mass of the German populace of the unavoidably inadequately shielded event because they were concentrating on the war, which they saw as a 'national' matter, and on the needs and sorrows associated with that."[18]

This citation emphasizes a passage from my book that refutes Habermas's claim that the two essays were not connected. A passage that seems more important to me from this piece about the mass murder of the Jews, one that makes explicit the link to the first essay ("Zusammenbruch im Osten" [Collapse in the East]) should follow directly, because here—as far as I can see—for the first time the various war projections of the German leadership in the Second World War are worked out in their idealized typology. The war "unleashed" in 1939 was for "a large part of the Nazi leadership, particularly for the SS . . . a means to settle once and for all the racial question and to carry out a racial reorganization of Europe by large-scale deportations and resettlements as was envisioned in the war goals of the pan-German party in 1914–1918." This contrasts with the ideas of the "large part of the German leadership elite . . . who were caught up in a demand for revising the Versailles system and saw the war purely as a political process aimed at gaining German hegemony over the European continent, in analogy to the German war aims of 1914–1918." Then followed the sentence that previously was cited in the discussion with Habermas: "Hitler's main aim was to advance the 'racial revolution' by the physical extermination of the Jews in Europe, because only through such a 'racial revolution' could permanence be lent to the 'world power' status of his Reich."[19]

In this piece about the mass murder of the European Jews, I had attempted to summarize the wide-ranging research in the field in the brief space that was available so as to show the reader of the first section the extent of the crimes of the National-Socialist regime in concentrated form. In the context of this article the crimes were repeatedly referred to but, though consistent with the selection of topic, could not be presented in extenso (although both complexes are closely associated). It was the aim of the first section, in anticipation of a larger presentation, to sketch relatively comprehensively the specific questions, tasks, and difficulties that face the historian interested in the topic "Zusammenbruch im Osten 1944/45 als Problem der deutschen Nationalgeschichte und der europäischen Geschichte" [Collapse in the East 1944–45 as a Problem of National History and of European History]. It was a conclusion—as Habermas's example has now demonstrated for me in a frightening way—of Alfred Heuß in his book *Versagen und Verhängnis—Vom Ruin deutscher Geschichte und ihres Verständnisses* [Failure and Doom—On the Ruin of German History and Its Understanding][20] that caused the idea to mature in me to make this topic the object of a longer lecture or an essay. According to Heuß, "the weak sensitivity about certainly the gravest consequence of the war [that is, expelling the Germans out of the eastern regions and the loss of these regions—A. H.] belongs to the oddest phenomena of contemporary Germany. It is perhaps similar to when a Frenchman thinks about the loss of Indochina."

I stood before the task of taking in the multilayered events of 1944–1945 sketchily from various perspectives. First in the narrative part I took the perspective of "critical sympathy" for the German populace, which became the victim of the impending catastrophe of flight and expulsion, of the attempts to save what could be saved. Then I wrote analytically, treating the current state of research, and with an awareness of the opposing war aims of Hitler and the Allies in the West and East. I wanted to mark the hopelessness in order to let the reader at least "sense the tragedy" that took place in the winter of 1944–45 in the East, as Hans Herzfeld put it in a lecture in the early 1960s. Finally I wanted to show the consequences growing out of the demise of the German East for German and European History.

Habermas sneers about the problem of identification that I mentioned at the outset. This problem gives the historian particular difficulties in the narrative part of his depiction. The philosopher arrogates the decision to himself, albeit without any "special expertise" about which perspective is legitimate for the historian and which is not. In his previously mentioned letter to the editor of August 11, 1986, he even says such a point of view is appropriate for the "memoirs of a veteran" but not for a "historian writing from the distance of four decades." Should a regulation be promulgated here—in contradiction to our liberal constitution—on what historians may and may not do? Here the arrogation[21] of an intellectual harassment becomes especially palpable, as it permeates Habermas's whole essay. It also permeates his discussions on these topics and notions of the three colleagues, which he "cooked up,"[22] just as he did the content of my book, so that they could be better suited for political attacks.

The philosopher as agitator thought up an especially evil "treatment" when he claims that I try to present my material from the view of the "brave soldiers, the desperate civilian population, and the 'tried and true' higher-ups of the NSDAP." In my article I clearly distinguish between the perspective that I chose for the first, introductory part (and only for this part) (not identification with Hitler and with the Red Army, but with the fate of the eastern populace), and the perspective that I chose for the subsequent survey (based on sources), which I present and evaluate with reference to the conduct of those who had regional or local responsibility in the East. In doing this I said in the text: "Among the higher-ups of the NSDAP many proved themselves in the emergency of final, desperate defense, of collapse and flight, while others failed, in part miserably." Although Klaus Hildebrand, in his article "Das Zeitalter der Tyrannen" [The Age of Tyrants], *Frankfurter Allgemeine Zeitung* of July 31, 1986,[23] has already called Habermas's attention to the grave difference between my statement and the distorted citation, Habermas, so hypersensitive in the other passages mentioned above, had the cheek to repeat the perversion of meaning of my text in his letter to the editor of the *Frankfurter Allgemeine Zeitung*, August 11, 1986,[24] where he claims "among those participants" with whose fate I identify, there are, in addition to "soldiers and civilians, also the 'tried and true' higher-ups of the NSDAP." I say, as my text makes unambiguously clear, absolutely nothing whatsoever about whether these higher-ups (on the basis of whatever accomplishments) were "tried and true" people. I merely render a judgment about their conduct in a situation of extreme emergency. Habermas, however, using his perversion of the sense of the sentence, wants to convince his readers that I identify with the people who "proved themselves" in and for the regime. It should and must be said about one of the leading ideas of history, the struggle for justice, that the line between "proving oneself" and "failure" in the final emergency is not the same as the line between party members and NSDAP higher-ups on the one hand and the remaining civilians on the other. This—not more and not less—was my intention. Habermas has in this case crudely abused the obligation to honesty.

When Habermas speaks of the "war-novel rhetoric" that he claims to have found in my first essay, then that statement, considering the moving events sketched there, condemns itself. The philosopher could hardly have occupied himself so intensively with military and war history on the lower or higher level that he could make an expert pronouncement on the "level" of my work. What remains is low-quality polemic. What I am supposed to do with "social science information" when I report about the excesses of the Red Army, not only in its penetration into eastern Germany but also into Poland, Romania, and Hungary, I do not know. I am not surprised that Habermas agrees with the anti-Prussia cliché that I described as the basis for the aims behind British war policy.

One thing must still be said: The author of the article is incapable or unwilling to report factually what I presented as the quintessence of the situation of the German *Ostheer* [Army of the East] in the winter of 1944-45. Of the four interwoven forces that I name—and it depends exactly on this interweaving—Habermas cited only one, with a scornful undertone and in an abbreviated way ("an umbrella of protection for a centuries-old German settlement area, for the homeland of millions who lived in the heartland of the German Reich"). This excerpt only makes sense in a context that illuminates the fourfold aspect of the war in the East in the winter of 1944–45 and lets it be seen as a tragedy.[25] "The remaining units of the German Army of the East with which Hitler had wanted to annihilate the Soviet Union now defended his rapidly collapsing Reich. Within its boundaries . . . the mass murder of the Jews was continued up until November 1944; in its concentration camps unimaginable crimes were carried out up until the last moment. But in precisely this situation the German Army of the East was also struggling . . . with its desperate defensive battle for preserving the independence and great power status of the German Reich. . . . The German Army of the East offered an umbrella of protection for a centuries-old German settlement area, for the homeland of millions of eastern Germans, who lived in the heartland of the German Reich—namely, in eastern Prussia, in the provinces of East Prussia, West Prussia, Silesia, East Brandenburg, and Pomerania. And the German Army of the East protected in a completely elementary sense the people in these Prussian-German eastern provinces who were threatened . . . by a terrible fate if their homeland should be overrun by the Red Army." If one is—as I am—convinced that the German eastern territories (east of the Oder and Neiße) are lost forever because of the conclusion of the war in 1945,[26] then the "encumbered remembrance"[27] applies here as well as the foremost duty of the historian.

Even if Habermas is no historian himself, one could have expected from him in this role as "enlightener" at least a breath of the tolerance that was characteristic of the great European Enlightenment—tolerance toward a historian who does not conform to his politics. I can detect no trace in him of Nathan the Wise, but all the more elements of that fanatical patriarch in Lessing's "dramatic poem," who in the face of all objections that he should keep this or that in mind always has the answer ready: "That does not change a thing. The Jew will be burned."[28]

Habermas's actual or feigned inability to take a historical text for what it is and to seek to understand its intention, that is, to present and analyze a complicated set of events, has its peak in the political conclusion: "The moral of the story . . . is obvious: Today at least the alliance of forces is the correct one." As if in my volume there were a single word about NATO! Habermas insinuates that my criticism from the historical perspective refers only to the politics and conduct of the Soviet Union, although the questionableness of the British-German policy was named at least as explicitly in my volume. Habermas is obviously against NATO—that is his concern—but what does that have to do with my work? How does he come to categorize my work as having so-called neoconservative tendencies? For decades I have never made any bones about my basic conservative position. Deeply suspicious as I am of all "leftist" and other world-improving utopias, I will gladly let the label "conservative" apply to me, meant though it is as defamation. But what is the meaning of the prefix "neo"? No one "challenges" this new "battle" label, so often seen these days, in order to turn this APO [Außerparlamentarische Opposition, the antiestablishment movement of the late 1960s] jargon against the inventor of the label. In the rest of it I see a striking contradiction between Habermas's aversion to NATO (against "a NATO philosophy colored by German nationalism," as he expresses it himself) and his incantation that a "reconstruction of the destroyed European Center"—also here the philosopher takes something of mine out of context[29]—includes the danger of becoming "estranged" from "the West." He is concerned about alienation from the West—as he calls it—to the degree that "the unconditional opening of the Federal Republic to the political culture of the West," which he describes "as the greatest intellectual achievement of our postwar period" (whose accomplishment?), might be reversed. Can "culture" and "politics" be separated in this way whether it is popular to do so or not or whether, as above, Habermas wants to prove the "opposite"? One could argue the contrary more convincingly: that the "Left's" loudly advocated aversion to NATO accelerates precisely the political and cultural process that Habermas pretends to want to hinder.

With this the political-journalistic field of the discussion has come into view. It is the sign for the total neglect of what is repeatedly demanded in *Die Zeit* when this weekly paper, which presents itself as liberal, allows itself to be used by the Habermasian aggression against four historians. The selection of letters to the editor in response to the article by Habermas, which the paper published in its edition of August 1, 1986,[30] shows that the echoes from the forest come back just as *Die Zeit* shouts into it. Aside from a few factual positions, these letters were a singular sequence of defamations of the attacked historians. The worst and most arrogant aspect of this was when the paper placed Ernst Nolte's reply in the middle of the letters to the editor. Attached to Nolte's reply was another letter from a student, Paul Nolte from Bielefeld, who was ashamed of his namesake and wanted most of all to forbid the four historians to teach: "For some time now, as a student one (has) only been able . . . to look on helplessly at the goings-on of the new revisionism in historiography." If only the editors of this newspaper were not too ashamed to publish this and other hatchet jobs of the same level!

Obviously a number of "leftist" publicists saw it as their duty to emulate Habermas on his "level" and, if possible, to outdo him in perfidy. It is difficult to decide whom to honor with the "crown." Brumlik in the Berlin *Tageszeitung* and Loreck in *Vorwärts* had the prospect of winning it, but that obviously did not let Wolfgang Malanowski rest until in *Der Spiegel* he had stormed the peak of infamy, breaking all other records. It is a scandal that he, as a historian with a Ph.D., was not even aware enough of his dependency on the statements of a philosopher playing the dilettante in history and was unwilling even to look at the text for himself to see if the quotations were correct. But such "independence" is indeed too much to ask.

What does Habermas want politically? In the foreground it looks as though he wanted to serve the SPD in the election campaign—how else is his appearance to be explained in the campaign event of SPD representative Duve on July 2, 1986? But probably more correct is what Frank Schirrmacher concluded in the *Frankfurter Allgemeine Zeitung* of November 7, 1986,[31] immediately after reading Habermas's article in *Die Zeit*. Schirrmacher said that the battle primarily had the value of a defense of his position, a position that has dominated over the leftist spectrum since 1968. The "unification" of the "image of history" that Habermas now supposedly sees on the horizon "is a reaction to making uniform the image of history, something Habermas has been doing for decades." He and his fellow travelers grasp a one-dimensional "image," formulated as an indictment of National Socialism and of "the" Germans in the "Third Reich."

Every differentiation of this image, which unavoidably occurs with research, ends up under ideological suspicion. Habermas and his friends spoke and speak a lot indeed about "pluralism." But this only means a "pluralism" within the "leftist" spectrum. Everything else is stamped with the word "reactionary." For some time now, "neoconservative" has taken the place of "reactionary." In this regard, still more exacting discussion can be expected. This can be valuable if the "level" of discussion can be kept above the "mudslinging" with which Habermas opened the match.

Joachim Fest with his article in the *Frankfurter Allgemeine Zeitung*[32] has already made a significant contribution to the return to a scholarly discourse. The problem of historicizing National Socialism[33] poses itself unavoidably. Embedded in it is the key question about the comparability or incomparability of the National-Socialist crimes, above all the comparability of the mass murder of the Jews in Europe with mass crimes of other regimes, in particular with those of the Soviet Union. The idea of comparability also applies to the question about the genesis of Hitler's will to annihilate and of its connection with the practices of annihilation in Bolshevist Russia. These questions cannot be supported by political-journalistic "calls to arms" and by defaming those who—with different scholarly impulses and provisional theses or hypotheses—touch actual or only seemingly tabooed zones. Sounding the alert and defaming those who touch on taboo zones are the tactics employed by Habermas and his fellow travelers and followers, who are beholden to a clichéd image of the Third Reich that long ago was supplanted by the more differentiated statements of scholarly discussions.

The great difficulties in unambiguously answering the key question referred to above so that a scholarly consensus would result are obvious. I see four individual problems of high priority.

1. The availability of the whole of the source material that has come down to us documenting the mass crimes of the National Socialists stands in contrast to the extraordinarily bad state of sources with respect to events in the areas under Soviet domination. This is a consequence of the strict secrecy of all events in the Soviet Union of the Stalin era (and thereafter). Here, at any rate, the Western research on eastern Europe has not undertaken the necessary efforts to present a coherent picture from the reports that have, despite everything, ended up in the West. This picture would have to be a mosaic assembled from very different components. It might well be a relatively clear mosaic image of diverse mass crimes in the Stalin era, at least to the extent that it is possible to piece it together, even though it would not be as well supported by sources. Thus the comparison remains burdened with many reservations in quantitative and qualitative respects.

2. The causes of Soviet mass crimes are confounded by history. If one sees Stalin's principle motivation as the prevention of the slavery that threatened everyone in the Soviet Union in the event of a German victory,

then the events, at least those amounting to mass crimes, that took place between 1941 and 1945 in the Soviet Union may be at least partially interpreted or half-justified as reactions promulgated to defend against the German attack. It was, after all, National-Socialist Germany, the country where the mass crimes were committed, that in 1941 carried the racially and ideologically motivated war of annihilation into the Soviet Union (including the territories acquired by the USSR in 1939–1940 in eastern Poland and the Baltics). In the Soviet Union at the same time, although during a much broader span of time, mass crimes were being committed. Thus widespread practices of annihilation were carried over to the great-power war unleashed by the German attack. Here at the latest, the purely statistical registry of crimes conceived of in 1 becomes impossible. Historians must decide whether they will judge more leniently the methods that the Stalin regime employed for the purpose of defense against the German attack than they will judge the crimes of the same "quality" that the National-Socialist leadership committed in the course of its war of annihilation.

3. The thesis, proposed early on (1945) and in the meantime almost ritualized, that the murder of the millions of Jews under the National-Socialist control is "singular" makes things difficult. The ritual of judgment places under moral suspicion those who on scholarly grounds report doubts about the singularity. This makes difficult the efforts of historians to test the comparability (which obviously has nothing to do with any "balancing of accounts"). Every event is in principle "singular," just as every event contains something comparable with other events. Ernst Nolte and, in a broader context, Joachim Fest (in his article in the *Frankfurter Allgemeine Zeitung* of August 29, 1986) have posed questions with provocative effect. Fest presented reflections that cause one to think.

4. Finally, it is not easy to say convincingly whether and to what extent reports about the events in "Jewish-Bolshevist" Russia in the early 1920s shaped Hitler's radical universal annihilation program, and to what extent his infernal hatred of the Jews resulted from his experiences during his time in Vienna before 1913, or whether individual psychic forces were not decisive, a thesis expressly advocated by the psychohistorian Rudolph Binion.[34]

Labeling such efforts with the term "revisionist" with the intent of morally wounding the historians in question complicates the scholarly efforts to approach this difficult terrain. "Revision" of current results is the norm of scholarship, anyway. The term "revisionist" is, at least in connection with the research of National Socialism and the Third Reich, already— mostly pejoratively—used for very different tendencies and directions of research. The term was used in the early 1960s regarding the work of Hoggan and Taylor, who sought in different ways to "exculpate" Hitler, and in the 1970s for those researchers who focused on the structures of the Nazi regime and not on Hitler's goals and motives. Since the end of the 1970s a group that stands on the political Right (organized around Alfred Schickel's

Research Center for Recent History in Ingolstadt) has characterized its work as revisionist. And now, finally, we four historians are placed under suspicion as revisionists by Habermas and his supporters. An end should be put to using this defamatory label as well as "neoconservative conspiracy," intimated in the *Zeit* article by Habermas.

In Habermas's letter to the editor of the *Frankfurter Allgemeine Zeitung* of August 11, 1986, the Bund Freiheit der Wissenschaft [Association for the Freedom of Scholarship] shows up—betraying his fears (by the way, it is also mentioned in another letter to *Die Zeit* published on August 1, 1986). Here he counts on the forgetfulness of the readers who no longer— or so apparently one hopes—remember that the Bund Freiheit der Wissenschaft was founded in 1970 as a defense against the extreme leftists in the West German universities amid the agitation and psychic terror unleashed against their non-Marxist colleagues by a few professors like Jürgen Habermas. If Habermas's goal is to create again that unbearable atmosphere that ruled in those years at West German universities, then he is deluding himself. History does not let itself, as fits the wishes of failed "prophets" and political agitators, be arbitrarily repeated.[35]

Source: *Geschichte in Wissenschaft und Unterricht*, December 1986, pp. 725–738

NOTES

1. Andreas Hillgruber. *Zweierlei Untergang: Die Zerschlagung des deutschen Reiches und das Ende des europäischen Judentums*. Berlin: Siedler Verlag, 1986.
2. Jürgen Habermas. "Eine Art Schadensabwicklung. Die apologetischen Tendenzen in der deutschen Geschichtsschreibung," *Die Zeit*, No. 29, July 11, 1986, p. 40.
3. So Michael Stürmer says, correctly, in a letter to the editor in the *Frankfurter Allgemeine Zeitung*, August 16, 1986.
4. Michael Brumlik. "Neuer Staatsmythos Ostfront: Die neueste Entwicklung der Geschichtswissenschaft der BRD," *Taz Magazin*, July 12, 1986, p. 14.
5. Jochen Loreck. "Kontroverse Darstellungen über das 'Wirken' Hitlers. Die Entsorgung der Vergangenheit," *Vorwärts*, August 9, 1986.
6. Wolfgang Malanowski, "Vergangenheit, die nicht vergehen will," *Der Spiegel*, No. 36, September 1, 1986, pp. 66–70.
7. Thus the report from Werner A. Perger, "Schlußstrich oder Schuldgefühle?" *Deutsches Allgemeines Sonntagsblatt*, No. 30, July 27, 1986, p. 3.
8. Joachim Fest, "Die geschuldete Erinnerung: Zur Kontroverse über die Unvergleichlichkeit der nationalsozialistische Massenverbrechen," *Frankfurter Allgemeine Zeitung*, No. 199, August 29, 1986, pp. 23–24.
9. Günter Zehm, ("Pankraz") "Pankraz, die Quellen und der neue Geßlerhut," *Die Welt*, No. 184–86, August 11, 1986.
10. Compare Jäckel's contributions in Eberhard Jäckel and Jürgen Rohwer, eds., *Der Mord an den Juden im Zweiten Weltkrieg: Entschlußbildung und Verwirklichung*. Stuttgart, 1985. Malanowski (in *Der Speigel*) also ascribes the allegedly "new" thesis to me.

11. Eberhard Jäckel. *Hitlers Herrschaft. Vollzug einer Weltanschauung*. Stuttgart, 1986, pp. 89ff. Quotation, p. 120.
12. *Frankfurter Allgemeine Zeitung*, August 11, 1986.
13. As in note 1, page 86. What strange consequences the "copying" from the Habermas article has as a result is shown in the essay by Rudolf Augstein, "Von Friedrich zu Hitler? Zum 200: Todestag Friedrichs des Großen," *Der Spiegel*, No. 32, 1986, p. 157, in that he also ascribes Dipper's thesis to me and connects absurd speculations to it.
14. As in note 1, p. 87.
15. Ibid.
16. Ibid., p. 89f.
17. As in note 12.
18. As in note 1, p. 97f.
19. Ibid., p. 89.
20. Alfred Heuß, *Versagen und Verhängnis: Vom Ruin deutscher Geschichte und ihres Verständnisses*. Berlin, 1984, p. 143.
21. The literary scholar Karl Heinz Bohrer allows himself an arrogation similar to Habermas's (*Frankfurter Allgemeine Zeitung*, August 16, 1986, Bohrer's letter to the editor, "Ins Schwarze getroffen").
22. *Frankfurter Allgemeine Zeitung*, August 16, 1986. Letter to the editor by Michael Stürmer ("Eine Anklage, die sich selbst ihre Belege fabriziert").
23. Klaus Hildebrand, "Das Zeitalter der Tyrannen," *Frankfurter Allgemeine Zeitung*, July 7, 1986.
24. As in note 12.
25. As in note 1, p. 64f.
26. Just this conception brought me energetic criticism from Herbert Hupka. (Compare *Das Ostpreußenblatt*, June 7, 1986, and July 19, 1986, and my position in the same journal, June 21, 1986, and July 26, 1986.) How mixed up the "fronts" are is shown in the fact that Hupka in his article of June 7, 1986, throws Hans-Ulrich Wehler, Michael Stürmer, and me in the same pot with regard to German political opinions.
27. Thus, the title of Joachim Fest's essay ("Zur Kontroverse über die Unvergleichbarkeit der nationalsozialistischen Massenverbrechen") *Frankfurter Allgemeine Zeitung*, August 29, 1986, p. 23f.
28. Act 4, Scene 4.
29. The connection is as follows: "Whether, beyond regional beginnings in Western Europe, a reconstruction of the destroyed European Middle—as a precondition for the reconstruction of the whole of Europe or as a consequence of such a reconstruction once it is in process—will ever be possible is, forty years after the collapse of the European Middle, as open as it was then." See note 1, p. 74.
30. *Die Zeit*, No. 32/1985, and August 1, 1986, p. 12. Letter to the editor under the headline "Streit um die Einmaligkeit der Hitlerschen Greuel—Geschichte ist auch eine Frage von Marktlücken."
31. *Frankfurter Allgemeine Zeitung*, July 11, 1986. "Aufklärung? Habermas und die Geschichte."
32. As in note 8. More details in Eberhard Jäckel. "Die elende Praxis der Untersteller: Das Einmalige der nationalsozialistischen Verbrechen läßt sich nicht leugnen," *Die Zeit*, No. 38, September 12, 1986.
33. Compare this also with the thoughts from Martin Broszat, which have an altogether different point of departure and certainly are not connected with the four attacked historians. "Was kann das heißen: Konservative Wende—

Zeitgeschichte, Wissenschaft, Tagespolitik," *Die Presse*, (Vienna) No. 30, August 31, 1986 (the "Spektrum" column).
34. Rudolph Binion, ". . . *daß ihr mich gefunden habt.*" *Hitler und die Deutschen. Eine Psychohistorie*. Stuttgart, 1978.
35. This article was complete on September 12, 1986. The factual and the—as is the case with Rudolf Augstein's extremely absurd article in *Der Spiegel*— polemic discussion could not be taken into account.

WALTER EUCHNER

The Nazi Reign—A Case of Normal Tyranny? On the Misuse of Philosophical Interpretations

It cannot be imagined any other way: The burden of the National-Socialist crimes weighs down German postwar politics. Luckily, after the collapse of the Nazi reign, there were men and women from all political camps who had opposed National Socialism and who were capable of uncompromisingly initiating political renewal. But the break with the National-Socialist past only succeeded to a degree. The first chancellor of the Federal Republic, Konrad Adenauer, not known as an overly sensitive man, was willing to tolerate people who also had held high offices in the Nazi period. But more decisive than this continuing presence of people with dubious backgrounds in high positions is the fact that, as Jürgen Habermas put it, "even those born afterward grew up in the context in which Auschwitz was possible." And even the "blessing of a late birth," which the present chancellor has claimed for himself, cannot save us from this. Nothing could be more foolish than to believe that the wounds that National-Socialist crimes have caused in other peoples have since healed painlessly. They can break open easily if German politics are not always influenced by a sense of collective shame and grief.

The present administration, however, sees this differently. Signs of the *Wende* (or conservative shift) are now expected to make their appearance in history (Susanne Miller, NG/FH 9/86, p. 836). And since, as Joachim Fest wrote in the *Frankfurter Allgemeine Zeitung* of August 29, 1986, "the public, despite all encouragement by political leaders, is nowhere near being out of the shadow that Hitler and the crimes committed under him have cast," the media have to push a little harder. The *Frankfurter Allgemeine Zeitung*, which appears to have decided to uncompromisingly place its editorial work in the service of the current government, is doing its best to achieve just that. The paper hardly omits a topic that proves that in National Socialism, too, life was normal and even human and that the criminal and illegal aspects of the regime's deeds can also be found in the political practice of other nations.

Anti-Semitism, as Karl Friedrich Fromme put it, "has existed through the centuries, and it still exists in the socialist countries, especially in the Soviet Union. Other nations are in a position to ask themselves whether sympathies can be forced upon them. The 'annihilation of the Jews'—the phrase belongs between quotation marks—took place in a discreet [*sic!* Fromme is truly a master of German euphemism] way. . . . Many Germans closed their eyes to monstrous deeds that they could not have changed anyway. They just wished not to be made responsible—and that is no less questionable than it is human." (*Frankfurter Allgemeine Zeitung*, February 28, 1986). The same author calls the fact that the district attorney at the State Court in Berlin dropped his investigation against judges of the *Volksgerichtshof* [Nazi People's Court] "a painful, also soothing, conclusion" (*Frankfurter Allgemeine Zeitung*, October 3, 1986).

Günter Gillessen attempted to make plausible the thesis, generally rejected by historical scholarship, that Stalin wanted to attack the German Reich in 1941—which, if this were really the case, would of course relativize the meaning of Hitler's actual attack on the Soviet Union (*Frankfurter Allgemeine Zeitung*, August 2, 1986). Klaus Hildebrand emphasized that not only Stalin and Hitler but also the British government planned far-flung war goals with great, even horrifying, shifts in territories and populations (*Frankfurter Allgemeine Zeitung*, July 31, 1986). Here the reader appears to be expected to learn that in the circles of the larger nations there is, as recent research has shown, many a sinner. No one has a reason to point his finger at others. And so now the time has arrived for a new German "national consciousness": "We all need a German national consciousness without hidden agendas and without arrogance" (Jean Marie Souton, *Frankfurter Allgemeine Zeitung*, August 20, 1986).

In order to avoid misunderstandings let me say that I am not trying to insinuate that the authors who are revising our image of recent German history are doing so with dishonest motives. The Bonn politicians of the *Wende* as well as historians and publications such as the *Frankfurter Allgemeine Zeitung* that follow the politicians in this direction are permitting their search for knowledge to be guided by an interest that shapes the direction of their statements. They will have to admit that the traditional German elites, on the whole, tolerated the experiment with Hitler and even went along to a degree—with the well-known result. But now, after German politics have creditably practiced liberal parliamentary democracy for a long while, they think that considering the Federal Republic's importance in the world economy and the Western alliance, the time has come to step out of Hitler's shadow and to develop a new sense of nation that is not influenced by the past. I do not share this view because it trivializes the mechanism so evident in German history that led to the disaster of National Socialism—in fact this view sweeps these objections under the carpet. And thus this kind of history writing is "apologetic"—as

Jürgen Habermas was quite correct in pointing out in his July 11, 1986, article in *Die Zeit*, in which he shook up the revisionists for a while to come.

To what results the attempt to step out of Hitler's shadow can lead is evident in the article in which Joachim Fest, in the *Frankfurter Allgemeine Zeitung* of August 29, 1986, discusses "the Controversy about the Incomparability of National-Socialist Mass Crimes." First of all, we have to ignore the sloppy use of the concepts "comparable" and "incomparable." By "incomparable" Fest means that events have so little to do with each other that they cannot be placed in a meaningful connection with each other. Proceeding from his revisionist intention, Fest also argues this in connection with National Socialism. The so-called singularity of Nazi crimes must be challenged so that the Nazi reign can be placed in a series with other tyrannies in history and in this way relativized. Thus, so the argument goes, Hitler engaged in racial extermination while Stalin was responsible for class extermination. Thus there is also no difference in the fact that the mass murders ordered by Hitler were carried out "in an administrative and mechanical form. . . . The gas chambers with which the executors of the annihilation of the Jews went to work without a doubt signal a particularly repulsive form of mass murder, and they have justifiably become a symbol for the technicized barbarism of the Hitler regime. But can it really be said that mass liquidations by a bullet to the back of the neck, as was common practice during the years of the Red Terror, are qualitatively different? Isn't, despite all the differences, the comparable element stronger?"

In this balancing act Fest is attempting to come to the aid of historian Ernst Nolte, who in his article of June 6, 1986, in the *Frankfurter Allgemeine Zeitung*, transformed the identity thesis into a mimicry thesis. The Gulag Archipelago, he argued, was "the logical and factual prius" to Auschwitz, and between both "a causal nexus was probable." (Also see *Die Zeit* of October 31, 1986.)

What Nolte is invoking here in this tightrope walk—that the Gulag Archipelago is "primary to Auschwitz," that is, that Auschwitz was not a direct response to the Gulag but that there was a connection—becomes a certainty in Fest's more concrete argumentation. Hitler, Fest argues, called the "practices of his revolutionary opponents of the Left lessons and models." The people who headed up the Munich Soviet revolutionary republic that went down in chaos and terror and among whom there were "more than a few Jews," strengthened Hitler's anti-Semitic obsessions. After all, he was willing, as he said himself, to "counter every act of terrorism by Marxism with a ten-times greater response."

Speaking of the terror of Marxism: Nolte, too, thinks that "the gigantic parades of the Social Democrats" terrified Hitler (*Die Zeit*, October 31, 1986). Of course I was not there, but I could imagine that military parades were more fearsome than the demonstrations of Viennese Social Democrats. People like Victor Adler and Wilhelm Ellenbogen, both Jews and educated humanists who set the tone for pre–World War I social democracy in Vienna, were supporters of the parliamentary system and fundamental civil rights. This was also the case with the mainstream of the German Social Democrats. Politicians like Karl Kautsky and Eduard Bernstein certainly did not inspire anyone to phantasies about annihilation. For these Hitler needed neither prewar Marxism nor the Gulag Archipelago. They were in fact a product of his insanity.

In the past, in *Faschismus und seiner Epoche* (1963), Nolte used more balanced tones in his analysis of these connections. What Hitler hated about Marxism, Nolte argued then, was "its bourgeois nature," which was about to hamstring "Germany's power and its preparedness to wage war." What Hitler disliked about communism, in other words, was the rejection of physical force, which in fact was characteristic for large segments of pacifist Social-Democratic Marxism. Moreover, he argues, Hitler's anti-Semitism, in its vehemence and absoluteness, by far exceeded even that of Streicher (p. 388). The annihilation of the Jews inspired by Hitler, Nolte went on, was different "from all other measures of annihilation both qualitatively and in terms of its intention" (p. 482).

The worst part of the whole identification and inspiration debate is the fact that it is by and large aimed at the person of Hitler and ignores the historical preconditions of Hitler's and Stalin's crimes. In Soviet Russia it was a matter of revolutionizing an economically, culturally, and politically backward country that lacked democratic traditions. The people who led this movement believed in the revolutionary force of the *terreur* in its model from the French Revolution. This and the Marxist teaching about the class struggle, combined with the activism of Russian social-revolutionary theses, removed the inhibitions to mass annihilations. The National Socialists seized power in a nation with an outstanding intellectual heritage but with a deficit in political culture. In contrast to the Bolsheviks, the National Socialists, whose ideology contained old folkish and anti-Semitic obsessions, were able to realize their political goals with the voluntary support of a substantial part of the traditional elites.

The complicity of National Socialism and traditional elites is the political scandal that has since that time besmirched the German name. But now it is this precondition for the Nazi seizure of power and reign that is no longer taken seriously when other acts of genocide, ranging all the way to the mass murders in Cambodia, are used for comparison's sake. And this is, or so I imagine, not an undesired side effect of the revisionist view of history. Thus there are a few points to remember: Civil servants and university professors who had worked without conflict with Jewish and Social-Democratic colleagues were willing to accept without protest that these people were fired from government service, driven into exile, or handed over to concentration camps. No one heard their calls for help. Jewish lawyers, artists, and scholars of world renown, highly valued members of society, were thrown out of their professional organizations and chambers without anyone so much as raising a finger for them. One-time constitutional judge (*Bundesverfassungsrichter*) Gerhard Leibholz, one of the great figures of postwar German history and a man of Jewish origin, remembered (of all places in the *Frankfurter Allgemeine Zeitung*, if I am not mistaken) that it was as if people at a dinner party were repeatedly hauled off and shot in the adjoining room while those who remained behind whispered "terrible, terrible" and continued to dine as before. And this transpired despite the education of the elites in German idealism, in the virtues of Prussianism, in the highly refined Catholic and Protestant theologies, in the immortal products of German art, literature, and music. People who still today admire German culture cannot understand that despite this cultural tradition Germans could have acted the way they did, becoming accomplices of the Nazis—and these people will never learn to understand how this happened if the efforts of revisionist historians are successful.

Fest's defense of historical revisionism culminates in a philosophical interpretation of the mass annihilations of the twentieth century. He describes all these crimes, including those of National Socialism, as part of regularly repeated acts of genocide. He toys with the "pessimistic" view that is not capable of perceiving much more in history than the murder and mayhem that always existed. This view sees history as dominated by hate, fear, and exterminations, without meaning and goal. But due to the technical innovations available today, history lives on with an unheard of passionlessness while demanding an endlessly greater number of victims than in the past. In this view, Auschwitz does indeed shrink to the status of a "technical innovation." He then counters this pessimistic view with an optimistic variant, that, as he says, has the weakness that it has to deal with a utopian "new man." Fest does not clearly decide between these two views, but the context shows that he considers the "insight that the act of genocide that Hitler set in motion was not the first and will not be the last" to be the realistic one. Habermas, whom he describes as "deeply rooted in the intellectual battles of yesterday and yesteryear" and whom he would have to count on the optimistic side, employs what he calls "fossil categories."

I do not want to participate in Fest's philosophical speculations. But I hope he does not consider them to be modern—for they are, after all, quite a bit more fossilized than the positions of the Enlightenment to which Habermas is trying to establish a link. And on top of that they are trivial. More important is the applicability that he sees in these ideas: that the feeling of shame for the crimes committed in the German name is understandable but inappropriate. "But does this attitude really make sense, even when such events happen again and again? Strictly speaking, this argument presumes the old Nazi distinction according to which there are higher peoples, and more primitive peoples who do not even know about the commandment against killing. Those who are more sensitive will recognize the arrogance in this master race attitude, even if it is concealed beneath a gesture of humility." What a mad dialectic! In any case, it will never lead us out of Hitler's shadow.

Source: Die neue Gesellschaft/Frankfurter Hefte, no. 12, 1986, pp. 1115–1119

Author's Note: This is the expanded version of a letter to the editor about Joachim Fest's "The Encumbered Memory"; the *Frankfurter Allgemeine Zeitung* refused to print it.

ERNST NOLTE

Letter to the Editor of the *Frankfurter Allgemeine Zeitung*, December 6, 1986

I have by no means "defused" my article of June 6, 1986, by publishing it in *Die Zeit*, as Christian Meier ("Not a Final Word," *Frankfurter Allgemeine Zeitung* of November 20) suggests. I simply cleared up a few errors and misunderstandings that were unavoidable in a precise reading by critics.

Source: *Frankfurter Allgemeine Zeitung*, December 6, 1986

Publisher's Note: The letter appeared under the title "Not Defused."

ROBERT LEICHT

Only by Facing the Past Can We Be Free. We Are Our Own Past: German History Should Not Be Retouched

From time immemorial people have been seeking an anchor in the past. This was a search for our ancestors: "And was thought to be a son of Joseph, who was a son of Eli, who was a son of Matthat, who was a son of Levi . . ." The genealogical tree of Jesus, recorded by Luke, runs through seventy-seven generations at a snail's pace, naming King David, then also the progenitor Abraham, and closing in the last verse of the third chapter: " . . . he was a son of Enos, who was a son of Seth, who was a son of Adam, who was in God." In Matthew, this genealogical tree begins with Abraham and goes the opposite direction all the way to Jesus.

In these texts early Christianity takes note of its history while sorting and interpreting its details, but the naked genealogical facts are less important for the authors, who are seeking signs of legitimacy. They desire to prove an especially auspicious lineage: from the patriarchs, from Abraham and David, from the first man, even from God. And they are willing to accept the fact that this patrilinear genealogical tree, and the virgin birth that endows legitimacy, do not quite fit together.

This is a conscious attempt to endow historical meaning. This early society did not write history for the sake of documentation. By talking about the past, they also speak about their present—and this in the light of the future. History does not merely offer these people empirical material. It provides them with the substance by which they can determine their own existence, gain orientation, and interpret their identity. Do we conduct our historical debates in a different way?

We conduct them in the same way—but with some differences. It is not only that the secularized world sees no possibility of deriving a future of salvation from a past that was fashioned to provide meaning. We Germans also have to bear responsibility for the fact that the first half of the twentieth century became the history of our disaster—in the catastrophe of the years between 1933 and 1945.

Eighty years after the beginning of the Christian era, Matthew and Luke were attempting to provide an interpretation. Whether it is forty or eighty years after the alleged "zero hour," or even much later, who knows whether we Germans will ever be capable of conclusively writing our history—that is, the history of National Socialism and its preconditions and consequences? Even though Franz Josef Strauß, motivated by the desire to increase our arms exports, angrily told us that Germans do not want to live much longer in the shadow of the past, we will do just that, whether we want to or not.

For this reason we will repeatedly experience disputes among historians similar to what we are seeing this year, similar to what happened last year on May 8 about Bitburg and Bergen-Belsen, or similar to a few years back with the TV series "Holocaust." This is a dispute that repeatedly forces us to interpret our present from the recent past and in this way to determine our future—that is, to look for what is right and to cast aside that which is wrong. There can be no unbroken, unreflected identity for us.

The longing for a historyless "normality" is understandable—precisely because what Germans did eludes comprehension. But any attempt to prescribe such normality, or even to desire it or to concoct it for political reasons, will cause the dispute to break out anew. In debates of this kind it becomes clear how inadequate all of our previous attempts to come to grips with the past have been.

Anyone who believed that historical events have some kind of half-life in which memory fades by itself, has deceived himself. Reparations to the survivors of the Holocaust from our newly acquired wealth were a moral imperative. But even if such reparations had been completely paid, they would not expiate the guilt for what happened. Democratic normality for over forty years—that has no doubt been a considerable achievement. But even that was not able to achieve one thing: it could not make us forget that democracy was not freely attained but came to us as the fruit of defeat. And even our resigned readiness to accept the consequences—the division of the German nation—will never be able to blur the reason it happened. On the contrary, this division repeatedly calls to memory the reason it happened. And even people who flee into denial can be recognized by their sideward glances, just as those born at a later date can be recognized when they insist on ignoring the facts.

We are currently experiencing a paradoxical development. As time runs down, what is fading is less the German catastrophe than the memory of the experience of founding the second republic. The government created by the Bonn Basic Law (*Grundgesetz*) was erected as a rational construct. With this, the West Germans achieved a connection to the political culture of the West with its constitutional traditions. The fatherland as a national, territorial, or even a mythical-mystical unity was deeply discredited. In its place came what Dolf Sternberger called "constitutional patriotism"—the "modern-day mutuality of minds and spirits." Where the Germans (and not even the majority) in theWeimar period had at best hesitatingly become, as Friedrich Meineke put it, "republicans of reason," they in 1945 established in the west a "republic of reason"—without roots in a secure tradition and based solely on historical insight and political rationality—and then only as a provisional territorial arrangement.

But such constructs of reason are always susceptible in political reality. Under the best conditions things may go well, at least as long as the experience related to founding the republic continues to affect the people. But as soon as the society enters a critical period (and our society is in a deep crisis that began with the oil shock and extends all the way to Chernobyl), as soon as the future appears uncertain, many people begin to feel the need for a transrational anchor, for a more deeply rooted identity, even for meaning mediated via endowed collective meaning.

Let's beware of this kind of thing. Let's recognize the risks inherent in all arbitrary attempts at creating a common identity. The desire for such an identity is currently causing a remarkable shift in political fronts. The progressives of all people are calling for a more precise analysis of our recent history, while the traditionalists are working on relativizing this history—whether because they want to evoke a more distant past or because they deny the singularity of the Nazi reign of terror.

Such tendencies toward relativizing recent history can be seen in the smallest circumstances, such as the speech about all the evil things done "in the German name"—as if the Germans had not done these things themselves but had hired a subcontractor. Tendencies like this, however, can also take on the crudest forms, for example, when Nazi crimes are diminished to a "logically consistent" reaction to Bolshevist atrocities. It was just this assertion by Berlin historian Ernst Nolte that precipitated the *Historikerstreit* in 1986. The endeavor to cast doubt on the singularity of the German years of 1933 to 1945 is doubly absurd. The attempt to portray Stalin as the real cause of Hitler is bound to fail for purely empirical reasons. And the desire to see the Nazi reign in an ameliorating parallel with other terror regimes before and after will, for moral reasons, not amount to much. For our responsibility and for our enduring liability, it is only important to know that the Nazi regime was unprecedented in our German history and thus singular. The "tu quoque" argument and the finger-pointing assertion "you did it, too" provide no ethical mitigation. Other people's crimes do not excuse our own. Anyone who nonetheless wants to insist on this argument is acting in an unhistorical way.

The meaning of the future arising from a disastrous past: What is the meaning of and why do we study German history? We can no longer naively make reference to our ancestors. And even if we were to go back seventy-seven generations, that would not change the fact that our legitimating traditions have been interrupted by the most recent generations.

A fragmented relationship to our own history is, of course, not a defect of our national identity—despite what all those say who want to convince us that they can drive away the shadows and help us forget. Quite the contrary: Only critical positions are appropriate for the present. Only by facing the past can we be free, as Hans Rothfels once said—not by looking away.

First, we must understand our history as arising from a dialectic of continuity and fragmentation. There are continuities that also led into disaster—without them Hitler and his regime would not have been possible. But the legitimizing traditions from which we still draw today were largely shattered back then. Today we cannot erect straight genealogical trees.

Second, only by using this kind of intensified consciousness may we risk the attempt to "historicize" the Third Reich—as Munich historian Martin Broszat has demanded. Anyone who—like Broszat—desires to remove the simple "moral isolation of the Hitler period" in favor of a moral sensitization of history in general must figure on that process being understood in everyday life as "let bygones be bygones." To understand all is to forgive all . . .

Third, in spite of that we must, as horrifying as the results were, piece together the in-part banal puzzle that makes up the preconditions of the Nazi period. Only in this way can we arm ourselves against repetition. The singularity of the German catastrophe—is only a certainty for the past. At the same time we have to examine the particulars of German history and try to recognize the general threat to humanity contained in it. That is at the heart of the critical question that Norbert Elias posed in a consideration of May 8, 1945, in which he generalized Hitler's war and the National-Socialist myth about societies: "Is this entanglement, this drifting toward war not perhaps inevitable precisely because the real substance of the conflict, which we might be able to discuss, is so exaggerated by emotionally laden social myths that we can no longer talk about the conflict? . . . Are these myths worth once again sentencing millions to death and making broad reaches of the planet unlivable?"

And thus it is just this broken relationship to history, this critical decoding of the past, that could give our present meaning. Doubtless, no one who was born at a later date can be guilty for the Third Reich. But in the history of peoples there is no possibility of forgoing a heritage of liability. We are all liable for the debits and credits of our national heritage. But if we do not honestly and openly accept this heritage, then we engender guilt in several senses.

It is, as Friedrich Nietzsche wrote, always dangerous to attempt to a posteriori give oneself the past from which one would like to have originated: "Since we are the result of past generations, we are also the result of their deviations, their passions and errors, even of their crimes. It is not possible to break the link that ties us to this chain. Even if we condemn these deviations and think of ourselves as having risen above them, we have still not done away with the fact that we originate from them."

Thus we also stand in the shadow of a history that we can no longer heal. And thus the imperative of the Enlightenment is all the more pressing. We cannot shape our history without retouching our past.

Source: *Die Zeit*, December 26, 1986

JOACHIM PERELS

Those Who Refused to Go Along Left Their Country in the Lurch: The Resistance Is Also Being Reassessed in the *Historikerstreit*

The dispute that Jürgen Habermas provoked (*Die Zeit*, July 11, 1986) concerning the historical assessment of the annihilation of the European Jews by the Nazi state has led to a revealing polarization. The historians and publicists (in particular Ernst Nolte and Joachim Fest, *Frankfurter Allgemeine Zeitung* of June 6 and August 28, 1986) who deny the singularity of the administrative mass murder of the Jews by comparing it to other—primarily Stalinist—forms of mass annihilation in the twentieth century have been put on the defensive. It became clear that, using this kind of comparison, the murder of the Jews in the human slaughterhouses of National Socialism has been inverted to become an element of a general historical process from which the peculiarities of German history are completely expunged. The role of the German perpetrators—ideological, administrative, and executive—was able to slip into the shadows. The attempt to change the treatment of the Nazi system so that painful questions can be replaced by exonerating interpretations has, at least for the time being, been stopped, thanks to decisive and convincing articles by Eberhard Jäckel (*Die Zeit*, September 12, 1986), Jürgen Kocka (*Frankfurter Rundschau*, September 23, 1986), Martin Broszat (*Die Zeit*, October 3, 1986), and Hans Mommsen (*Blätter für deutsche und internationale Politik*, no. 10, 1986).

In a balanced article in the *Frankfurter Allgemeine Zeitung* Christian Meier sided with the critics of Nolte and Fest. He focused on the singularity of the mass murder of the Jews and showed how this event was anchored in German history (*Frankfurter Allgemeine Zeitung*, November 20, 1986). But it is incomprehensible how Christian Meier in the end arrives at the point where he attests that Joachim Fest's article possesses "thoughtful argumentation." This, after all, is an article that goes far beyond what is allowed in an objective dispute and slanders Jürgen Habermas, accusing him of "academic dyslexia" and of "scholarly and possibly personal character assassination," which he is said to have practiced on his conservative opponents.

The fact that this reassessment and relativization of the annihilation of the Jews has not yet prevailed in public opinion says nothing about the profound effects the theses of Nolte and Fest are having in nonpublic opinion. This is being influenced by a perspective that, in addition to strengthening already widespread denial, allows the participation of countless Germans in selecting, "deporting," and systematically killing the Jews to be swallowed up by the general horror of world history.

The current discussion must be seen in the context of a planned change of the anti-Nazi system of coordinates in which the Nazi reign had previously been comprehended (cf. M. Buckmiller, *Vorgänge*, no. 6, 1986). Refashioning this system of coordinates is what is at the heart of the debate whose conclusion is still completely open. On the one side the view of the resistance against the Third Reich—including the perspective of the conspirators of July 20, 1944—is declared to be inappropriate for historical analysis of the Nazi reign. On the other side, the positions of the Allies who fought against the National-Socialist system is also seen as a barrier to the historical understanding of the crumbling Nazi reign. This tendency can be seen in Andreas Hillgruber and Ernst Nolte, but also in Christian Meier.

Andreas Hillgruber writes, "The observer stands before the dilemma of those who had to act back then. On the one side there was the stance, based on an ethic of conviction, of the men of July 20, who, despite a hopeless foreign policy situation, decided to go ahead with their assassination attempt on Hitler in order to signal to the world that there existed an 'other Germany.' . . . On the other side there was the stance, based on an ethic of responsibility, of the commanders, district chiefs, and mayors from whose point of view everything depended upon constructing at least a veil of secure points on the East Prussian border in order to prevent the worst from happening: the impending orgy of revenge by the Red Army" (A. Hillgruber, *Zweierlei Untergang: Die Zerschlagung des deutschen Reichs und das Ende des europäischen Judentums*, Berlin, 1986, p. 20f.). Hillgruber opts—in 1986!—for the so-called ethically responsible stance of the commanders, district chiefs, and mayors in the East and thus discards the political alternative of the conspirator group of July 20, which represented conservatives, Christians, and Social Democrats. By declaring the stance of the men of July 20 to be one based merely on an ethic of conviction, Hillgruber implicitly evaluates their undertaking as politically irresponsible—corresponding to Max Weber's classic differentiation: "There is a fundamental difference between acting according to maxims based on an ethic of conviction—in religious terms, 'The Christian acts righteously and gives God the credit'—or according to ones based on an ethic of responsibility, that one is responsible for the (foreseeable) results of his actions"

(Max Weber, "Der Beruf der Politik," in Weber, *Soziologie, welthis-torische Analysen, Politik*, Stuttgart, 1956, p. 175). By insinuating that the conspirators of July 20 were engaged in an attempt based on an ethic of conviction, Hillgruber forgets that their stance resulted from a specific connection between an ethic of conviction and one of responsibility: The revolt of the conscience was aimed at a system of lawlessness and was also intended to end the war.

Ernst Nolte uses other reasons to problematize the evaluation of the Third Reich from the perspective of the resistance. Nolte asks, "whether with this nonpassing of the past interests were and are at play . . . the interests of the persecuted and their survivors in attaining a permanent status of privilege and distinction" (*Frankfurter Allgemeine Zeitung*, June 6, 1986). The legitimacy of the interests, of the affliction of those persecuted by the Third Reich are denied, while on the other side Nolte is quite capable of precisely immersing himself in Hitler's psyche in order to explain the Holocaust as a result of Hitler's obsessions.

Finally, in an essay in the *Frankfurter Allgemeine Zeitung*, which, instead of glossing over the Nazi mass crimes shifts them into our consciousness, Christian Meier disqualified the perspective of the resistance against Hitler as an alternative to the prevailing affirmative mentality. Meier writes, "One can hardly hold it against the Germans that they carried out their duties punctually, properly, and competently, or that they risked their lives. How and why should they leave their country in the lurch because of the regime?" (*Frankfurter Allgemeine Zeitung*, June 28, 1986). With this question the Nazi regime is blithely identified with our country, with the result that refusing to go along with and joining Hitler's *Wehrmacht*—and there are impressive examples of individual socialists and Christians who did refuse—is seen as forsaking one's country. Meier considers the alternative of resistance, but his comments make resistance appear to be a politically impossible stance: "Even then it is difficult to determine whether one [in cases of resistance or sabotage], by taking the measures necessary to seem normal, does not contribute more to the regime than one can harm it through resistance" (ibid.). Did Hans von Dohnanyi, Dietrich Bonn-hoeffer, or Julius Leber, in opposing the clique of Nazi murderers, contribute more to the regime than if they had gone along with it? This question needs no answer. This is completely unfair to those who sacrificed their lives in the struggle against planned despotism because it indirectly places the martyrs of the resistance on the side of the regime.

Andreas Hillgruber goes even farther. He draws a strict line of demarcation against the Allies, without whom the yoke of Nazi despotism would not have been broken. He does this under the viewpoint of that part of the military forces with which historians can identify: "Identifying with the future victors—and in the case of the East, that meant with the Soviet

Union, the Red Army—was unthinkable. The notion of liberation implied this kind of identification with the victors. Of course, the concept is completely justified for the victims of the Nazi regime liberated from concentration camps. But for the fate of the German nation as a whole it is inappropriate" (A. Hillgruber, as quoted above, p. 24). In this comment, the "fate of the German nation as a whole" appears as an entity that can be viewed separately from the victims of the Nazi regime. But then what about the victims of National Socialism who were liberated from the concentration camps—Eugen Kogon, Martin Niemöller, Kurt Schumacher, or Emile Carlebach—do they have nothing to do with the "fate of the German nation as a whole?" This possible consequence arises from a rightist conservative view that identifies with certain elites of the Nazi power structure—especially with the *Wehrmacht*—that extend all the way to individual "higher-ups of the NSDAP" (A. Hillgruber, p. 37). Thus this view must consider the positions of decisive opponents of the Nazi regime to be questionable. And this includes the resistance and the Allies.

The fact that the stance of the opponents of National Socialism is placed in doubt as a point of reference for analyzing the Third Reich has to do with the prevailing self-understanding of the Federal Republic, the stability of which certain conservative historians are concerned with preserving. This stability was in part possible because a large part of the military, administrative, and judicial elites was uncritically incorporated into the constitutional state that was the early Federal Republic. Only if the role of these elites in the period of the Third Reich appears in an unproblematic light and the German and Allied opposition to the Nazi system can be rejected as a political alternative can the birth defect of the early Federal Republic—constructing a democracy based on the rule of law, but using elites from a totalitarian regime—remain in the dark.

The Federal Republic constituted itself via two essentially contradictory legitimation principles. These make it impossible to construct an unbroken political identity for the Bonn republic. The Federal Republic defines itself as the negation of the Nazi reign. This fact finds its clearest expression in the basic rights of our constitution, which are supposed to make despotism impossible. But for a long time the Federal Republic has also defined itself as a political order that is in principle just and legal. Gustav Radbruch's concept of legal injustice, aimed at core principles of National-Socialist rule, hardly had any practical significance for the administration of justice in the 1950s, 1960s, and 1970s. To provide an example: On the one side there are annual official commemorations for the men of July 20. On the other side the same state, in a 1956 decision of the Supreme Court, affirms that the resistance of Bonnhoeffer, Hans von Dohnanyi, and others is high treason. Thus their murder, ordered in early 1945 by an SS military court in the concentration camp Sachsenhausen, can be viewed as legal in principle (cf. G. Spengel, *Rechtsbeugung als Rechtssprechung*, Berlin 1984, pp. 89ff.).

Thus the rule: Something like a democratic identity in our country can only be shaped by serious discussion about the hereditary encumbrance of National Socialism.

Source: *Frankfurter Rundschau*, December 27, 1986

Authors Note: The text originally bore the title "Relativization of the Resistance against the Nazi Regime?"

IMANUEL GEISS

On the *Historikerstreit*

A dispute about recent German history has been raging in the German public sphere for months. The history of German scholarship—by no means lacking in such events—has yet to see anything as intense as this.

It all began with an article by Jürgen Habermas in *Die Zeit* (July 11, 1986) called "A Kind of Settlement of Damages." In it, the social philosopher of the Frankfurt School accused historians Ernst Nolte, Andreas Hillgruber, and Michael Stürmer of engaging in cold-blooded trivialization of the Third Reich and its crimes by normalizing German history in a neoconservative way. After numerous contributions to the discussion, most of which appeared in *Die Zeit* and the *Frankfurter Allgemeine Zeitung*, Rudolf Augstein used his essay in *Der Spiegel* to intensify Habermas's attack to the point of accusing Hillgruber of being a "constitutional Nazi."

The main argument against the "revisionists" (Habermas) is the thesis that Auschwitz, the high (or low) point of National-Socialist crimes, was so unique in world history that no kind of relativization should be permitted because such a thing would amount to trivializing the Nazi regime and its crimes. The understanding of the singularity of Nazi crimes is tightly bound to the consensus of progressive historians of the German *Sonderweg* that led to the Third Reich and its crimes. For this reason, Habermas and Augstein seek to fend off all comparisons of the Nazi regime with communism, from the Russian civil war and Stalinism to Pol Pot.

Habermas and Augstein are certainly driven to their sharp polemics by legitimate concerns that should be taken seriously. But they also have to submit themselves to the question of whether the methods and the tone of their polemic are not more harmful than helpful to their cause. The following countercritique seeks to address political and historical dimensions that can lead beyond the controversy and out of the labyrinth of this otherwise sterile professorial dispute.

Habermas imputes to the "revisionists" the intention to create a neoconservative *Wende*, or political shift, among historians. That would amount to a recourse to a stronger emphasis in German history writing on national identity. Habermas, in contrast, proposes a "universalist orientation of values" and a "constitutional patriotism" that is bound to the West. Moreover, he, as a German, wants to prevent his sense of shame about the Nazi crimes being somehow driven out of him. Those are honorable positions that I share. But I cannot go along with Habermas's (and Augstein's) tone and style of argumentation. The polemics of both of these men are too crude and emotional, and in a central point, Habermas gets entangled in an insoluble contradiction. With a topic as complex and emotionally charged as this one, a line of reasoning needs to be more refined and differentiated. *Terribles simplificateurs* of the one or the other color can only cause unassessable damage due to the polarization they bring about, which causes existing difference of opinion to escalate to conflicts. The point is to limit the realm of controversy and to at least emotionally defuse the dispute by employing objectivity.

First of all we must distinguish between the positions of the historians. Since 1963, Nolte has been saying that fascism—and thus also Nazism—has historically represented a reaction to the Communist revolution in Russia. The simple chronology (1917–1919/22/33) speaks for the idea of a sequence of action (October Revolution) and reaction (fascism). Then of course there is the fact that in Germany from 1918 on, the extreme right-wing forces were dead set against including the moderately leftist Social Democrats in the government.

But this chronological sequence and a historical categorization of both systems by no means supports the conclusion that the crimes of each of the systems can be placed in an analogous sequence, as Nolte suggests (Gulag before Auschwitz). This kind of localization cannot be supported by scholarship and must be rejected morally. Whether Nolte intended this or not, it amounts to balancing one set of crimes with another and in this way invariably leads to German-nationalist apologetics. Two important points deserve to be looked at in more detail:

First, Nolte does not deny the Nazi crimes, as Habermas suggests. Second, one must allow authors—in a scholarly as well as in a political sense—to speak about the crimes of communism as well as those of National Socialism, if not in the kind of causal chain suggested by Nolte.

Nolte expressed his assertion in an essay published in England (and apparently also orally to an Israeli historian): namely that due to Chaim Weizmann's declaration at the beginning of the Second World War, the Jews became a warring party. Thus the deportations of Jews was justified. This is hair-raising nonsense, even if we ignore the moral aspect. In 1939 the Jews were not at all a warring party because they had no government that was recognized by international law. But even if they had been a warring party, valid international law (the Hague Convention) forbade any kind of reprisals against noncombatants—that is, the Jewish population.

The matter is quite different with Hillgruber. He tends to be a rather conservative historian who is a product of German-national traditions. But in the course of his some thirty years of scholarly activity, he has, influenced by the facts from source materials and the literature, proved to be extraordinarily adaptive. This is particularly true of his extensive reception of Fritz Fischer's research on the Kaiserreich and the First World War and of his fair evaluation of GDR research in this field. The two Hillgruber essays that Habermas took for the focal point of his attack are, each on its own, respectable summaries of the most recent research on two aspects of the Second World War. Both in terms of form and of content, they display weaknesses that Habermas and Augstein were able to exploit mercilessly.

Dragging together two essays that had appeared elsewhere and publishing them in the slim volume (*Zweierlei Untergang: Die Zerschlagung des deutschen Reiches und das Ende des europäischen Judentums* [Twofold Fall: The Destruction of the German Reich and the End of European Jewry]) is irritating enough. But it took Habermas to establish a negative connection in the words "*Zerschlagung*" [destruction] and "*Ende*" [end]), which he achieved partially by malicious insinuation and partially by over-interpretation.

Hillgruber's first essay on the collapse of the German East Front in 1944–45, however, was a point of vulnerability. He abandoned the sober explanation of the constraints—which no doubt existed—on those in charge on the German side in favor of a voluntaristic demand that one had to decide for one side or the other. This weakness, however, does not justify the merciless severity, almost in the tone of an old testament prophet, with which Habermas goes after this dissident historian. This is particularly true where Habermas distorts Hillgruber's text. Heinrich-August Winkler was justified when, in an article in the *Frankfurter Rundschau*, he recently removed Hillgruber from the firing line of progressive criticism.

Michael Stürmer's position must be judged as different again. For twenty years he has been one of the few really good, eloquent German historians. As a commentator in the *Frankfurter Allgemeine Zeitung* and a political adviser to Chancellor Kohl, he has openly taken positions on the politics of our country—which is his right. In his writing, Stürmer represents a centrist and intelligent variant of the governing camp. His work shows traces of the antinationalist historiography of Fritz Fischer. Stürmer's attempts to rediscover a collective—and thus national—identity in our "problematic fatherland" (Heinemann) are neither inherently reactionary nor repugnant. In cases like this, criticism must strive to be concrete.

But it also is not justified to simply dismiss any consideration of the geographic position of the Germans in Europe as mere "ideology of Central Europe that our revisionists are once again warming up with their geopolitical drumbeat" (Habermas). Geography, with its influences on history, is so elementary a factor that the—largely progressive—*Annales* school in neighboring France has made it the basis of its analysis. Center and periphery, centers of power and power vacuums are indeed indispensable categories for any historical study of power politics and foreign policy—and thus also for Germany and the German question in Europe.

That is not even close to being "geopolitics." Geography as a historical explanation does not become geopolitics until it is used to provide arguments for offensive, expansionist power politics.

When Habermas even contemptuously refers to Stürmer's search for a position as "nationalist NATO philosophy" in the style of primitive anti-Americanism, then he ends up contradicting his much-invoked linkage of the Federal Republic to the West—to which, after all, NATO also belongs. Furthermore, the linkage of the Federal Republic to the West, heatedly debated by Habermas and Stürmer on the theoretical level, can only be maintained on the basis of a clear analysis of German history—a history that, after all, took place in the center of Europe, increasingly in the polarization of East and West.

More dangerous for our system are the consequences that go beyond the controversy. Habermas has already intimated that the "neoconservative revisionists" had already abandoned the basis of our democratic constitutional order by their morally repugnant apology for the Third Reich and its crimes. With his caustic expression "constitutional Nazi," Augstein explicitly places Hillgruber on the wrong side of the line that defines constitutional legitimacy.

The public and moral execution of the "revisionists" by Habermas and Augstein also indirectly marks everyone who thinks like Hillgruber and dares to contradict the moral caretakers of our republic—guilt by association.

Their hypersensitive antifascism perceives the stirrings of fascism in every corner and identifies large parts of our society as, if not unmitigated Nazis, then at least "constitutional" ones. But the expression "constitutional Nazi" inevitably provokes the counterexpression "constitutional Communist." Habermas and Augstein's brand of friend-or-foe thinking thus irrevocably polarizes our society into clans of the Right and of the Left. But then what remains of our democratic and liberal Federal Republic? As a consequence of their actions, Habermas and Augstein, whether they want to or not, are destroying our social order because their kind of attack further escalates polarization, and their "historical moralism" (H. Fleischer), if given a chance, would cut off free discussion coming from the Right.

One of their chief errors was not distinguishing between effect and possible intentions of the historian-"revisionists" they attacked. Of course the "revisionists" reflect and influence—in what for complex societies is the normal swing of the pendulum between Right and Left—the political development of the Germans over the forty years after the end of the Second World War and the fall of the Nazi system. Even the geographically small Federal Republic is seen in economic terms as a world power and it really is a world power in military and political terms. After decades of German horror about German misuse of power in two world wars, the Germans, too, have to relearn to reflect in a historically rational way about power and power politics so that they might use their new power in a wiser and more humane way.

And thus it should also be possible for German historians to analyze the explosion of the First World War without emotional and moralizing recourse to terms such as "war guilt." Certainly Germans must never be allowed to forget Auschwitz. In fact they should make Auschwitz, as I argued in this magazine over two years ago (cf. *Evangelische Kommentare*, 12, 1984, p. 673ff.) a starting point to achieve a positive collective identification with their society. But that is not possible without reexamining the history of those inconceivable events. Nor is it possible without historical comparisons and thus without some kind of relativization.

A historical comparison of National-Socialist and Communist crimes must be permitted if the topic demands it. This is particularly true when one keeps in mind that comparing things does not mean equating them (this is a common error of people who do not think precisely). The Nazi crimes are a unique peak of cruelty. But they are also comparable to the Communist crimes. There is a danger that the crimes of one side might be balanced with those of the other. This danger arises from the simultaneity of Nazi and Communist crimes, and it must be opposed energetically. But the "neoconservative revisionists" have attempted nothing of the kind, and only Nolte can be accused of such an attempt, and then only implicitly.

The political-ideological discussion of these days could force even us Germans to address the crimes of communism. The historical crimes of German fascism still today serve Communist agitation as a preferred argument in support of the ideological conflict between East and West— without itself openly and directly dealing with its own crimes.

Any attempt at classifying the Third Reich and its crimes is inevitably a tightrope walk between apology and distortion on both sides. And thus a rational discussion of the entire problem complex has become necessary— one without prohibitions and without generalizations and defamatory insinuations. Habermas and Augstein's kind of attacks inspire the impression that they are claiming a monopoly to interpret German history for themselves and their supporters. And thus they are destroying the pluralism that is absolutely essential for our system to survive.

In the end, their thinking is of a dualist-fundamentalist type that only knows categories such as good and evil, friend and foe. Their fundamentalism is secularized and enlightened. It is of little consolation that in our worldwide crisis situation, religious dualism is experiencing a worldwide renaissance with fundamentalist trends in the various religious communities.

Source: *Evangelische Kommentare*, No. 2, February 1987

APPENDIX
Notes on the *Historikerstreit*

JÜRGEN HABERMAS

Note, February 23, 1987

The first reactions to my July 11, 1986, article in *Die Zeit* made it evident how Hildebrand, Stürmer, Hillgruber, and Fest intended to handle the accusation that they were engaged in the kind of revisionism that seeks to trivialize its object. They denied the facts and the political context. They disputed that the activities of the historians I had mentioned had anything to do with each other. And they insinuated that I had fabricated the quotations I used. I would have been willing to overlook even the most threadbare element in this defensive strategy—the accusation of scholarly dishonesty—if Hillgruber (in K. D. Erdmann's journal *Geschichte in Wissenschaft und Unterricht*, 12 [1986], 725–38) had not taken it up again— this time in an unusual way.

Apparently neither Hillgruber nor Hildebrand made the effort to check their quotations—nor did their historian colleagues who passed along the accusation that I had falsified quotations. Otherwise they would have noticed the only serious error that slipped by me. I should not have illustrated the style with which Hillgruber plays down the annihilation of the Jews in *Zweierlei Untergang* [Twofold Fall] (Siedler, 1986) by writing that the gas chambers had been described as a "more effective means" of liquidation. On page 95 the author makes clear by the use of quotation marks that the expression "effective" is borrowed from Nazi jargon. I regret this error all the more because I could have easily found many other equivalent examples. How much this general accusation that I had manipulated quotations is used as a pretext is illustrated by the fact that not one of these historians mentions this one, demonstrable error. The three or four specific accusations that I found in the various texts, however, will not stand up to such a test.

1. Michael Stürmer has the chutzpah to simply deny his own position: "Endowing meaning?"—so he asks in a letter to the editor (*Frankfurter Allgemeine Zeitung*, August 16, 1986) and provides the astonishing response: "It (history) should leave endowing meaning to others." In the article that he himself refers to ("Dissonanzen des Fortschritts" [Dissonances of Progress], 1986), one can read: "It appears necessary to abandon the merely apparent difference between social history and cultural history and to understand that at the end of the twentieth century humans residing

260

in industrial cultures must more than ever before seek and comprehend their historical identity in order not to lose themselves." I had continued to attribute to Stürmer the conviction that history was called upon "to endow meaning." Martin Broszat (in *Die Zeit*, October 3, 1986) proved with four Stürmer quotations that this was no "imaginative invention."

2. In a letter to the editor (of August 11, 1986) I have already briefly responded to an additional accusation by Klaus Hildebrand (*Frankfurter Allgemeine Zeitung*, July 31, 1986). The principals from whose perspective Hillgruber (in *Zweierlei Untergang*) would like to portray the events of the war—the German Army in the East, the navy, the German population (p. 24)—are here joined by commanders, regional officials, and mayors to whom Hillgruber attributes an ethic based on responsibility (p. 21). Thus in this story "higher-ups of the Nazi party"—without quotation marks, by the way—appear, some of whom "proved themselves" while others failed (p. 37). That justifies my drawing the conclusion that Hillgruber is seeking to "portray these events from the perspective of the brave soldiers, of the desperate civilian population, but also of the tried and true higher-ups of the Nazi party" (*Die Zeit*, July 11, 1986). Using the usual rules of logic one cannot conclude with Hildebrand that in my argumentation Hillgruber was asserting or implying that back then there were only brave soldiers or only tried and true Nazi party officials.

In *Geschichte in Wissenschaft und Unterricht* 12 (1986), p. 731, Hillgruber criticizes the same sentence under a different aspect. He insists on the distinction, which I may have not considered in sufficient depth, between those who were "tried and true over a long period" and "those who proved themselves at that time." But doesn't the person who proves himself in extremis deserve the description of being a "proven, or tried and true man"? And in any case, this ridiculous dispute about words and secondary virtues just confirms Hillgruber's lack of objectivity about this entire sphere. This is a case of praising the fire department that set the fire.

3. Finally, Hillgruber asserts that I had misrepresented his text by attributing to him ideas that were not his. That, too, is incorrect. In one place (p. 86), Hillgruber retraces a thought experiment by Christoph Dipper and appropriates the substance of these thoughts. In conclusion, he casts doubt on a certain thesis from Hans Mommsen (p. 87). I correctly reproduce those thoughts as an opinion that Hillgruber supports. And I make the thesis recognizable as a view that Hillgruber criticizes—without naming Dipper and Mommsen by name. Hillgruber's farfetched demand is that I, in my necessarily brief summary of his only marginally scholarly train of thought, should have pointed out whose views the author is at any time supporting or criticizing. The editors of a weekly newspaper even strike out the much more important documentation of quotations. Hillgruber appears not to be able to differentiate between these types of text. He should know that a newspaper polemic is not a term paper for a history

seminar. In a polemic essay for a newspaper the correctness of quotations is only measured by whether the reproduced text segments do justice to the thought process or the style that they characterize.

4. I cannot judge the way Hillgruber himself deals with texts since I know only the popularized compilation of the two of his essays that appeared with Siedler. But little confidence is aroused by an assertion (made in *Geschichte in Wissenschaft und Unterricht*, 12, 1986, p. 736) that I just happen to be able to judge. There, Hillgruber says that I had exerted a "significant influence on the agitation unleashed by the extreme leftists at West German universities and on the psychic terror aimed at individual non-Marxist colleagues." One expects from historians, and I do not mean just this historian, that they take the relevant and in this case easily accessible documents and research into account before allowing themselves to be taken prisoner by the resentments stemming from their unquestioned life story. My behavior is well documented in J. Habermas, *Kleine politische Schriften I-IV*, Suhrkamp, 1981. Also see Rolf Wiggershaus's *Die Frankfurter Schule*, Hanser, 1986.

ERNST NOLTE

Concluding Note, April 15, 1987

I was unable to sustain my objection to the subtitle of this volume* because I did not want to be responsible for any possible delays in publication. My suggestion, one that I think is far more appropriate, is "Documentation of the Controversy Surrounding the Preconditions and the Character of the 'Final Solution of the Jewish Question.'"

---

*[Nolte is here referring to the subtitle of the German-language edition: *Die Dokumentation der Kontroverse um die Einzigartigkeit der nationalsozialistischen Judenvernichtung* (The Documentation of the Controversy Concerning the Singularity of the National-Socialist Annihilation of the Jews).]

JOACHIM FEST

Postscript, April 21, 1987

Several observers have termed the *Historikerstreit* "superfluous." Anyone
who examines the substance of the differences of opinion expressed in this
debate could easily come to this conclusion. For no opponent has ever
doubted or even contested the crimes committed against the Jews. No one
attempted to relativize these crimes or to balance them with the crimes of
other peoples. And it took the ever-astonishing excitability of a Rudolf
Augstein to invent the formula of the "new Auschwitz lie." This is, as we
now know, clearly a form of journalistic dyslexia. Not even Ernst Nolte
challenged the singularity of the Nazi crimes—although he is now being
accused of just that. It is also uncontested that these crimes have a singular character for the Germans themselves. These mass murders are an
elementary component of the Germans' past and will continue to be,
perhaps for generations, a part of their future.

In its substance, the dispute was initiated by Ernst Nolte's question
whether Hitler's monstrous will to annihilate the Jews, judging from its
origin, came from early Viennese impressions or, what is more likely, from
the later Munich experiences, that is, whether Hitler was an originator or
simply being reactive. Despite all the consequences that arose from his
answer, Nolte's question was in fact a purely academic exercise. The
conclusions would probably not have caused as much controversy if they
had not been accompanied by special circumstances.

One of these is Nolte's tendency to draw sharply pointed arguments,
which he brings to an extreme and often speculative head and on which he
at the same time casts doubt by using rhetorical questions. As a result, the
arguments quickly become recognizable as experimental figures of rhetoric
and thought. Closely related to that is the often-posed objection that this
kind of argumentation should not have been published in a daily newspaper. But the one as well as the other is part of the same tradition in the
search for knowledge. This is related to the recognition that truth can only
be approached through a protracted process, which nothing can move
along better than public dispute. I myself do not agree with Nolte on the
central point of the controversy. But I am also of the opinion that particularly problematic considerations, inasmuch as they do not violate the
political and moral general consensus of the post-Hitler period, should be

made accessible to everyone. No one is served if these ideas remain obscured from the general public. After more than forty years of historical enlightenment about the character of the Nazi regime and of being tested in democracy, the society in the Federal Republic should be capable of debating such topics openly and objectively.

If the *Historikerstreit* was important despite everything, then, it was important because it taught us, not unlike the shameful prehistory of this book, that gentle public debate is not possible. It is not without a sense of melancholy that one notes the fracture that runs through the discipline of history and divides it into two camps.

Standing on the one side, to simplify, are those who want to preserve Hitler and National Socialism as a kind of antimyth that can be used for political intentions—the theory of a conspiracy on the part of the political Right, to which Nolte, Stürmer, and Hillgruber are linked. This becomes evident in the defamatory statements and the expansion of the dispute to the historical museum. It is doubtless no coincidence that Habermas, Jäckel, Mommsen, and others became involved in the recent election campaign in this way. Many statements in favor of the pluralistic character of scholarship and in favor of an ethos representing a republic of learned men reveal themselves as merely empty phrases to the person who has an overview of these things.

On the other side are, disinterested and without recognizable party preference, the representatives of a scholarly pursuit that, far (sometimes too far) from all concerns of the day, arrives at new questions, presents its theses, and subjects them to public debate.

Strictly speaking, Nolte did nothing but take up the suggestion by Broszat and others that National Socialism be historicized. It was clear to anyone with any sense for the topic—and Broszat's opening article made it evident that he too had recognized it—that this transition would be beset with difficulties. But that the most incensed objections would come from those who from the beginning were the spokesmen of historicization—this was no less surprising than the recognition that yesterday's enlighteners are today's intolerant mythologues, people who want to forbid questions from being posed.

Nonetheless, the process of historicization will continue. It cannot be stopped. For it has the most powerful imaginable force on its side: time. Not the kind of time that makes us forget, but the kind that can lead from new questions to an enhanced sense of morality. That Habermas and the partisans of domination-guided discourse are not only pleading for a static image of the Nazi regime but are also at loggerheads with changing times—this makes them the advocates of a hopeless cause.

MICHAEL STÜRMER

Postscript, April 25, 1987

Jürgen Habermas has provided the legitimation problems of late Marxism with examples:

1. the invention of fact-free scholarship;
2. the unification of knowledge and interest;
3. the portrayal of dominance-free discourse.

Ad 1. In regard to my texts, Habermas insists on the kind of distortions and falsifications that have motivated him for over a year. This book provides an opportunity to examine the relationship between poetry and truth. But what about Habermas's deeply felt expression—encouraging but surprising—of support for the Federal Republic's ties to the West? After all, he is able to formulate no worse a reproach than that of a pro-NATO historian—whatever that might be. And what does this fearful indictment have to do with neonationalism? Even an important social philosopher should know that the North Atlantic system, at least for the German participants, is and always was of a supranational nature and leaves no space for national ambitions. His assertions are either absurd or a kind of ideological counterfeit.

Ad 2. Habermas conceals from us that the alarmed statements that initiated this quarrel agree in tone and content with what he, invited to a committee hearing on July 2, 1986, by the SPD-fraction of the German Bundestag, had to say *urbi et orbi* on the theme of the proposed German Historical Museum in Berlin. Three of those unmasked by Habermas had nothing to do with this project. He was apparently unable to discover any quotable citations on the Nazi regime from the fourth, me. The Hamburg weekly [*Der Spiegel*], which loyally printed the words of the master thinker of Frankfurt, was tactful enough to skip over the special partisan provenance. In the national election campaign, the practice of anti-Fascist agitation—exposing anyone who disagrees with you as a Nazi (how else are we to understand the term "neoconservative apologist")—played an obscene role and is destined, if Habermas and his ilk have their way, to continue to play this role.

Ad 3. Habermas, in his inimitable way, put Piper Verlag under pressure. Only he demanded a postscript, which he then transformed into an

266

invective. If the publisher did not agree, he would not allow his articles to be printed. In this way he forced others and myself into the embarrassing position of having to once again get involved with his disinformation campaign.

Jürgen Habermas has achieved a lot: mistrust, personal animosities, the loss of language. I congratulate nobody on that.

"It is an ill wind that blows nobody any good."

ANDREAS HILLGRUBER

My Concluding Remarks on the So-Called *Historikerstreit*, May 12, 1987

Jürgen Habermas's reply of February 23, 1987, to my article "Jürgen Habermas, Karl-Heinz Janßen, and the Enlightenment in the Year 1986" which was published in the magazine *Geschichte in Wissenschaft und Unterricht*, 37 (1986), pp. 725–738 (it is reprinted in this volume) is once again a revealing illustration of the peculiar way this philosopher deals with texts. In my article I demonstrated that Habermas had extensively misrepresented my statements and manipulated them with quotations in a way that solely served the purpose of politically "enlightening" the readers of his article "A Kind of Settlement of Damages" (*Die Zeit*, July 11, 1986) about allegedly "apologetic" tendencies in my book *Zweierlei Untergang* [Twofold Fall] (Siedler Verlag, Berlin, 1986). By comparing my text in the Siedler book with the "quotations" in the *Zeit* article by Habermas and my reply (which refers to the Siedler book) in the article in *Geschichte in Wissenschaft und Unterricht*, any reader can see for himself whether my accusation that Habermas had engaged in scholarly dishonesty is justified. His response of February 23, 1987, is a persistently arrogant attempt to vindicate himself by again attacking the historians he had attacked in his *Zeit* article. He does this with evasion, diversion, sophist hair-splitting, and—once again—by misrepresenting my statements. This practice deserves a clear and fundamental rebuke.

In his essay in the newspaper *Die Welt* "He Who Wants to Escape the Abyss Must Sound It Precisely" (reprinted in this book), Klaus Hildebrand spoke of a "Habermas method" that opened the floodgates for all forms of capricious behavior in dealing with texts. Just how justified this characterization is—even beyond this individual case—became fully clear to me in recent months when I read the numerous letters that reached me and when I talked with numerous colleagues (in history and philosophy). Habermas, and this is evident from a large number of reviews of his works by authors of varying political affiliations, tends to descend upon these texts, even if they are philosophical texts (even classics such as the works of Kant and

Hegel are not excepted), in a way that is no different than what he did to my historical essay. He does this with more or less grotesque distortions of quotations, excerpts that twist meaning, and quotations transplanted out of their context in order to provide the kind of confusion that causes the reader to be blinded and dazzled. If one knows this, then it is perfectly evident how unfruitful any continued scholarly discussion with Habermas is—for example on the basis of the February 23, 1987, reply. Thus I have no intention of once again wasting time and energy on a response, as was unavoidable with my essay in *Geschichte in Wissenschaft und Unterricht*. A further response would only mean going along with his obvious and expressed need for publicity. And it would only provide him with an opportunity to again respond with new excesses.

It will always remain a riddle to me how some of my historian colleagues, instead of rebuking this dilettante, could entirely or in part support Habermas's "arguments." It was only in this way that the Habermas scandal became a *Historikerstreit*. I also have very little understanding for the opinion expressed (in the *Mitteilungsblatt des Verbandes der Historiker Deutschlands* [Bulletin of the Association of German Historians], 1, 1987, p. 3) by association chair Christian Meier ("On the So-Called *Historikerstreit*") that "no special knowledge was necessary" to "participate in this dispute." Historical scholarship will have been done a tremendous disservice if extraordinarily important historical topics are abandoned to the "Habermas method" that then, by referring to the philosopher Habermas, can be "applied" by publicists like Rudolf Augstein and exaggerated to an absurd degree and made into defamation of the worse kind. In contrast, the last great public debate about an important historical problem, the so-called Fischer Controversy about the responsibility of the leadership of the Second Reich for precipitating the First World War, led to a remarkable scholarly gain. And this took place despite the powerful emotional character of the material being discussed. The reason is that this dispute was carried out by professional historians. The *Historikerstreit*, however, with the exception of a very few objective contributions and balanced considerations by colleagues in the field, degenerated into a boundless public palaver whose end is not yet in sight.

ABOUT THE AUTHORS

RUDOLF AUGSTEIN, born in 1923, is the publisher of *Der Spiegel*.

KARL DIETRICH BRACHER, born in 1922, is a professor of political science and current affairs at the University of Bonn.

MARTIN BROSZAT, born in 1926, is the director of the Institut für Zeitgeschichte (Institute for Modern History) in Munich and an honorary professor at the University of Munich.

MICHA BRUMLIK, born in 1947, is a professor of education at the University of Heidelberg.

WALTER EUCHNER, born in 1933, is a professor of political science at the University of Göttingen.

JOACHIM FEST, born in 1926, is copublisher of the *Frankfurter Allgemeine Zeitung*.

HELMUT FLEISCHER, born in 1927, is a professor of philosophy at the Technical University in Darmstadt.

IMANUEL GEISS, born in 1931, is a professor of modern history at the University of Bremen.

JÜRGEN HABERMAS, born in 1929, is a professor of philosophy at the University of Frankfurt.

HANNO HELBLING, born in 1930, is the director of the editorial page section of the *Neue Züricher Zeitung*.

KLAUS HILDEBRAND, born in 1941, is a professor of modern history at the University of Bonn.

ANDREAS HILLGRUBER, born in 1925, is a professor of modern history at the University of Cologne.

EBERHARD JÄCKEL, born in 1929, is a professor of modern history at the University of Stuttgart.

JÜRGEN KOCKA, born in 1941, is a professor of modern history and social history at the University of Bielefeld.

ROBERT LEICHT is assistant editor-in-chief of *Die Zeit*.

RICHARD LÖWENTHAL, born in 1908, is a member of the board of directors of the Research Institute of the Deutsche Gesellschaft für auswärtige Politik [German Society for Foreign Policy] in Bonn.

CHRISTIAN MEIER, born in 1929, is a professor of ancient history at the University of Munich.

HORST MÖLLER, born in 1943, is a professor of modern history at the University of Erlangen.

HANS MOMMSEN, born in 1930, is a professor of modern history at the Ruhr University in Bochum.

WOLFGANG J. MOMMSEN, born in 1930, is a professor of modern history at the University of Düsseldorf.

THOMAS NIPPERDEY, born in 1927, was a professor of modern history at the University of Munich until his death in June 1992.

ERNST NOLTE, born in 1923, is a professor of modern history at the Free University of Berlin.

JOACHIM PERELS, born in 1942, is a professor of political science at the University of Hannover.

HAGEN SCHULZE, born in 1943, is a professor of both modern history and the theory and methodology of history at the Free University of Berlin.

KURT SONTHEIMER, born in 1928, is a professor of political science at the University of Munich.

MICHAEL STÜRMER, born in 1938, is a professor of modern history at the University of Erlangen.

HEINRICH AUGUST WINKLER, born in 1938, is a professor of modern history and current affairs at the University of Freiburg.

AFTERWORD TO THE *HISTORIKERSTREIT*

Ernst Piper

This book documents the dispute that began early in the summer of 1986 and became known as the *Historikerstreit*. This debate was sparked by the publication of a lecture that Ernst Nolte had been scheduled to deliver at the Römerberg Talks in Frankfurt (p. 18 in this book) and by an essay in which Jürgen Habermas (p. 34 in this book) takes to task Nolte's lecture text and a recently published book, *Zweierlei Untergang* [Twofold Fall] by Andreas Hillgruber. Preceding these texts is an essay of 1980 (p. 1 in this book) in which Nolte delineates his position on further history writing about National Socialism. This essay has never been published in Germany in its entirety.

It is characteristic of the altered political climate in the Federal Republic that Nolte's theses caused a sensation neither when they were delivered in a lecture at the Siemens-Stiftung—and following that they were published in excerpts in the *Frankfurter Allgemeine Zeitung*—nor when the complete essay appeared in an English anthology. But things were quite different with the lecture that Nolte did not deliver at the Römerberg Talks.

This text stands at the beginning of the liveliest dispute among German historians since the Fischer Controversy of the 1960s about German guilt for the outbreak of the First World War—but the *Historikerstreit*, unlike the Fischer Controversy, has expanded well beyond the guild of historians.

To preserve the character of the documentation, all texts have been reproduced in their entirety—that is, as they originally appeared. Despite the necessity for quantitative limits, one can say that the most important contributions to the *Historikerstreit* can be found in this volume. The reader who is interested in additional comments on this controversy will find many of these discussed or at least mentioned in the published articles. The editorial deadline was late January 1987. We were not able to print anything that appeared after this date. Most of the essays that appeared later are less contributions to the *Historikerstreit* than comments about it.[1] Moreover, the published volume represents a compromise between the naturally divergent desires and opinions of the authors; it is not the product of a specific editorial conception. Many of the people who contributed to this book linked their permission to publish to conditions that the book should contain certain other texts, by themselves or by others.

The question of who would bear editorial responsibility remained contested. Some expressed the desire to have an editor in charge—several names were mentioned—while others, particularly Jürgen Habermas, rejected this idea. Habermas wrote:

> I believe that there can be no nonparticipants in this question and thus I can think of no one who would be authorized to rise above the dispute. In any case, no one will have the last word—that is an old hermeneutic wisdom.[2]

My function in creating this book was thus that of a moderator. This was not always easy, particularly because during the debate unfortunate personal antipathies developed between the participants.

Not atypical for the climate of the discussion were the repeated complaints of several authors from both camps that the articles of the opposing side were in the majority. The compromise we achieved was temporarily endangered when it became known that Habermas wanted to add a lengthy footnote to his third text (p. 162 in this book). Fortunately, we soon found another compromise: This footnote would be placed at the end of the book[3] and the four people attacked in it by name would also be accorded opportunity to respond. These five "annotations," contained in the Appendix, are the only original—not previously published—texts in this volume.

One of the compromises that had to be made to assure the publication of the book was to omit my introductory foreword to the material. Despite all attempts at neutrality, several contributors had objections to my text.

It was relatively easy to come to an agreement that all foreign contributions to the *Historikerstreit* should be omitted. Due to the complexity and extreme diversity of the foreign discussion, agreement would have made editing and publishing the book so complicated that it would have been impossible.

In light of the great interest demonstrated abroad, the Foreign Office sent a detailed documentation of the *Historikerstreit* to all German embassies on November 6, 1986. The accompanying letter said:

> This controversy shows how our public sphere, against the backdrop of the Nazi period, is struggling for the meaning of history and an understanding of history in the Federal Republic. In part the debate links the fortieth anniversary of the end of the war and President Reagan's visit to the military cemetery at Bitburg in 1985. The discussion is also related to the preparation of a plan for two museum projects, the House of the

History of the Federal Republic of Germany in Bonn and the German Historical Museum in Berlin.

Questions treated are

- Should history provide meaning, be a bearer of national identity, and if so, how?
- Is history being misused as an instrument of political debate?
- What self-understanding and what image of history should the Federal Republic have?
- Are we striving toward a patriotism oriented toward the constitution ("constitutional patriotism") or a patriotism oriented toward a sense of nationhood ("national patriotism")?
- Are the crimes of the Nazi period unique, or are they comparable to other mass annihilations of history such as those in the Soviet Union?
- Should the discipline of history "historicize" or "moralize"?
- Is there a "causal nexus" between the crimes of the National-Socialist regime and those of the Russian Revolution and Stalinism?
- What was the function of the German Army in the East in the winter of 1944–45?
- Was Germany "liberated" in 1945?
- Is the destruction of the German Reich a response to the crimes of the Third Reich?

In addition to these questions of substance, historians participating in the *Historikerstreit* also debated our political culture, the scholarly pluralism of German history, reciprocal misinterpretations by historians, and scholarly conscientiousness when quoting other authors.

In the Bundestag electoral campaign of 1986–87, the question of the National-Socialist past was one that the Bavarian minister-president [Franz Josef Strauß] placed in the center of his campaign statements.[4] The basic tenor was that the German people must step out from behind the shadow of the past. In an interview, he said about his campaign speeches: "You should hear the hurricane of applause from people who do not want to be constantly accused of the Third Reich."

None of the authors represented in this volume can be made responsible for these partisan opinions. At no time did such an opinion have a political majority on its side, as is shown by the Bundestag debates about the statute of limitations [for Nazi war crimes] of 1965, 1969, and 1979, the speeches of Chancellor Kohl and President Richard von Weizsäcker on the fortieth anniversary of the end of the war, and also the Bundestag's anti-Semitism debate of February 27, 1986.

Young academics have followed the *Historikerstreit* with great interest and sensitivity. At many universities, the student body organized special lecture series, and, of the some 65,000 copies of the German original edition of this book sold to date, a disproportionate number were purchased in university towns.

Thus I feel there is reason to hope that coming generations of historians will take note of the French historian Marc Bloch, who was shot by the Gestapo in 1944. Bloch said that it was the task of the historian to organize a dialogue between the living and the dead. And who among the dead could be closer to us than those who were victims of German deeds?

MUNICH, OCTOBER 1991

NOTES

1. In the meantime, a number of books on the *Historikerstreit* have appeared: for example, Jürgen Habermas's *Eine Art Schadensabwicklung*, Frankfurt, 1987; Christian Meier's *Forty Years after Auschwitz. The German Recollection of History Today*, Munich, 1987; Ernst Nolte's *Das Vergehen der Vergangenheit: Antwort an meine Kritiker im sogenannten Historikerstreit*, Berlin, Frankfurt, 1987; Hans-Ulrich Wehler's *Entsorgung der deutschen Vergangenheit? Ein polemischer Essay zum Historikerstreit*, Munich, 1988, and *Ist der Nationalsozialismus Geschichte? Zu Historisierung und Historikerstreit*, ed. Dan Diner, Frankfurt, 1987. Other works are in preparation. In this context we must also mention Ernst Nolte's *Der europäische Bürgerkrieg 1917–1945: Nationalsozialismus und Bolschewismus*, Berlin, 1987. In this book, on which Nolte worked parallel to the *Historikerstreit*, he discusses in detail his disputed theses.
2. Letter to the author of December 16, 1986.
3. In the German original edition only the first part of Habermas's footnote is reproduced. It appeared in its entirety in Habermas's *Eine Art Schadensabwicklung: Kleine Politische Schriften VI*, Frankfurt, 1987, pp. 149–158. This complete text is printed in the English-language edition, which, at least in this respect, surpasses the German edition.
4. Franz Josef Strauß, "Entscheidung für Deutschland," *Bayern-Kurier-Report*, January 17, 1987, pp. 1f.

INDEX